ECONOMIES OF  N

Sara Miller McCune founded SAGE Publishing in 1965 to support the dissemination of usable knowledge and educate a global community. SAGE publishes more than 1000 journals and over 800 new books each year, spanning a wide range of subject areas. Our growing selection of library products includes archives, data, case studies and video. SAGE remains majority owned by our founder and after her lifetime will become owned by a charitable trust that secures the company's continued independence.

Los Angeles | London | New Delhi | Singapore | Washington DC | Melbourne

ECONOMIES OF DESIGN
GUY JULIER

Los Angeles | London | New Delhi
Singapore | Washington DC | Melbourne

Los Angeles | London | New Delhi
Singapore | Washington DC | Melbourne

SAGE Publications Ltd
1 Oliver's Yard
55 City Road
London EC1Y 1SP

SAGE Publications Inc.
2455 Teller Road
Thousand Oaks, California 91320

SAGE Publications India Pvt Ltd
B 1/I 1 Mohan Cooperative Industrial Area
Mathura Road
New Delhi 110 044

SAGE Publications Asia-Pacific Pte Ltd
3 Church Street
#10-04 Samsung Hub
Singapore 049483

Editor: Michael Ainsley
Editorial assistant: John Nightingale
Production editor: Imogen Roome
Copyeditor: Solveig Gardner Servian
Proofreader: Sarah Bury
Indexer: David Rudeforth
Marketing manager: Lucia Sweet
Cover design: Jennifer Crisp
Typeset by: C&M Digitals (P) Ltd, Chennai, India
Printed by CPI Group (UK) Ltd, Croydon, CR0 4YY

Library of Congress Control Number: 2016948132

British Library Cataloguing in Publication data

A catalogue record for this book is available from
the British Library

ISBN 978-1-4739-1885-6
ISBN 978-1-4739-1886-3 (pbk)

At SAGE we take sustainability seriously. Most of our products are printed in the UK using FSC papers and boards.
When we print overseas we ensure sustainable papers are used as measured by the PREPS grading system.
We undertake an annual audit to monitor our sustainability.

CONTENTS

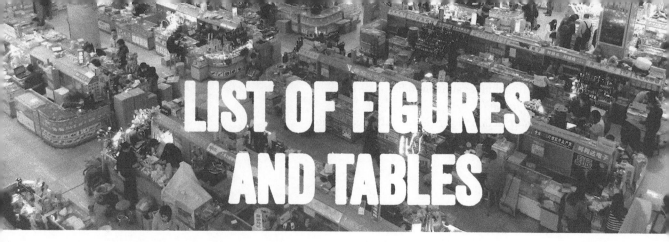

LIST OF FIGURES AND TABLES

FIGURES

TABLES

LIST OF ILLUSTRATIONS

ACKNOWLEDGEMENTS

The research for this book has gathered pace through many years. Back in that fateful year of 1986, the economic and social historian John Styles had a considerable influence on me in thinking about the triangulation of design, production and consumption. I thank him for introducing me to this approach and for his enthusiasm then and since. By the 1990s I had considered writing an account of design in the context of Thatcherism and Reagonomics. During this period, my research on design and marketisation in Spain, Hungary and elsewhere also made me realise that many other local developments were taking place within global processes of neoliberalisation. Transitions were going on within transitions. Time passed until thinking about economics, design and the dynamics of change began to lurk more heavily in the background as I wrote revised editions of *The Culture of Design*. Julia Hall and then Mila Steele at Sage Publishing were thoroughly supportive commissioning editors through its three iterations.

Like so many commercial products, this book could not have come into being without state support. My role as the University of Brighton/Victoria and Albert Museum Principal Research Fellow in Contemporary Design has allowed me to devote paid time to it. I thank my colleagues in both institutions – particularly Anne Boddington and Bill Sherman – for agreeing to my prioritisation of this project.

Parts of this text have been developed through more focused articles and book chapters. Some of the earlier sections in Chapter 2 took shape in an essay I wrote for the accompanying book to the V&A exhibition 'British Design since 1948'. Approaches to the idea of the neoliberal object have been shaped in various ways elsewhere, including a chapter in *Designing Mobilities, Mobilising Design: intersections, affordances, relations* (Spinney et al., forthcoming). Fragments of Chapter 8 appear in articles for the journals *Knowledge Technology and Policy*, *City*, an article co-written with Malene Leerberg for the *Finnish Journal of Urban Studies* as well as a chapter in *Human Smart Cities: Rethinking the Interplay between Design and Planning* (Concilio and Rizzo, 2016). The Design Culture Salon that I have convened at the V&A has been a particularly fertile ground for ideas, some of which I have blogged separately but have also worked their way into this publication.

Three Arts and Humanities Research Council funded projects have influenced this book. 'China's Creative Communities: Making Value and The Value(s) of Making' (AHRC Newton Fund, 2016) produced valuable, first-hand viewpoints that underpinned part of Chapter 7. I thank Cat Rossi and Justin Marshall who led this excursion. The issues around *shanzhai* innovation and its relationship to open innovation and governmental policy in China were unfolding very rapidly as this book was finalised. The findings presented here are thus very much a snapshot in time. The other two projects 'Mapping Social Design' (2013–14) and 'Developing Participation in Social Design: Prototyping Projects, Programmes and Policies' (2015–16) led to material that appears in Chapter 8.

Through these latter two projects, Leah Armstrong, Jocelyn Bailey and Lucy Kimbell have been stalwart colleagues. Leah Armstrong dependably undertook some background research for this book as well. Lucy Kimbell has been a critical friend, providing immensely useful comments as my text developed. In addition, anonymous reviewers have supplied important feedback on early plans and drafts, while Michael Ainsley and Delayna Spencer at Sage Publishing have masterfully coordinated these. Viviana Narotzky has also generously provided constructive and clear-sighted advice. Carolyn Burke, Ian Cochrane, Mark Green, James Mair, Simon May, Sabina Michaëlis and Jeremy Myerson shared important insights from their various backgrounds in the design professions. My thanks also go to Divia Patel at the V&A, who introduced me to *jugaad*. Ultimately, however, any shortcomings in this book are entirely my responsibility.

INTRODUCTION: CONTEMPORARY CAPITALISM AND THE RISE OF DESIGN

Since the 1980s there has been extraordinary growth and visibility of design throughout most of the world. This is connected to fundamental developments in capitalism. This period may otherwise be termed 'neoliberalism'. Chapter 1 explains some of the ways by which the rise of design and neoliberalism are connected. In particular, it shows how neoliberalism is played out in multiple ways and, relatedly, how design is varied in its practices and outcomes. The reach and complexity of design objects has also extended in the era of neoliberalism and some of this chapter considers the new kinds of artefacts that have emerged. The overall approach of this book and its chapters are also explained.

Economics and design have never been particularly good bedfellows. One suggests certainties and statistics or, at least, attempts to get a clear understanding of what is going on in the big picture of world events or the smaller one of firms and individuals. The other proposes sensations and aesthetics, opening up myriad ways of doing things, of living, of functioning *in* the world. One tries to demonstrate the knowable, the other is constantly pushing towards the unknowable. Putting these together creates a seemingly impossible nexus.

This book is concerned with the various economies in contemporary capitalism that make design and the ways by which design contributes to the making of economies. In so doing, it seeks the complex and varied meeting grounds of these two fields. Some interrogation of their terms and conditions may help to set the scene.

'The economy' (singular) is a construct. It is an idea that is made up to fit a dominant way of organising the economy of a location – usually emanating from the respective politicians who are in power. 'The economy is ... booming/in need of stimulation/needs a lower taxation regime and public spending cuts' are all declarations that express political and spatial interests. 'The economy' means various things. But in its reduction to a singular entity it comes to express an homogenised view of financial and commercial arrangements that conforms to, basically, how politicians and those who agree with them see that they should be run. It then becomes unchallengeable, unalterable, immutable it seems.

Design, meanwhile, is also presented as a singular idea. Although less talked about than 'the economy', design is frequently presented as if it were a coherent whole (e.g. Nelson and Stolterman 2003; Cross 2006; Heskett 2008; Verganti 2013). It is common for headline speakers at design conferences to claim that 'Design is ...' followed by a few sentences of unerring certainty that place this pursuit fairly and squarely into a particular worldview which itself is not actually declared but lurks beneath the surface.

As a starting point for this book, here is my definition of design.

Design is far too variegated in its practices, far too widely deployed and far too diverse in how it is understood and used for us to be able to express a singular definition for it. Instead, we have to take into account the different temporalities and territories that it operates in. We have to understand its various and, sometimes, conflicting purposes. We must recognise the many formats it appears in and the conjunctions of objects within these and between them. No object is an island. No one definition of design is enough.

Economies (plural) sit in, overlap with and operate outside that construct of 'the economy'. Inside 'the economy', there are activities that usually do their best to thrive within the legal structures that are set by it. They make their money, pay their taxes, calculate their loss and profit and find ways to operate formally and informally without breaking the rules or messing up. Sometimes grey areas are sought, though. This is where spaces open up to do something; that is, it takes advantage of the structures of 'the economy' while also doing something counter to or alternative from its overarching aims. And then there is wilful distancing from them.

Thus, to talk of 'economies of design' is to pursue the different contexts and processes where design functions and investigate the different ways it does this. At times, these may become 'design economies'. In this change of emphasis, we find design to be more clearly and self-consciously central to activities – where design is the driving force of the way that a context is organised. It is where design is a project in itself that garners various motivations, interests or forms of investment.

The historical parameters for this book are built around two related factors. One is an understanding of the priorities and impacts of neoliberal economic practices from the 1980s. The other is the growth of the multiple ways that design practices have grown, accumulated and intensified through the same period. Putting these together, I would argue, has received little attention in design history, design studies or elsewhere. It necessitates an analysis of the economic processes that take place within design practices, those around it and how each of these interact.

Broadly speaking, design works in two ways in relation to neoliberalism. First, it makes stuff that is used within its systems. Products are fashioned for sale, environments are configured for use, images are formed for viewing, services are designed and rolled out and so on. These form part of the neoliberal pressures of marketisation and differentiation. Second, design also plays a more symbolic role. As a thing that is intended to be at the leading-edge of cultural production, it points towards the possible. It shows what it is *in potentia*. It materialises the probable. Design plays a semiotic role in making change appear reasonable.

To briefly expand on this secondary, semiotic, role of design, the signalling of transformation may be carried out in various ways. This symbolism produces subjectivities that are disposed to particular economic processes and logics (Jessop 2004). Getting excited about a new design also infers getting excited about economic transformation. In the public sphere, for example, a new urban design scheme works as part of a neighbourhood regeneration scheme in order to tidy streets up. It also shows to property investors or companies looking to re-locate that this area is 'on the up' and worth considering. The academic specialism of cultural political economy provides some theoretical starting points for thinking here (Best and Paterson 2010; Sum and Jessop 2013). We can take political economy to involve the relationship of politics, economics and law. This might include the study of such things as civic resource allocation, legal frameworks, trade agreements or taxation systems. Cultural political economy is more concerned with the *meanings* that are formed through policy and business and how and for whom these meanings function. How design works to get us used to certain economic processes and ambitions is a question at stake here.

This process of habituation to ways by which contemporary capitalism functions may work in quieter ways as well. Artefacts come into use and become part of routines. In this, they may seem very ordinary – their apparent significance may fade a little. Nonetheless, through repeated contact and use the meanings of things go deeper, are performed, get re-enacted and embodied. Thrift (2008: 187) goes further to describes this within a processes of *microbiopolitics* – small-scale actions that are undertaken in tiny slices of time but which are, nonetheless, sensed and that connect to a broader disciplining of the self (Foucault 2008). Thus it is important to think about the influences of design objects at various levels, from the bigger narratives to intimate actions in everyday life.

The next section considers the ways by which design has developed in this neoliberal age, drawing further attention to its diversity and its porosity in relation to other practices. There follows a section in which I describe some of the overarching qualities of neoliberalism, again opening up its unevenness, its hybridity and functionings. Neoliberalism is seen more as a process of change than as an end – hence it is more accurate to talk about *neoliberalisation*. Further detail is given thereafter where I break down this process into four key components: deregulation, new economy, financialisation and austerity. How design is entwined into these is briefly opened up. Some of the kinds of design objects that I am mostly interested in paying attention to in this book are then pursued further before finishing this chapter with an outline of the succeeding chapters.

THE RISE OF DESIGN: QUANTITIES AND QUALITIES

Design is on the exponential rise. Copious graphs and tables – such as in Table 1.1 – demonstrate the growth of design around the world over the past three decades. Indeed, the quantifying of design professionals and turnover has become a minor industry in itself. Local and national governments, transnational groups like the European Union and even the United Nations have all taken part in this as well as institutions dedicated to promoting the design profession and consultancies whose job it is to inform business and policy (see Julier 2014: 24–5).

Table 1.1   Top design exporters in developed and developing economies (UNCTAD 2010)

Exporter	Value (in millions of US$) 2008	Market share (%) 2008	Growth rate (%) 2003–2008
China	58,848	24.32	15.45
China, Hong Kong SAR	23,874	9.87	5.01
Italy	23,618	9.76	10.35
Germany	16,129	6.67	16.71
USA	12,150	5.02	14.25
France	10,871	4.49	13.11
India	7,759	3.21	18.57
United Kingdom	7,448	3.08	10.93
Switzerland	6,938	2.87	16.09
Thailand	4,474	1.85	10.80
United Arab Emirates	4,464	1.84	49.80
Belgium	4,339	1.79	8.72
Poland	3,855	1.59	13.72
Japan	3,783	1.56	17.21
Netherlands	3,773	1.56	13.91
Turkey	3,543	1.46	11.72
Malaysia	3,186	1.32	12.87
Viet Nam	2,687	1.11	23.44
Mexico	2,535	1.05	1.40
Singapore	2,392	0.99	16.21

With this have come debates as to how to identify and quantify what design does. Who and where are the designers? The United Nations has side-stepped this by referring to 'design intense' products such as fashionware, souvenirs and toys; they have then looked at global trade statistics to track the growth of exportation of these items, and then concluded that this must mean that there is more design around in the world than ever (UNCTAD 2010). However, this can only deliver a very partial picture as the analysis only refers to product-based design. Where is graphic or interior design here, for instance?

Other problems arise when we quantify design by counting the number and output of professional designers. How do you identify designers? Professional associations provide lists and contacts for researchers to survey, but these will usually only cover their membership. Furthermore, these are often limited by the particular reach of that association. Legions of designers who work in-house for companies or as freelancers are often missed. And in any case, there are constantly emerging design specialisms which are either unknown or overlap with other professional activities so much that it is difficult to disentangle them. A service designer may also be a strategist, a business consultant, a digital technology developer or an ethnographer.

The key point here is that emphasis on quantities in the rise of design often misses fundamental developments in its qualities. It has become an orthodoxy to talk of the growing complexity of design in our 'complex world' (e.g. Thackara 2006; Norman 2010). But it is important to not just accept this notion as a given, but to try to unpick what the constituent parts of this 'complexity' are. Let us consider what these might be.

First, the growth of design has by no means meant 'more of the same'. Until the 1980s, its mainstay had been in its sub-sectors of industrial, graphic, fashion and interior design. Since then, as Table 1.2 illustrates, the design profession has constantly atomised into more and more specialisms. Unlike, for example, law or architecture, design has never been subject to normative curricula or any kind of externally certified professional attainment levels. The downside of this has been that, historically, it has always struggled for recognition outside. The upside is that this has meant that design education and the design profession has been able to move swiftly, inventing new sub-sectors and approaches as it goes along.

Table 1.2 The accumulation of design specialisms

1970-	1980-	1990-	2000-	2010-
interior design	corporate identity packaging	branding		
textile design fashion design				
interior design	retail design exhibition design	leisure design experience design		
graphic design	multimedia design	web design		mobile application design
	design management	user-centred design participatory design	interaction design service design design thinking design activism	social design design for social innovation strategic design design for policy
furniture design			design art critical design	
industrial design engineering design	green design	concurrent design sustainable design		
transport design				
building design		urban design		

Second, and as already intimated, the boundaries between design and other professional disciplines have become ever more porous. This has largely been in response to market and technological changes. In the 1980s, this porosity was driven by commercial considerations, in particular around corporate identity and retail design where increased efforts were made to present a unified design language across visual, material and spatial elements. This was consolidated in the 1990s, in particularly through branding, where in addition to coordinating the physical attributes of a service or product offer, digital presence became increasingly important and greater attention was paid to customer experience; thus issues such as staff training and management styles began to be mixed into the branding equation. The increased overlapping of design disciplines has also been driven by ethical considerations, such as environmental sustainability. Design for sustainability in its early days of the 1970s to the mid-1990s focused principally on material questions such as recyclability (e.g. Papanek 1995). Latterly it has incorporated more complex questions of social arrangements and participation in the design process itself that enhance carbon neutrality (e.g. Manzini 2015).

Third, in its intensification design has become more knowing of itself, more reflexive and more self-conscious in its various ways. Aside from the proliferation of design webzines, blogs and print publishing we must also note the growth of semi-formal gatherings of designers through talks and panel discussions at, for example, trade fairs and design festivals. The fora that are available for the debate of design have grown with it. We must also note the growth of design schools, design research and attendant conference circuits, symposia and peer-reviewed journals.

Fourth, the temporalities within which design operate have become more varied. At one extreme, the processing of design has speeded-up. Not least, this has been facilitated by technological change. Computer systems allow for far more rapid development, negotiation and deployment of designs. It has also been driven by increasing velocities in the global economy as a whole. This is not usual to the whole of design practice, though. At the other extreme, many designers have moved into much longer-term relationships with their clients or users. This means that they might work in more iterative ways, developing successions of designs and projects with them that go deeper in terms of their contact points. Typically in commercial contexts, they may be involved in the design of a wider suite of objects that encompass both the 'above the line' features that the public see and 'below the line' aspects relevant to the internal workings of the client, such as training manuals or brand guidelines. In more socially oriented design practices, there has been a move to building long-term processes with stakeholders. Here, the designer engages in deep understanding of the make-up of organisations or populations and what constitutes their specific cultures.

Fifth, the territories of design have altered since the 1980s. An obvious example of this has been in growth of design in the former Soviet bloc or in so-called emergent economies such as in East Asia and Latin America. These come with their specificities in terms of their material and technical resources but also in their politics as to the uses of design or in the economic structures within which they operate. Beyond this, we must also consider the transnational, border-crossing that takes place on the one hand, while on the other, movements occurred where a very conscious relocalisation of economies and design has occurred.

Sixth, and to combine points four and five, in many contexts design has taken up a role not just in providing goods and services to satisfy current requirements, but has increasingly functioned to indicate sources of future value. Design is used to leverage value outside itself – to build on other assets and/or to point towards these. Further, many forms of design have become just part of networks that are under continual adjustment and modification. An example of this is in smartphone technologies whose running systems, apps, handsets and signal provider systems are under constant redesign in relation to each other. In this, the objects of design are often 'unfinished' while the broader 'culture of design' of a location, a design specialism or a corporation, for example, can also be said to be in an ongoing state of becoming. Here, there has been a rise in maintaining or even protecting the 'territories' within which design operates through time against the competition. Hence, intellectual property (IP) has taken increased prominence in the discourses of design.

Through these six points I have focused on the design supply side. It is important to appreciate, however, that this is also about how design is experienced, consumed or known in the every-day routines and experiences of work, leisure, mobility, survival, disappointment or aspiration. Where and how design is encountered; for how long one engages with a product or service of notable designerly input or the time taken between discovering a desire and its realisation; what one thinks or knows about whoever designed it: such factors have become more intensified and variegated as they have become more numerous and widespread.

Studying economies of design involves an investigation into the multiple ways that design is configured within different economic processes. At the same time, it pays attention to the broadening and deepening of design's meanings and functions.

The next section considers a firmer theoretical foundation through which we can understand this unfolding of design. Specifically, it does this by consolidating an understanding of the processes of neoliberalisation.

NEOLIBERALISATION

'Neoliberalism' is a relatively recent term. It is generally attributed to the economist Alexander Rüstow who, in response to the German economic crisis of the 1920s and 1930s, advocated that the marketplace should be free of any direct state involvement; rather, the state should be strong in setting the rules within which market operations take place (Hartwich and Razeen 2009). It wasn't until the 1970s that the capitalist world fully returned to consider this idea. In the meantime and in the aftermath of the Second World War a different global economic landscape emerged that – in the capitalist world – was concerned to engineer a balance of state, market and democratic institutions to ensure peace and wellbeing. The so-called Bretton Woods agreement of 1944 and afterwards aimed at a stable system of global trade where the US dollar worked as the reserve currency against which others were fixed.

In 1971, President Nixon unilaterally pulled the USA out of the Bretton Woods agreement by ending the convertibility of dollars to gold. The costs of the Vietnam war and public spending programmes were producing America's biggest deficit of the twentieth century and the 'Nixon Shock' performed a fiscal shuffle to stabilise the national economy. In short, this meant that international currency exchange rates could no longer be pegged against reserves and ceased to be subject to internationally agreed controls. Currencies could now be traded more openly and flexibly in the financial markets which, in turn, would determine their value. In the longer term, this would usher in a new era wherein a liberalised marketplace, in terms of trade of goods, services and finance, would dominate the expanding capitalist world.

Marxist geographer David Harvey makes the case for the years 1978–80 in the acceleration of neoliberal policies (Harvey 2005). This is when Chinese premier Deng Xiaoping began the process of liberalisation of his country's economy in competition against the rise of Japan, Taiwan, Hong Kong, Singapore and South Korea. In the UK, Margaret Thatcher was elected as Prime Minister in 1979 with a mandate to curb trade union powers, liberalise the labour market and break a decade's economic and inflationary stagnation. In the USA, Ronald Reagan was elected as President in 1980 who, likewise, looked to a series of deregulationary measures on trade, agriculture, industry, mineral extraction and labour protection. Such measures led Harvey to provide the following, succinct definition of neoliberalism:

> Neoliberalism is in the first instance a theory of political economic practices that proposes that human wellbeing can best be advanced by liberating individual entrepreneurial freedoms and skills within an institutional framework characterized by strong private property rights, free markets, and free trade. (2005: 2)

As a term in common usage, however, 'neoliberalism' has only circulated more widely in the last decade (Peck et al. 2009). In particular, the global financial crisis of 2008 has provoked closer inspection of neoliberalism by academics in order to understand its complexities and contradictions. To extend from Harvey's definition, neoliberalism is typified by the following features:

- the deregulation of markets and the privileging of market forces, free of state intervention;
- the privatisation of state-owned enterprises;
- the foregrounding of financial interests over others (e.g. communitarian, civic, social, environmental etc.);
- an emphasis on competitiveness and on individual, entrepreneurial practices.

Harvey (2005) points out that it is more accurate to see neoliberalism as 'a theory of political economic practices' rather than a complete political ideology. *Neoliberalisation* as a transformative and variegated process might more accurately describe this. Indeed, neoliberalism has been deployed across a range of political frameworks (witness, for example, its vigorous application within Pinochet's dictatorship in Chile from 1973). Thus, neoliberalism is slippery. Indeed, just as designers 'dodge and weave' to find new marketplaces for their skills, create new needs and desires, so neoliberalism is constantly on the move, finding new territories and combinations. Neoliberalism, like design, is a process of change more than an endpoint.

Neoliberalisation is commonly associated with globalisation. It certainly depends on the easy movement of finance, goods and services across national borders, unhindered by legal constrictions. It takes advantage of the integration of technological supports around the world, some common cultural understandings and aspirations, the dissemination of knowledge and strong infrastructures, such as transportation, to facilitate the movement of goods. This paints a picture of an even, homogenised world. And yet, neoliberalism '*necessarily* operates among its others' (Peck et al. 2009: 104, emphasis in the original). It is parasitical in that it attaches onto a variety of localised contexts as a transformatory process rather than an end. As such it is always hybrid, messy, diverse and unfinished. It claws into places in different ways, finding points of resistance, friction, slipperiness and ingress. Jamie Peck puts this patchiness more poetically:

> Chronically uneven spatial development, institutional polymorphism, and a landscape lit-
> tered with policy failures, oppositional pushbacks, and stuttering forms of malregulation
> are all consequently par for neoliberalism's zigzagging course. (Peck 2013: 140)

Finally, for this section, neoliberalism as a programme emerged in the 1970s and 1980s, thus giving it more than four decades of activity, spreading irregularly across seven continents. In this, we
must see it as uneven in its historical trajectories through different geographies. But just as design
has accrued specialisms that appear in various conjunctions through these years, so a series of
overlapping and accumulating neoliberal policies and practices have occurred. The next section
explains these and the role of design therein.

DEREGULATION, NEW ECONOMY, FINANCIALISATION, AUSTERITY

Neoliberalisation is indeed varied in its processes and outcomes. However, there are four historical, structuring elements that have been important to it. These have emerged into dominance in
the West roughly in the order of deregulation in the 1980s, New Economy in the 1990s, financialisation in the 2000s and austerity from 2010. In other geographies, this decade-by-decade
development is not so clear-cut. Similar accumulations have taken place in different timeframes
and with varying emphasis, though.

The 1980s saw successive waves of **deregulation** in the West as the result of the influence of
so-called Reagonomics in the USA and Thatcherism in the UK (Ehrman 2006; Peck and Tickell
2007). 'Deregulation' is a term employed in the context of political economy to describe the
relaxation of legal constrictions regarding finance, trade and commerce. Part of this has included
privatisation of state industries and services. It has presented a multitude of new possibilities for
design. Global trade, for example, has been subjected to progressive deregulations that undermine economic protection of territories. In turn, this has produced new locations for design to
thrive in as places respond to global competition. We may also read deregulation to be active in
labour relations. The growth of flexible working and project-based employment has been a key
aspect in the supply end of the creative industries in general and design work in particular. There
have been other processes going on that are linked to these, such as the consumer and credit
boom, shifts towards homeownership or the greater presence of women in the workforce. These
have been indirectly enabled by changes in national and international laws and, subsequently,
have had profound effects on design. Equally, the speeding up of digital communications have
produced new ways by which design ideas are circulated and new audiences created for them.
Thus, we may read deregulation as both an output of political economy and an input of social
practice, with design working between them.

These rapid historical shifts set the scene for the emergence in the 1990s of the so-called 'New
Economy'. This term was coined in the magazine *Newsweek* in 1995, a year that coincided with
the establishment of Amazon.com and eBay.com. Around the **New Economy**, the employment of
digital information technology networks for inventory and supply was crucial. After all it was during the 1990s that the World Wide Web was established. Between 1993 and 2000, it is estimated
that the amount of information moving through two-way telecommunication that was carried
globally by the internet (as opposed to other means such as surface mail) leapt from 1 per cent to

51 per cent; this figure had risen to 97 per cent by 2007 (Hilbert and López 2011). The internet made recording and analysing consumer preferences, sourcing and communicating with suppliers, controlling stock and tracking delivery processes easier. In other words, a more flexible and tighter system of provision could be ensured. Thus, New Economy practices are centred around the notion of 'faster, better, cheaper', a slogan that has its origins in American defence spending policy of the Reagan era (McCurdy 2001). This mantra was adopted into the New Economy: 'faster' meant the compression of the supply chain to deliver 'mass specialisation'; 'better' meant that with more distributed and supple supply chains, companies could concentrate on their core capabilities through design, innovation and brand building; 'cheaper' meant that new manufacturing and service bases in Eastern Europe, the Indian sub-continent and the Far East could be exploited for their cheaper labour and material costs. In short, the geographies and temporalities with which designers would engage would change radically. This also meant significant changes for the ways by which they worked. 'Faster, better, cheaper' also transformed the expectations and practices of creative labour.

The roots of **financialisation** can be traced back to the early 1970s, but were accelerated through the deregulation of banking and stock market systems in the 1980s. It was in the late-1990s and 2000s, however, that this mode of economics became most dominant and intense in the West. Deregulation and New Economy combined the flexibilisation of labour and infrastructures for the production and distribution of goods as well as service provision in a global context with the affordances provided by digital information technologies. Likewise, financialisation involved swifter and more complex transnational movements of finance. Briefly, it is typified by greater emphasis being laid on strategies being played to maintain the value of shares, brands, real estate or capital flows. This is done in three ways: first, through the rise of shareholder value within corporate governance; second, through the rise of profit through financial rather than commodity production systems (e.g. deferring on pension systems, sub-leasing a truck fleet, liquifying the real estate of a corporation to lease it back while investing the capital elsewhere); and third, through the rise of financial trading (Froud et al. 2000; Froud et al. 2006). In all these, there is a constant exchange between tangible and intangible assets and this is where design must be understood in three corresponding ways. First, it helps to shape those fixed, tangible resources to add value. Second, it plays a symbolic role in pointing towards sources of future value – things whose worth can be leveraged. Third, design is employed in the actual systems and technologies that facilitate processes of financialisation. Furthermore, it is not surprising to learn that intellectual property has grown as an asset and process alongside financialisation. Design is used strategically to differentiate and provide protection on assets through law. It is therefore also something that generates future value through the licensing out of designs for others to use or through its use in the protection of corporate assets. Design may also be mobilised in the more private sphere, for example, in improving the value of domestic real estate. Thus while financialisation is associated with jargon-heavy practices in banking and investment, it also finds its ideological way through to many other levels of everyday life (Martin 2002).

Austerity springs from financialisation as financialisation emerges from New Economy and New Economy derives from deregulation. Classically, we associate it with the measures introduced by governments around the world in the wake of the 2007–8 global financial crisis. Briefly and bleakly, this largely came out of over-leveraging – financial institutions, including government ones, raise money against assets. If, for example, the value of that asset falls, the cost of borrowing rises and drops in productivity impede the ability to pay down debts (as happened in 2007–8), this provokes financial crisis and economic recession. Governments then attempt to reduce their deficit and stimulate the private sector by making heavy cuts in their own spending. This is austerity. In recessionary periods, it might be understandably assumed that designers suffer strong pressures as commercial operations reduce their costs. The austerity programmes of governments in the 2010s produced two responses within the very broad rubric of 'social design' (i.e. socially-oriented design for collective benefit that deals largely with non-commercial clients): one has been for service designers to specialise in helping local, regional and national governments develop cheaper and more user-focused services; the other has been in a strengthening of politicised, activist design practices that propose alternative economic and social frameworks to austerity.

It is tempting to view these four components as discreet 'moments' that conveniently fill out respective decades from 1980 onwards. Economic practices are uncertain and uneven, however. Evidence of all four was discernible in the UK and the USA during the 1980s. They bottlenecked into the 1990s in Central and Eastern Europe. Versions of these coursed and lurched through several Latin American economies in the 1990s and 2000s. And so on. So while they do exhibit some sequencing in terms of how they were most intensively practised and talked about in Western capitalism, we may also see them as accumulative, iterative or even kaleidoscopic, depending where else you look. The schema in Table 1.3 is meant as a guideline, seen from a mostly Western viewpoint and to be rearranged and challenged according to where you are as a reader.

The next section follows up on this view by identifying three clusters of design activity that weave across the four components of deregulation, New Economy, financialisation and austerity. These are sourced from Nigel Thrift's opening salvo in *Knowing Capitalism* (2005) and are then developed further in terms of the chief forms of design that articulate these. In the context of this discussion of economies of design, they each confirm a distinctive conceptual challenge presented by this book.

DESIGN OBJECTS OF CONTEMPORARY CAPITALISM

Beyond the accumulation of more specialisms in design since the 1980s that is presented in Table 1.2, there have been more general changes in the culture of design, its objects and the practices that course through it. These changes coincide with what geographer Nigel Thrift (2005: 5–10) argues are three crucial arenas through which contemporary capitalism has developed and continues to do so. Below, I explain them and develop on their significance in terms of design.

The first is in the discursive power of what Thrift calls the 'cultural circuit' of capitalism. In particular, he refers to the critical appraisals of capitalism that are produced through business schools, management consultants and gurus, and the media. These dissect the log-jams, vagaries, inefficiencies or other challenges that hinder business. Their critiques feed back into ways of 'doing capitalism' that modify it, add to its repertoires but also provide further orthodoxies for it. Design is also replete with its gurus, blogs or institutions that do this work. Books, webinars and master-classes provide no end of advice to design managers, practitioners and students.

This cultural circuit extends to the actual things that bridge between singular analysis and multiple or serial implementations. By this I refer to the more meta-level activities that produce brand guidelines, corporate visions, best-practice handbooks, procurement manuals, design method

Table 1.3 Features of neoliberalisation, examples in everyday life, relevant design disciplines and examples

Economic feature	Key components		Examples in everyday life	Relevant design discipline	Examples in design
deregulation	• privatisation of state-owned industries and services (e.g. transportation) • elimination of global trade and financial barriers • elimination of state regulatory controls e.g. on finance, property, transportation media content • competitivity as commercial and civic driver	1980-	• growth of consumer credit • growth of out-of-town shopping as leisure activity • growth in home ownership • drop in relative cost of consumer goods	retail design corporate identity	• shopping malls • own brand clothing stores • corporate reports
New Economy	• reduction of stock inventory and move to just-in-time production and delivery • globalisation of manufacture and distribution • online inventory and purchasing • adoption of 'best-value' principles in public sector (New Public Management) • increased outsourcing and subcontracting of commercial and public sector operations	1990-	• further drop in cost of consumer goods • online shopping • growth of international travel and short break vacationing • rise of more flexible working patterns • rise of creative industries as career option	branding digital design concurrent design experience design	• brand strategy for multiple goods and services • fast fashion • placebranding • creative and cultural quarters
financialisation	• the dominance of shareholder value within corporate governance as the central force • the rise of profit through financial rather than commodity production systems • rise to dominance of the finance industry • real estate closely bound into global flows of capital and speculation • strategic use of intellectual property rights to produce value	2000-	• housing and education seen as 'investments' for the future • gentrification of neighbourhoods • personal financial planning • growth and consolidation of tax havens • private finance initiatives (PFIs) to produce public-private partnerships for welfare and education	urban design strategic design design art	• urban design as part of regeneration processes • product design detailing driven by shareholder value • design art as investment opportunity • exploitation of intellectual property rights (IPR) • crowdsourcing of creative labour
austerity	• further privatisation and outsourcing of state functions • further shrinkage of welfare state • increased wealth of elites • further consolidation of financialisation processes	2010-	• civil society (NGOs, charities, neighbourhood groups) filling government policy void • growth of 'sharing economy' • alternative currency systems	social design design for policy design activism	• participatory design methods in social innovation • design and innovation labs in government policy making • hacktivism, craftivism

toolkits, masterplans and local design statements. These do the work of codifying, organising and mediating analysis and expertise in relation to various scales and publics; they are developed to provide organising principles for specific, but multiple contexts of application. Thus they play a 'meta' role in being designed as systems and understandings that script design further downstream. Design criticism has a tendency to focus on the 'finished objects' of production – chairs, posters, interiors, uniforms and so on. This book frequently goes back upstream to consider the role of design in shaping certain business principles and outlooks through those codifications. These play a discursive role in that they reinforce certain overall conventions of, for example, how a firm concerns itself with the interface between its internal culture and how it is seen from outside in the case of brand guidelines. They circulate, are read, acted on or even legally enforced, thus feeding back into the wider operations of design and the operations of capitalism.

Second, there are new forms of commodity and commodity relations. Thrift (2005: 7) claims that these forms are 'intimately bound up with the increasing mediatization of everyday life'. This can be an unhelpful reading as it runs the risk of stating the obvious that, simply, we spend more time looking at screens than before. Certainly, mediatory technologies such as smartphones, tablets and plasma screens are more pervasive, as is their interconnectivity. Thrift goes on, here, to identify the ubiquity of brands as well as increased attention given to the affective register in goods and services that constitute the 'experience economy' (Pine and Gilmore 1999). It is here that we can push further in terms of thinking about design's role in commodity relations.

Certainly, as Thrift asserts, the boundaries of many commodities are redefined. Thus, for instance, goods such as mobile phone applications or computer software require routine upgrading which makes their usefulness time-limited. However, these are also contingent upon other objects (for example, app stores, operating systems, memory capacity in the hardware, data networks, wireless hotspots, electrical provision) (Julier 2014: ch. 11). Objects are unfinished in that their performance is contingent on complex linkages that are forever shifting (Knorr Cetina 1997). This means that there is never a fixed meaning of the object (Folkmann 2013: 141). Rather, objects form part of a series of open-ended systems that are dynamic and constantly subject to incursions and modifications. Sometimes these multiplicities are unified within the singularity of a brand (Lury 2004). Object constellations also reposition the consumer. A product website featuring a short video where its designer talks about their inspiration for it; an SMS that gives you tracking information on the delivery process of something you have bought online; the service designer's mapping of a customer journey before, during and after their use of an amenity: these all purport to forge closer, distinctive and routine relationships between people, things and organisations. It is this relational function of design – both in how it fashions individual parts and orchestrates these as unities – where many newer design specialisms have emerged, including service design and brand strategy.

The third significant development of contemporary capitalism for Thrift (2005: 8–10) is in the construction of new spatial forms. This may straightforwardly be through the subcontracting of goods production and service delivery to form new systems of provision. Outsourcing may produce new geographies where supply lines stretch across and between territories. This other spatiality may also include shopping and leisure centres or new housing developments that are premised on easy mobilities. Notions of time–space compression enter into the frame here (see Julier 2014: ch. 8). Logistics and the analysis and ordering of the movement of things, finance and people is also a feature here.

In design terms, this new spatiality produces gated communities, tax havens, privatised waterfront developments, business parks, technological development zones, creative quarters – all manner of 'clusterings'. These are transformative of places due to their connectivity to others rather than, perhaps, their co-location with other urban functions. In other words, their function and value is realised because they are like, or *seem like*, other such spaces elsewhere in the world. Again, then, the design of these spaces works to give form to them in terms of providing their bricks and mortar, glass and brushed steel, signage and benches; and it also works semiotically to signal an asset. By association with other such iterations elsewhere, it works competitively to align that place, to help it appear to 'go up a league' or to place it in an international order.

Having established that neoliberalisation involves a drive to ongoing transformations, that contemporary capitalism is uncertain and multifarious and that design is equally multi-coloured and variegated, the task now is to consider how the rest of this book is structured in order to provide at least some narrative.

ECONOMIES OF DESIGN: STRUCTURE AND APPROACH

How do we make sense of this intensity and diversity? How does this book progress an argument to contribute to our understanding of the interrelationships of economies and design?

In *The Culture of Design* my chief aim was to open up a cross-disciplinary approach to understanding, largely, the cultural processes and meanings of design. In so doing, I was able to centre much of the book around specific design examples, starting with them and then opening out onto different viewpoints, taking in varying emphases given the economic work of designers, the systems of production, mediation and distribution and the world of consumption and social practices. By starting with the object, I was able to reveal its polyvocality, its multiple meanings and contexts.

In this book, I am treating design objects the other way around, mostly. Here, my approach is to build up a consideration of different forms and processes in economies, hanging design examples onto these. At times, I use what I call 'counter-factual' examples: cases where deliberately alternative design approaches are taken that throw dominant activities into relief. This is done in part to disrupt any narrative that accepts the absolute dominance of any singular models of design practice or of economic frameworks.

Chapter 2 primarily focuses largely on the cognitive processes that are active in neoliberal, capitalist context. In particular, it makes a case for a specific 'design culture turn' that took place in the 1980s. It features an analysis of a range of design objects and spaces that emerged, specifically around 1984–86. These, I argue, illustrate a particular set of activities and expectations concerning discreet, experiential environments, expectations and measurement and the rise of the individual sovereign consumer. Here I am distancing myself from accounts of design drawing from cultural studies that emphasise identity construction within postmodern and post-structuralist readings. Instead, I bring issues of cognition and social practice in line with key economic trends of the time. In this way, the overarching aim of the chapter is to drive links between macroeconomic policy, micro-economic practices and their enactment in everyday life.

Chapter 3 takes up the question of working in design. It picks up on the networked, cognitive qualities that the previous chapter focuses on to explore the specificities of design work in contrast to academic and policy approaches to creative and cultural industries. In particular, it discusses two aspects of design labour: one is its intensely performative characteristics where expectations of what it means to 'be creative' or 'designerly' are played to; the other is in the downward pressure on design to cut costs, thus reproducing themselves as a precariat. The economic and geographical disparities that exist more broadly in capitalism are also to be discovered in design.

Chapter 4 focuses on issues of globalisation, trade and mobilities and the volatility and unevenesses that these produce. Rather than take globalisation to be an homogenising process, I show how design functions in two different but related ways. One is in the production of intensities, where a tight fit of design, production and sometimes consumption cluster around locations. The other is in design's role in extensities: serially reproduced systems and nodes that encourage easy flow of goods, people and capital.

Chapter 5 considers how design functions in relation to assets. Design is often rolled into various versions of 'capital', such as social, cultural and creative capital; it is used to indicate the wellbeing of a location in terms of knowledge economies. Beyond this, we see how design is entwined with financialisation. Noticeable, yet highly readable design features are incorporated that maintain the interest of shareholders in the case of mobile phones, or future purchases in the case of private homes. The role of media is important here. From this we go on to look at how the design of shopping centres is handled to align with the requirements of institutional investors. These provide destinations for surplus liquidity that circulate in the global flows of finance.

Chapter 6 considers the uneven relationship of design to intellectual property rights (IPR). The growth of global corporations works in parallel with the competition of monopolies. Brands and technologies are developed to ensure differentiation and so intellectual property is a guiding principal here. This logic works in smaller scales within economies as well. Design works both to shape the content of IPR and communicate it. However, differentiation is unstable and short-lived, which is why designers are embedded into temporal cycles of product renewal. These cycles are structured by external forces such as trade fairs. At the same time, there are elements of performativity going on as business orthodoxies format standard ways of doing things.

Chapter 7 takes us outside more 'official' forms of practice to discuss design in informal and alternative economies. The former is where practices lie partly or wholly outside legal, governmental constraints. Here, we see how copying and 'tinkering' takes places within looser attitudes to intellectual property. What happens when this develops towards more officially recognised economies of design is considered here. The chapter progresses to review more politically charged approaches to using design in alternative economies and how it is dealt with in horizontalist self-management approaches and within timebanking systems.

Chapter 8 pursues the role of design in the weakening of state bureaucracies. Government has given way to governance in which politics has become about managing the interfaces between private and public interests. Design has been implicated into the presentation of policy but, increasingly, it has also been a tool to be used in its very formation. This finds its way into 'behaviour change' approaches in public policy which draws, in part, from 'choice architecture' of the marketplace. However, more explicit use of design has emerged in the growth of governmental policy design labs that use design thinking and strategic design. While these place much emphasis on putting the users of policies before the systems that format and deliver public services, their strategic role in delivering public sector cost-savings shouldn't be overlooked. More radical forms of governance can take place, such as in participatory budgeting or planning where citizens have a more direct role in policy priorities and planning. This may open onto forms of 'design citizenship'.

Chapter 9 pulls the main themes of the book together to build on some of its key arguments and suggest directions for further study of economies of design. It begins with a critical discussion of design management, arguing for the need for more grounded and situated analytical approaches to be taken through the fields of design culture and economic sociology. It then reflects on three questions that have sat behind preceding chapters. First, it recapitulates on the the broader relationships of design and neoliberalism. Second, it discusses some of the ways that design functions in terms of the qualitative elements of economics. Third, we review how design works to materialise finance.

Some of the text that follows involves historical analysis so that we might develop a sense of the some of the origins to the state we're in. However, in its thematic approach, this book is not intended to provide anything near a complete design history of neoliberalism. In dealing with the dynamics of change in design and economics, I tend to adopt something of a 'backward glance' as advocated by Thrift (2005: 2). This involves projecting oneself into the future and then looking back at the present, picking up on what I see as some of the key contemporary trajectories to hand while also understanding their historical formation. Just as the historian opens out the complexity and contradictions of the past, so we must be alive to the unsettled, dynamic multi-directionality of the present.

2

DESIGN CULTURE AND THE NEOLIBERAL OBJECT

Is there such as a thing as a 'neoliberal object'? How does design function to change the way we operate as economic beings? Chapter 2 begins by exploring shifts in consumer culture and design practice in the neoliberal age. It argues that a particular 'design culture turn' has taken place. This isn't just about the growing pervasiveness of professionally designed goods and services. More generally, the domains of design, production and consumption have been brought into closer, more intense relationships. At the same time, particular design objects have been brought into being that change the ways we act in and feel about our economic lives.

It is tempting to think of the everyday workings of much of contemporary capitalism as being dematerialised, deterritorialised, invisible or even purposefully hidden. Finance flows around the world through unseen cables, between unknown servers (MacKenzie 2014). Goods – US$17.5 trillion worth in 2012 (Manyika et al. 2014) – are moved across borders in anonymous containers (Martin 2013). Of global money held, over 90 per cent is held digitally rather than in ready cash. Some of it – nearly US$1 trillion in 2014 (Kar and Spanjers 2014) – moves illicitly out of developing countries. Other amounts are hidden away – US$7.6 trillion are sequestered into the 82 tax havens that are littered across the world (Zucman 2014). And then, closer to home and more prosaically, many of us go work in anonymous buildings – odourless glass boxes that enclose offices in city centres (Grubbauer 2014) or low-sitting warehouses on industrial estates (Pawley 1998).

This all seems far away from the notion of the material that demands the direct commitment of our senses. The objects of capitalism are to hand, however. This chapter focuses on how certain design artefacts and processes are active in habituating people to particular ways of being and acting that align with and, indeed, produce neoliberal behaviours and dispositions. This isn't a brainwashing effect. It's a simple set of affects that adjust the senses to the rhythms, concerns and purposes of contemporary capitalism. Is there a certain form of design culture that is specific to the workings of neoliberalism? What is the neoliberal object? And is there a neoliberal cognitive style?

There are objects that give themselves over more obviously to this affective domain of neoliberal action than others. Most blatantly and brutally, a plethora of books and digital products exist for children to learn the arts of saving and investment. Bochner and Bochner's *The Totally Awesome Money Book for Kids* (with cartoon, games, riddles and quizes) (2007) and Catzky's *Not Your Parent's Money Book* (with advice on 'making, saving and spending your OWN money') (2010) are just two examples of these. But the affective domain of neoliberalism works in other ways, too.

There are the five basic senses: seeing, touching, hearing, smelling, tasting. We can push further, though, into other sensorial subdivisions of counting, calculating and timing, for instance. Or, moving through, moving around, moving into, moving away from. Speeding up and slowing down. Distancing it; nearing it; becoming it; being it. These are everyday actions that, at times, can reinforce what it is to be in the contemporary, capitalist world.

This is all part of a general disciplining to a 'technology of the self' (Foucault 1988). It is where individuals learn – often in tacit or unconscious ways – acceptable forms of conduct in accordance with how best they want to be perceived within a power system. It is where they learn to regulate their behaviour. It is where subjects not only discover what to do with their money, but 'a way of working that money' and thus work on themselves (Martin 2002: 16–17; Allon 2010).

Some of this chapter discusses the design of environments and devices that are active in financialisation such as the offices and equipment of stockbrokers or the layout of high street banks. Some of it shows how the design profession itself developed to both produce and engage in the demands of neoliberal systems. Some of it, however, steps back to consider objects that produce a kind of 'financialist sensorium' – the fine-tuning of cognitive assets that allow people to function better in the wider world of contemporary capitalism.

By beginning with an historical approach to these issues, this chapter charts the confluence of developments in design, changes in political economy and the affective order from the mid-1980s. In effect, this covers the domains of design, production and consumption that make up cultures of design. Indeed, I would argue that it is precisely this constellation, its intensity and dynamic relationships between its parts that make up what we understand as design culture in the contemporary age, framed, as it is, by neoliberal, capitalist systems. Around this, reflecting and informing it, are particular academic viewpoints that have emerged in relation to the changes and developments that exist here. They provide significant and important intellectual markers onto this historical development.

Ultimately, then, the aim of this chapter is to push against any notion that economics is just about abstracted data of statistics. Instead, it makes a case for paying greater attention to the material, visual, spatial and temporal qualities of design that bear onto economic action and thinking at a most intimate and very real level.

The next section goes back to some of the broad academic discourses that were in use in the 1980s, showing an alignment of cultural analysis, selfhood and economic change. Some resonance with this was also to be found in the design profession. The section that follows therefore focuses on very specific developments in the London design scene at this time. It shows how design processes were made quicker while becoming even more attuned to commercial demands of profit. To some extent, these were responding to emerging opportunities, particularly those afforded by changes in shopping and consumer practices. The chapter then returns to a series of design objects of the mid-1980s that, I argue, had a more intimate and direct role in the construction of neoliberal sensibilites among citizens. Contemporaneous academic discourses, partly emanating from analyses of digital culture, are then discussed in order to explain this process further. I then 'fast-forward' to more recent scholarly considerations of the devices that are employed in financial and other forms of trade. This then provides a conceptual grounding in and alertness to how some design artefacts might be functioning as neoliberal objects. As such, it prepares the way for many of the arguments in subsequent chapters.

POSTMODERNISM AND POST-FORDISM

During the 1980s it was particularly fashionable in the arts and humanities to talk about 'postmodernism' or 'postmodernity' (e.g. Foster 1985; Huyssen 1986; Umbral 1987). The rigours of mid-twentieth century life, with its beliefs in a shared destiny and adherence to structure, had finally given way to a world of surfaces, fragmentation and multilayering, it seemed. Subsequently, a new emphasis would be placed on identity and the role of taste and consumption as vehicles for its construction (Campbell 1987; Miller 1987; Hebdige 1988). These provided important departures for thinking about the interface of design and everyday life as alternatives to discussions that focused primarily on the work of designers.

However, while their approaches varied, these texts rarely considered the economic processes of consumption itself. How labour was structured and rewarded, the availability of expendable income, financial priorities: these considerations were largely absent.

A related narrative was emerging, though, that paid more attention to a move in economic practices from mass manufacture, Fordist systems to flexible, just-in-time or post-Fordist processes (e.g. Sabel 1982). This account wasn't limited to changes in productive systems, however. It also included the considerations of transformations of the self, of social practices and relations and new ways by which personal and collective aspirations are played out in this process.

In October 1988, a special edition of the UK-based magazine *Marxism Today* on these 'new times' appeared. The aim of this much celebrated edition was to reflect on the trajectories of capitalism that had been instigated from the 1970s. This involved a discussion not only of its economic processes but of cultural and political ones. In it, cultural theorist Stuart Hall argued that post-Fordism involved not just a changing economic system, but that the self was and would also be more subjective, more incomplete, more multiple, dissipated and fragmented (Hall 1988). Of particular influence here was the work of Laclau and Mouffe (1985) in connecting a post-Marxist analysis to cultural change (Bowman 2007). As labour would involve more multi-tasking, as production would be more flexible to produce specialist batches, as the state would move from being concerned national to a greater variety of territorial scales, so individuals would adopt more subject-positions (Hebdige 1985; Moulaert and Swyngedouw 1989). In this account, then, the 'freeing-up' of economies through deregulation also entailed a freeing-up of the self.

The economic, cultural and social developments that were instigated in the 1980s in the USA and Western Europe have been described in other ways. One has been to term this process the 'end of organised capitalism' or otherwise 'disorganised capitalism' (Offe 1985; Lash and Urry 1987). In such accounts, the transition from more state-regulated and unified economies to independent and fragmented business practices is part of a wider shift away from a dominance of the state, large-scale primary material extraction and industrial production. The democratisation and liberalisation of Latin American countries in the 1980s, the break-up of the Soviet socialist states into the 1990s or the economic liberalisation of China – leading to more widespread market-based business practices – may also be read as extensions of this process.

Design would play a greater role here. It would shape shopping centres to make them places you went to spend time rather than just buy things. It would package products to make them more desirable, wherever they came from. It would make companies look more competitive in their outward appearances and in their internal communications. New ways were taking shape by which design would come to bear on and configure people's lives. People themselves were discovering new uses and meanings of design. There was, in other words, a design culture turn going on.

At that time, none of these things was labelled under 'neoliberalism'. It would take nearly 30 years for this term to enter into more frequent use, but all of the examples mentioned above were central to an intensified way of operating in the world that was emerging in the 1980s. There would be successive developments of the locations, technologies, practices and structures of neoliberalism in the ensuing decades and through each of these, new emphases would be laid. The design profession has grown and become more complex with these, adopting new roles while maintaining old ones.

This is not to say that this mid-1980s deregulation turn has led to a 'free-for-all' in which the commercial marketplace or subjective identities are unleashed to invent themselves. The rise of design doesn't mean untrammelled and unending fashioning according to whims and shifting tastes. Indeed, much of this chapter and the next will show that design is embedded into the shaping of disciplining structures, whether in its own processes or in many of its objects.

The next section reviews the fundamental changes of the mid-1980s in more detail. Around these, the more macro-context of Western governments' deregulation of financial and trade sectors needs to be understood alongside changes in the design industry itself.

LONDON 1986

Neoliberalism and design culture are both global in their reach. And yet, by reviewing the confluence of their consolidation in a very specific location and time – London 1986 – we can understand their qualities and relationships in greater depth. On the one hand, the case of the UK capital presents, here, a particularly intensified and dynamic version of these. The changes taking place in the political economy under the prime ministership of Margaret Thatcher at the time were hugely influential across Europe and, later, much of the rest of the world (Hall 1988). At the same time, London was and remains home to the largest concentration of designers and creative industries' specialists in the world (Freeman 2011). The micro-stories of London design in the mid-1980s fed into and off larger structural changes in the economy while also being, ultimately, highly significant in themselves for the way we conceptualise design culture.

On 26 September 1986, the world's first weekly design magazine appeared on newsagents' stands. Aptly titled *Design Week*, it provided news, analysis, gossip and commentary, mostly centred on London's burgeoning design scene. It was also the only design magazine that addressed all design sectors. Costing £0.80, its mainstay was its classified ads. Here, in this pre-internet environment, consultancies could seek designers at short notice to work on cross-discplinary design projects as they came in. This was a pivotal moment for the design industry. The magazine ads facilitated the speeding-up of design processes with an increased project-orientation of multidisciplinary teams (Myerson 2011).

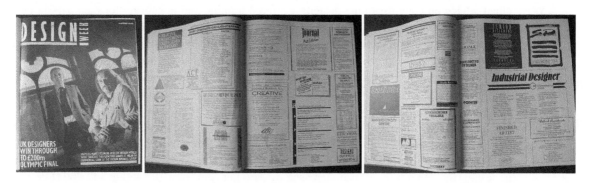

2.1   Cover and classified ads section of first edition of *Design Week*, 26 September 1986 (Photos: Guy Julier)

On 27 October 1986, there was another pivotal moment – more significant in global terms. This was the deregulation of the London Stock Market. Thenceforth trading commissions were no longer fixed, overseas investors could operate on the London markets, the roles of broker and market maker were merged and deals could take place by telephone and computer. In short, money could be moved quicker, further and easier. Money could move in new ways. With the Big Bang, turnover on the London Stock Market practically doubled overnight while face-to-face trading dropped to a quarter of previous levels through 1986 (Clemons and Weber 1990).

Each of these events were tied up in new working practices. They signalled longer, more flexible hours, a speeding-up of transactions and a loosening of divisions between specialists.

But beyond the ways by which design or finance were done, these were significant moments because they formed part of a series of fundamental changes taking place in the West: changes that not only meant the emergence of new ways of doing business, manufacturing and distributing products, configuring services but also how the world was viewed and understood.

Between the first edition of *Design Week* and the Big Bang, the Business Design Centre was opened. This former agriculture hall was converted into a permanent building to house 124 design product showrooms, 2,300 square metres for design exhibitions, conference facilities and three restaurants, parking for over 300 cars. It was intended as a 'one-stop shop for designers and their clients'. It had been estimated that designers spent 40 per cent of their time sourcing products rather than liaising with clients or actually designing and this environment would speed up their job (Blackwell 1986: 8). More importantly, the initiative represented the provision of infrastructural services to the design industry on an expanded and more entrepreneurial scale.

The opening of the Business Design Centre coincided with the establishment of the Design Business Association (DBA). This organisation was a direct spin-off from the Chartered Society of Designers (CSD) but its foundation suggests a new orientation in how design was thought about. Since its inception in 1930, the CSD's chief commitment was to the professionalisation of design. This was a largely inward-looking strategy that emphasised the establishment of professional 'codes of conduct' within the design industry in order to gain recognition and respect outside itself (Armstrong 2015). Contrastingly, the DBA sought a more dynamic, commercially oriented relationship with potential design clients in promoting the interests of its membership. Thus it compiled and published a directory of design consultancies and their services; it provided client advice on commissioning design; it offered training and mentoring for members to help them deal with the commercial rigours of running a design business. Just as the Design Business Centre was created to build a physical infrastructure to bring designers and clients closer together and foster more efficient modes of working, so the Design Business Association provided a professional environment that was less concerned with normative identities for designers and more encouraging in promoting more flexible ways of operating for and interfacing with clients.

As the UK design industry expanded rapidly through this period so, at least for a while, CSD membership rose steeply to peak at 9,800 in 1989. It is telling that after this date membership declined rapidly through the following decade, only returning to its 1963 level of around 2,500 by the early 2000s (Armstrong 2015: 349). By comparison, between 1994 and 2001, employment in design (including fashion) had increased by 31.6 per cent from 108,400 to 142,700 (Creative Industries Task Force 2001). A key factor in this was the proliferation of new modes of design practice against which the CSD seemed outdated. In 1989, the CSD only provided for six categories of design (product, fashion and textile, interior, graphic design, education and design management), while specialisms such as retail, exhibition, packaging or corporate identity design, for example, were becoming increasingly prominent and subject to their own specific skills and knowledge bases. As these emerged, so traditional thinking around how the sectors within design would be termed and accounted for became continuously challenged, subsequently (e.g. Fairs 2005). The evasion of normative procedures and professional identities by the design industry is in no small part the result of its constant adherence to 'following the money' by inventing new specialisms to exploit technological and business opportunities.

The mid-1980s also saw movements within the internal operations of design consultancies themselves towards a sharper focus on accounting and workflow. A few of the larger, more well-known design consultancies had already declared a starker adherence to focusing on turnover and profit by floating themselves on the stock exchange. These included Allied International Designers (floated 1980), Fitch (1982), Michael Peters Group (1983) and Addison (1984) (Julier 2014: ch. 2). In turn, this led, for some, to their massification in terms of numbers (Fitch employed 300 in 1987) and expansion in terms of reach. Capitalisation programmes allowed these to add competencies such as consumer or futures research.

With this massification within design studios came further challenges in their management. Prior to the 1980s, most design consultancies worked on a pretty much laissez faire way with regard to their accountancy systems. With larger-scale projects, particularly for retail design that involved the coordination of graphics, interior and product design, so the design process had to be managed across several individuals and teams in the studio. Timesheets, hitherto anathema to the long-hours but more 'relaxed' culture of studio practice, were introduced. Workflows had to be devised and managed. Specialist teams within the studio became cost centres. New employees had to be inducted into the design consultancy's particular way of processing projects. The profit-motive was no longer to be a backroom issue for the account handlers. Rather, greater efficiency and quicker turnover of design projects became imperative. A new environment of 'commercial reality' took centre-stage (Southgate 1994; Cochrane 2010).

During the 1980s, many clients were experiencing work with a design consultancy for the first time and thus the need for designers to explain what they were doing (and thus charging for) was paramount. The retail design consultancy Fitch, for instance, coined its 'Perception, Concept, Action' structuring of projects for the sake both of client understanding and for its own staff training (Cochrane 2010). It is difficult to say whether or not this shift in working practices had an effect on the finished look of objects and environments, but it did ensure quicker turnaround of projects and an easier outflow of volume in design projects. It also helped build trust with clients and streamline the processing of projects. British design, one might say, was being increasingly packaged for its clients.

The year 1986 represents a watershed moment for the UK design industry, centred on London. The big things that were happening within larger design consultancies – flotations, mergers and acquisitions, streamlining and efficiency measures, enhanced client-focus – set the standard for the much longer 'tail' of small design studios. This was not least because these developments were being reported through *Design Week* as they happened, or gossiped about at the Design Business Centre.

If design moved up a gear – if there is a design culture turn here – this was in the intensification of linkages between designers, producers, clients and consumers. This resonates with wider changes in commercial working practices, in particular as found in changes in the reorganisation of stockbroking and banking activities. The professional environment and aspirations of design mirrored the increased flexibility and speed afforded by the Big Bang for the financial sector. More directly, some designers speculated on how the Big Bang would provide client growth for them as a halo of law and accountancy firms as well as management consultancies that were expanded around the stock market and financial services industries (Blackwell 1986).

The move from manufacturing to an economy dominated by service industries at this time changed the priorities for designers. The decline of manufacturing in Britain from the 1970s had seen the growth of its service sector. Employment in manufacturing dropped in the UK from 38.4 per cent in 1960 to 22.5 per cent in 1990; Britain's share of world manufacturing exports dropped from 14.2 per cent in 1964 to 7.6 per cent in 1986 (Barberis and May 1993). Nonetheless, during the 'Thatcher decade' of 1979–89, employment in the service sector grew by 2 million, roughly the same figure as the decline in manufacturing employment. Output in the services sector grew by 28.8 per cent as against nearly 10 per cent in manufacturing (Wells 1989). Concurrently, in the USA, between 1980 and 2005, hours worked in service industries grew by 30 per cent while those who laboured in production and craft dropped by 38 per cent (Autor and Dorn 2013).

To draw the focus more tightly on this growth of service industries and how this affected design thinking, let us consider the design of banks. Hitherto, high street banks had occupied architecturally prominent buildings that emphasised their historical pedigree and importance. The majority of their interior space was given over to backroom offices and archiving. Two important changes took place for banks in the 1980s. The first was in the move of accounting information to more centralised, digital storage facilities away from individual banks, thus freeing up space in branches (Wilkinson and Balmer 1996). The second was in the deregulation of banks. The Building Societies Act 1986 allowed building societies to operate as banks. In turn, this introduced far greater competition for customers and diversification in terms of the services offered by both banks and building societies. As a result, banks were redesigned to be more outward-facing. Fitch's redesign for the Midland bank branches in the mid-1980s made them look more welcoming – places to browse new financial products as much as undertake transactions. These featured the introduction of soft furnishings, a brighter colour palette, multi-directional circulation (rather than the standard 'bank queue') and greater visibility of bank staff.

More broadly in this period, we find new forms of material, visual, spatial and temporal organisation of designed environments. This was most detectable in the ways by which shopping centres, retail parks and supermarkets were reworked (Fitch and Knobel 1990).

The design culture turn has involved an increased emphasis on ease of movement within real and virtual spaces, the manipulation of different temporal rhythms within these, the 'softening' of the relationship between consumer and service provider and the more general greater emphasis laid on the semiotic field.

There was, in short, a cognitive shift taking place at this moment in history. This was to do with changes in the shopping environment, but, as we shall see in the next section, a number of other design objects and environments are indicative of this as well.

OBJECT ENVIRONMENTS, INTENSIFIED MOVEMENT, EPISODIC MEASUREMENT

In 1986, the Nintendo Entertainment System (NES) was introduced in Europe, having been tentatively rolled out in the USA the year before and in Japan in 1983. This followed a slump in video games console sales, 1983–85, hitting many producers, in particular Atari. The NES included a much advanced control that was more ergonomic, comfortable and intuitive. Video gaming at home became a more embodied activity as compared to earlier consoles that were clunky and difficult to manage. This, combined with its graphic language, meant that games developers could design much more sophisticated, episodic games (Kim 2010). The NES was released with Super Mario

Bros., which became a significant entry-level game for consumers. A further development was in opening up games design to third-party developers, thereby stimulating creative enterprise and a diversity of games within a prescribed digital format. The NES provided home computer gaming that upped the stakes in terms of bringing bodily action into the object environment of Super Mario Bros. It promised a gaming space in which progress was clearly calculated. Each of its episodes would be a measured experience. The overall game was broken down into audited parts, just as cost centres in some design consultancies (as seen earlier) had become.

In 1985, Philips introduced the Magnavox, the first universal remote control that could interact with both TV and VCRs. The spread of the use of the TV remote from the mid-1980s had serious implications for how the green-eyed monster in the corner of the room was used. While multiple cable stations and pre-recorded programmes were available, the universal remote facilitated 'grazing behaviour' and 'zapping' that in turn re-structured TV scheduling and advertising approaches, and contributed to the integration apparatus and entertainment corporations such as through the merger of Sony and Columbia in 1989. The TV remote was to be found in 27 per cent of US households in 1985; by 1993 it was in 90 per cent (Bellamy and Walker 1996). Again,

2.2   Nintendo Entertainment System and Super Mario Bros. game, 1985 (Photo: Emilio J. Rodríguez-Posada, Wikimedia Commons)

product use became more immediate, more embodied, more about the user's agency in determining the narrative. Like the NES, hardware and software were brought together with the key point being at the interface, be it the TV remote or the games console control.

In 1985, the Silicon Valley company Adobe Systems introduced the first version of the PostScript computer programming language. This meant that in computer graphics, for the first time, text and image could be combined on one page, on screen. Previously, these would have to be generated separately to be laboriously and literally cut and pasted onto paperboard. Second, it streamlined PC-to-printer communication so that these no longer needed separate drivers and protocols. Most importantly, PostScript instigated 'what you see is what you get' between what was on the PC screen and what was outputted through the printer. This provided the means for desktop printing, revolutionising the entire print industry by cutting out the artisanal stage of typesetting that was carried out by printers. Graphic design to print would be quicker and cheaper. It also meant that designers could begin to play more inventively with fonts on screen, without the burden of specifying and explaining to a third party. In 1986, Adobe released its Type Library, it thereby becoming a digital type foundry and opening up the range of fonts available (Pfiffner 2002). Such developments were wrapped around the appearance of Apple personal desktop computers such as the Macintosh 128k (1984), the Macintosh Plus (1986), the Macintosh SE (1987) and the Mac II (1987). Like the TV remote, new, more deeply entangled relationships between hardware and software were being forged wherein technical and commercial barriers between these were being removed. Faster and more direct engagement between bodily action and outcome were being fostered. Movement between creative conception (of a page layout, for example) and its realisation into print was shortened and intensified. Feedback loops of input and output were shorter.

2.3   Macintosh Plus computer, 1986 (Photo: SP, Wikimedia
Commons)

In the mid-1980s, across Western Europe and beyond to Japan, interior design moved up a gear. This is most forcefully seen in the design of a number of bars, restaurants and clubs by a small but influential set of architects. Crudely, these signalled an intensification of visual references within the interior. Walls, floors, ceilings and fittings were dramatically packed full with elements taken from mass media – real or imaginary. Rather than focusing visitors on a dominant feature (the bar, tables or the dance floor) that afforded a central activity to the location, they moved through a scenography. This included Eduardo Samsò's design for the nightclub Nick Havanna in 1986 and Alfredo Arribas's Network Cafè in 1988, both in Barcelona. These were dedicated to layering-up the narratives in these spaces with multiple references to film and TV (Julier 1991: ch. 4).

The most renowned example of this type was Caffè Bongo, which opened in Tokyo in 1986 and was designed by the British architectural studio Branson Coates. In 1986, monetary policy in Japan shifted gear, with low interest rates stimulating credit and consumerism. This created what is know as the 'Japanese bubble economy' that lasted until 1991 (Kerr 2016). Caffè Bongo was a clear signifier of this change. Situated on Tokyo's busiest crossroad, it presented a collage of tangled Roman classical architectural forms, held together by bent girders and crumbling brickwork. On the outside, it seemed that an airplane had crashed through the building, its wing and engines poking out into the street. Through these lavish and exaggerated forms, the architecture of this bar was like a chaotic avant-garde theatre space (Coates 2012). As such, these became semi-immersive spaces to move through – scenographies for the night-time economy. Writing in 1988, Nigel Coates fittingly acknowledged the need, in his words, 'to reactivate the otherwise empty social stage, which television as a phenomenon (but not as a language) appeared to have forced us to abandon' (1988: 98).

How best do we sum up these shifts of the 1980s? In his theorising, Coates saw his own design work, and society in general, as 'post-TV' in the sense of it not being about the passive reception of such media. Rather, media environments were things to be and move *in*. Or, as Scott Lash later described, 'Culture is now three-dimensional, as much tactile as visual or textual, all around us and inhabited, lived in rather than encountered in a separate realm as a representation' (2002: 149). The universal TV remote allowed easy flow between channels, between devices and between the viewer and the apparatus for viewing. The video games console bridged between the player and the games setting, itself configured as a set of episodic events where skill is measured by speed, scores and progression through these. Computer graphics software increased the sense of speed and power of the designer while also moving the production of print into the office or home, further breaking down professional and productive demarcations.

Coates further claimed that 'We ... have been deprogrammed from the constraints of a manufacturing society towards one which manipulates excess' (1988: 98). The multi-channelled possibilities of cable TV, video games, computers or designer bars may be read as providing access to excess but also a kind of lightening against the deadweight of traditional industry. They also increased the notion of individual agency, albeit limited to highly bounded settings.

The examples that have been discussed in this section share three qualities with different emphases. These qualities connect to a set of economic priorities and practices that were emergent at their time. These are aggregated into Table 2.1.

Table 2.1 Summary of cognitive effects of neoliberal objects

Quality	Example	Cognitive effect
Object environments	shopping centres narrative architecture TV universal remotes games consoles digitally mediated stock exchange	new sense of embodied action where movement is 'virtualised' new forms of technology–human interfaces multidirectionality in bounded spaces
Intensified movement	desktop publishing customer-facing banks	concentration of interactions speeding up of processes
Episodic measurement	computer games cost centres	breaking down of tasks to measurable sections emotionality and calculation are combined (counting becomes exciting) multilinear narrative structures

This 1986 convergence of things, actions and possibilities may otherwise be thought of, in their assemblage, as an atmosphere. Baudrillard (1995 [1968]) understood the notion of 'atmosphere' as something made through the collectivity of signs carried in images, objects and spaces (or, indeed, colours, materials, textures and so on) that produce a structured whole. More recently, others have pushed atmosphere as an affect (McCormack 2008; Anderson 2009; Ruddick, 2010; Ash 2012). Anthropologist Kathleen Stewart calls this meeting of atmosphere and affect 'a force field in which people find themselves … not an effect of other forces but a lived affect or capacity to affect and to be affected that pushes a present into a composition, an expressivity, the sense of potentiality and event' (2011: 452). Thus an atmosphere does not sit dormant. Part of its production is in the living and feeling of it. Therefore the intensifications of 1986 may be seen as generating a cognitive and experiential shift. A new somatic memory was required here, linking body to informational space and different vocabularies of affect.

Let us go one step further. Certain objects get you thinking and acting in certain ways. The way they are configured to be used in particular modes – otherwise, their scripting (Akrich 1995; Fallan 2008) – 'programme' highly internalised physical and psychological states that, nonetheless, are sympathetic to certain economic dispositions. Väliaho (2014) discusses the idea of somatic memory and digital information in relation to 'the neoliberal brain'. He shows how visual-kinetic representations, particularly to be found in video games, and their affect produces certain dispositions and forecloses others. In turn, this brings into line certain economic behaviours. They contribute to the anticipatory practices that attempt to rationalise and preempt future events within a logic of calculation (Ash 2010: 661; Stiegler 2010: 18; Ash 2012: 7–9). In the context of video games, Väliaho writes about the live map that often appears in the corner of the screen. It helps you see where you are but also plan your next movements. The map therefore becomes a space of anticipation. Generalising from this observation, he observes that 'At the heart of finance capitalism lies a model of neoliberal brainhood that is centered on imaginative mappings of future possibilities and pre-emptive measures' (Väliaho 2014: 58). Things are active in constituting people as calculating and rational in relation to financial decision-making and action, or, in other words, in the production of *homo œconomicus* (Foucault 2008).

HUMAN–MACHINE INTERACTION

The way by which a concentration of new media forms produces new forms of cognition had been pursued by Marshall McLuhan in the 1960s. McLuhan had developed the argument that media forms impact on bodily dispositions and outlooks in his 1964 book *Understanding Media: The Extensions of Man*. He argued that these had profound social effects, transforming people to have a greater emotional depth and sense of inter-connectedness. New media transforms the mind and the central nervous system, facilitating new ways of perceiving and knowing the world and its people, he posited. The effect isn't just one-way, though: media become 'extensions of man', ways by which our senses get externalised. Twenty years later, this view became even more apposite.

It seems not to be coincidental that Donna Haraway wrote the first version of her 'Cyborg Manifesto' (2006 [1985]) in this mid-1980s period we have been discussing. Here she noted the loosening of the boundaries between animal and human, animal-human and machine, and the physical and non-physical. Fascinated by the economic and technological changes that were taking place – and, moreover, their effects on social life, including gender roles – she argued against the idea of essential properties of objects, wanting to draw more attention to how artefacts are absorbed into networks and systems which, in turn, function to facilitate movement between different types of materiality, lived experience or identities.

Along with Haraway, several other authors were concerned during the mid-1980s with the relationship of artefacts to humans; in particular they were spurred on by how advances in digital culture were changing this connection. Sherry Turkle had already published *The Second Self: Computers and the Human Spirit* (1984), in which she callenged the division between the physical and the social. Here the term 'interaction' appears not just as something that is exclusive in terms of human-to-human communication, but also that happens between human and machine. In this, humans get 'rewired', their cognitive processes become adjusted to encompass the language and processes of digital technology. They become hybrid with these machines.

Similarly, Lucy Suchman (1987) argued that cognition was situated and contextual. This means that far from being fixed, it is formed in ever changing ways according to dynamic interactions that take place between humans and their material environments. Meanwhile, Winograd and Flores (1986) were also concerned with the functioning of the interface. Again, they saw this as being about a dynamic relationship rather than a separate realm. The user is *in* it rather than a separate viewer *of* it. In this way, the analysis breaks from Cartesian dualism where the experience of external phenomena is assumed to largely engage the mind rather than the whole body.

Apart from Haraway, these authors were primarily concerned with understanding the relationships of technological and human processes. After all, Suchman was working as an anthropologist at Rank Xerox in Palo Alto, California at this time; Winograd and Flores were both working at Stanford University and closely engaged with advances in the digital industries of Palo Alto as well. Nonetheless, the coincidence of their work with the kinds of developments that are described in the previous section are stunning.

It is as well to note that these authors were also being speculative, casting forward along the vectors that were being unleashed in multiple ways at this time. Equally, they were providing general observations and insights on socio-technical change; they were less concerned with how the human–machine interface was applied. What kind of interactions take place when using numeric data as compared with video gaming, for instance? And how does materiality function in different modes? In the next section we shall develop this question of the human–machine interface, in particular in relation to financialist processes.

THE NEOLIBERAL SENSORIUM

If, to return to McLuhan's maxim that a transformation of the mind and the central nervous system takes place and that the senses get externalised in devices, so we must turn to a more detailed understanding of what this means in terms of the content of different sensorial epochs.

Let us fast-forward the debate a bit. As the influence of financialisation began to take even greater hold in the 2000s, so social scientists turned their attention to a detailed understanding of the world of stockbrokers, fund managers and bankers (e.g. Knorr Cetina and Preda 2004). For the sociologist Donald MacKenzie (2008), this would include close study of the material environments that they use and inhabit: cables, screens, office chairs and other paraphenalia come under close study. Part of what he achieves is a clear understanding of how 'market devices', such as algorithms and multiple screens for tracking market trends, guide the decision-making processes in stockbroking. MacKenzie's work is important to thinking about the material culture that is specific to workers in financialisation. It shows how it is active in creating a specific *habitus* and sets of dispositions in stockbroking.

The work of Karin Knorr Cetina also engages close observation of the environments and devices that stockbrokers use, but perhaps takes the analysis closer to thinking about their affective elements. In the first instance, she shows how screens are 'epistemic things': they show information but also do some of the 'thinking'; they carry knowledge but also do some of the work of interpreting that knowledge (Knorr Cetina and Bruegger 2000). They are also always partial and unfinished, not least because the information they carry is subject to constant updating. However, in a more complex sense they are also partial in that they pertain to complex networks – other computers, stock markets, brokers and so on – whose participation in these creates an ever changing constellation that each part is responding to (Knorr Cetina 2001). They are 'global in scope' but 'microstructured in character'; in other words, they are networked around the world but are highly detailed and focused in their constituent elements. Thus they are 'apresent' in that they do not necessarily 'fit' their immediate vicinity but are connected to other nodes around the world that are equally apresent. As such they are active in a highly refined 'timeworld' where temporal coordination between other stockbroking nodes is vital for their functioning (Knorr Cetina 2003).

In a wider-reaching study, Nigel Thrift picks up on this question of the relationships between devices, space and the senses in contemporary capitalism (Thrift 2008). Thrift identifies the notion of 'qualculation' as central to everyday practices, a term developed by Callon and Law (2005). This involves the qualitative assessment of phenomena through data, digital or otherwise (as in 'How's my driving?' or 'How many *likes* did it get?'). Thrift argues that this kind of continual assessment at every encounter is rife in modern life. Cochoy (2008) takes the example of pushing a trolley around a supermarket, constantly making calculations as to value-for-money versus quality. The shopping list, the trolley and packaging information, for example, all work as devices that inform this process. More generally, in everyday life, Thrift lists five processes that involve a changed sense of evaluation of one's relationship to space and data. These are: the prosthesis for cognitive assistance (think: Google maps on a smartphone); provisional spatial coordination (think: continual tracking of parcel delivery); continual access to information (think: newsfeeds at railway stations and in airports); an opening up of metrics (think: the multiple measurement systems in exercise apps); that places are less places of return (think: continual adjustments of supermarket aisles or updating of smartphone apps).

There is a danger of taking Thrift's claims to be technologically deterministic – that it is such devices alone that shape social and cultural behaviours. At the heart of his argument, however, is an attempt to try to understand how cognitive processes have altered as part of economic, cultural and technological change. More prosaically, he shows that, for instance, our sense of touch has altered as technological devices and economic structures and processes have come to bear on ordinary lives. Manual performances alter. 'Push', 'hit', 'stroke', 'caress', 'seize': their meanings change (Thrift 2004: 598). In this, we need to accept that cognition is embodied and not a purely mental act. This runs counter to Cartesian conceptions of a mind–body split, as, indeed, Winograd and Flores (1986) had already noted. Computer games and shopping centres, for example, involve bodily responses within calculative, episodic architectures.

By extension, we may see this different corporeal action as part of a performance of wider economic processes. The loosening of trade and financial regulation in the 1980s implied a heightened sense of mobilities. It also meant a greater sense of flexibility – in which direction one might go, what hours one might work, where one might invest surplus finance. The growth of the use of internal accounting procedures within companies where each section becomes a cost centre required to make its financial case implies a sharper attunement to the calculation and demonstration of value.

It is useful to seek other examples of the various arguments put forward by Knorr Cetina and Thrift in order to explore further design manifestations and everyday practices that demonstrate and generalise their viewpoints. One clear example is in the design of objects that are concerned with coordination, temporality and ordering, such as the Filofax. This analogue, leather-bound personal organiser that involved paper inserts of calendars, addresses, notepaper and other supports for capturing and ordering data originated in the USA in the 1910s but was branded as the Filofax in the UK in 1921 (Hall 2010). It was not until the mid-1980s that sales multiplied. Indeed, it became closely associated with the acquisitive Yuppie generation of that decade (Campbell and Wheeler 1988). The Filofax may be viewed as the forerunner to the digitally-based personal organisers that replaced it by the end of the 1980s. These would include the personal digital assistant (PDA), first released by Psion in 1984, and subsequent versions through to the many smartphone apps from the 2000s that undertake this task. The Filofax therefore encouraged habituation to the interactions that would become more routine with digital information technologies (McMurdo 1989).

The Filofax and the PDA played roles in a general shift towards calculating, allocating and coordinating time-slots. Through much of the twentieth century, it was, arguably, more commonplace to view time in everyday life as a continuum. Cotidian tasks would not necessarily be assigned to particular moments in the day or week, lasting a certain duration of time. Instead, activities tended to unfold from one to another. The late twentieth century saw a shift towards thinking more in terms of units of time that often have to be coordinated with other people's units of time (Southerton 2003). Indeed, this lends to a perceived shortage of time even though, in actuality, this has not been the case for most people in the West, at least, in recent years (Sullivan and Gershuny 2004). Finding a 'window' in one's diary, billing for hours spent on a task, synchronising a meet-up with friends to undertake a leisure activity are all examples of this practice of 'time squeeze'. The bubble of Filofax sales in the mid-1980s evidences a shift towards object-environments that take part in the qualculation of time. More lately, digital platforms conspire in this process.

Flicking through one's iCalendar or booking a gym session via a website engage those bodily activities that are at the heart of neoliberal dispositions. Just as stockbrokers coordinate temporally between global marketplaces or calculate delivery times on commodities, so these kind of activities are often reproduced in our leisure practices.

Neoliberalisation involves a transformation of ourselves and the way we design our lives.

Contemporary capitalism requires a productive, efficient, healthy and sane population. This is partly created through continuous and routine management of the human body and is where Foucault's notion of 'biopower' is useful (Foucault 1998 [1976]). Biopower reaches into mundane aspects of human life, such as relationships, communication, creativity, problem solving. It involves a wholesale mustering of the self, not in a submissive or coerced way, but in a way that both promises liberty and holds individuals accountable to those structures that promise that liberty. In terms of contemporary capitalism, it could be argued that the specific 'type' required here is that of a flexible, adaptable and self-organising subject (Picard 2013). The neoliberal sensorium, and its devices, do some of the work in producing this type. Neoliberal devices can work at different scales, as we shall see in the next section.

BUDAPEST 1996

In mid-September of 1996, I happened to be in Budapest. I was there to continue some research I was conducting on the impact that the post-Soviet transition to a market society was having on design in Hungary. My visit to the Hungarian capital coincided with a public debate regarding a proposal to do a 'gift-wrap' of one of the city's most historically important bridges that spanned the Danube. The Hungarian subsidiary of the Coca-Cola Company was offering, to the General Assembly of the city authorities, to do a Christmas makeover of the Chain Bridge for free. Rather than put up more billboards or run TV ads, Coca-Cola wanted to take a more 'public relations' led approach in Central and Eastern Europe and this was their first go at it (Fejos 2000). The 'goodwill plan' would brighten the city and be seen as a generous act, they reckoned.

Rumours were circulating as to what this 'goodwill plan' would mean. One was that it would be decorated in red, white and green – the colours of the Hungarian flag – but the red would be in the hue of Coca-Cola, not Hungary. Whatever the plan, it was clear that, for many Budapest citizens, this was an affront to local sensibilities. Here was a multinational company packaging up the city for business, infiltrating its public space with disregard for its local and national heritage, identity and environment (Harper 1999). In the event, the proposal had already been rejected by the Budapest General Assembly while the public debate raged on.

A Hungarian friend of mine and I sat in a café discussing this affair. Kati also saw this as part of a general invasion of corporate capitalism into the streets of Budapest.

'But isn't this just the same as having those statues to Lenin and Marx all over the city as you did during the Soviet period?' I asked.

Kati looked at me aghast.

'No!' she exclaimed. 'When we saw those statues we could just put them out of mind and not think of the Communist regime. They were separate from us. But this is different. Coca-Cola. We see an advert. We see it in a shop. We have it in our fridge. We drink it. It's all around us. And then we *become* it.'

In this brief and heated remark, I realised that Kati wasn't just summing up her views on Coca-Cola, she was talking about the aesthetics of capitalism. In a country going through rapid change from a state-controlled economy to marketisation, the signs of multinational corporations looked even more stark and impactful on the streetscape. But it also reached right into everyday lives, our homes and even our own bodies. It was a magic potion to be drunk, a subtle adjustment of the prism, a texture to be felt and, in the deep recesses of cognition, something to be known.

One might leave this episode as a straightforward illustration of the claim that 'we live in an increasingly visual world, where the saturation of images in everyday life operates', a claim that is so often repeated among scholars of cultural studies or visual culture. However, I want to go further with this. I want to push the notion that meaning and habituation are more than about looking: they involve more embodied acts that work deep into muscle memory, taste buds and neural pathways.

The design culture turn isn't homogenous, just as processes of neoliberalisation aren't. Different speeds, relationships and discourses are active in distinctive locations and moments in history. In Budapest, for instance, the changing conditions of political economy and design culture triggered related discussions that revolved around national identity, the public realm and the environment.

This Chain Bridge/Coca-Cola anecdote connects private perspectives to public debates. It shows how design functions in 'normalising' economic change. It's just what happens. It is simpler than the other kinds of neoliberal objects I have discussed earlier in this chapter. It shows that design culture can work at different depths. Its objects can structure neoliberal-friendly ways of being and acting in sophisticated ways. Or they can just help you get used to it.

CONCLUSION

Neoliberalism has had various beginnings. The end of the 'golden age' of rapid global growth in the late 1960s, the collapse of the Bretton Woods agreement in the 1970s, the breakdown of the Soviet bloc in the 1980s, the debt crises in Latin America through the 1990s: these are all starting points (Saad-Fiho and Johnston 2005).

For design in the West, neoliberalism really gets going in the mid-1980s. This is when many design studios begin to pursue profit in more strategic and organised ways. It is when its labour market becomes more flexible, more governed by the demands of individual projects and client contracts. It is when technological and organisational ways are found to speed up the design process. It is when retail design and corporate identity begin to develop in line with the growing finance and service sectors in the West. Other parts of the world would go through these changes, variations of these and/or their own processes at different times and at different speeds.

In differing formats, this is where we find a design culture turn taking place. The notion of design as something that is more commonplace and 'all around us' gives rise to a new set of conceptions of what design is in everyday life. Following on from the observation regarding the rise of retail design and corporate design, we might think of design here becoming more spatialised and relational. Instead of the idea of design being conceptually attached to the serial production of manufactured objects, we find it inhabiting a range of other registers. Shopping centres, corporate reports, hotel and retail chains, bars and restaurants: these, and many other, service sector formats distribute the serial reproduction of symbols. With this notion of design culture, however, I want to go further. This goes beyond the objects of design themselves to consider the greater intensification and visibility of the links between those objects and the people, institutions, resources and commercial organisations that are directly and indirectly involved in their shaping, materialisation, circulation and consumption.

In the next chapter we see how design work has evolved from this moment on, considering how it plays out particular forms of labour in contemporary capitalism. Again, we should remain mindful that this history of design is uneven, as is neoliberalism – different moments and locations produce different objects and possibilities.

DESIGN WORK

The development and promotion of the creative industries have become important features of economic policy in many countries. But what is distinct about design work here? And how do designers see their own professional identities? Chapter 3 analyses the status of designers in their studies, work and aspirations. This can be understood at two levels: one is in terms of their everyday working practices; the other is in terms of how design work functions symbolically for wider ideas of employment in the conditions of contemporary capitalism. The chapter ends by considering how the globalisation of design and digital networks have created particular forms of design work.

Much of the last chapter was devoted to broader cultural and cognitive issues where design works with and in neoliberal processes. Within this, a change of pace in the way design has been undertaken and a change in the spatial relationships within the design industries were noted. This shift includes a quickening of the tempo of design – it responds to client and public demands more rapidly to fashion objects, images and environments of greater variety, closing gaps between conception, execution, distribution and consumption.

Designing is rearranged accordingly. I'm not making a claim for the rise of design, or the creative industries in general, as being historically exclusive to this era. Rather, I want to note a step change in how design, at least, is transformed in terms of its economic practices. Design studio sections as cost centres, flexibilisation of hiring and firing employees, the rise of freelance work, easing the flow between digital and physical outputs or systems that make the procurement of materials easier: these developments have shaped the ways by which designers make their way in this neoliberal world. As we shall see, it's a slippery, fluid and breathless world at that.

This chapter therefore looks more closely at the qualities of design work. Since the late 1990s, there has been plenty (perhaps a surfeit) of scholarship that has analysed the creative industries in broad terms. Much of this has alighted on varying definitions of what these entail – each one having implications for how we account for their economic impact and understand their practices. At the same time, it has been argued that insufficient attention is given to the particularities of each of its components and, moreover, what the specificities of working in its various parts are (Nixon 2003; Hesmondhalgh 2007).

We can go further with this argument, however. If, as shown in Chapter 1, the design industry itself is subject to successive fragmentations and widening of the scope of its professional undertakings, then how does this result in various registers of its practice? In other words, what are design's different working norms? How does this result in dominant or variable forms of professional self-identity or notions of autonomy? How do designers respond to global economic and technological changes or adjustments in commercial spatialities?

These questions are tackled in a layered way. I use the career progression of imagined individuals, from student to junior designer and beyond, as an organising trope to move the argument through different contexts for the consideration of design work and its meanings. In doing so, I recognise what is at play through different moments and in different locations to produce diverse and often conflicting accounts of what design work is.

We start, therefore, by considering the design student and how certain historically-constructed, institutional norms of the art school produce discussion of creative autonomy. We then contrast this with academic and policy conceptions of the creative industries to force a more nuanced and varied set of contexts for designers into consideration that is not so much mediated by the object of design as by the relationships that designers enter into. This relationality and, indeed, sociality is what drives professional identity, I argue. Nonetheless, within the heterogeneous fields of design, there is a strong degree of performativity – a playing out of what is expected that the designer should be. As the designers' careers unfold through time, some drop by the wayside, some struggle on, others triumph. The strongly relational characteristics of design work (or, more prosaically, the 'dodging and weaving' that goes on) puts designers in a peculiar position with regard to economic fluctuations. Designers' responsiveness to changing commercial contexts results in rapid reinventions of the professional field – a constant redesign of design itself. If stark variances take place through time, so there are also variances in space. We therefore consider the role of sociality in design and how clustering of designers into locations produces both positive and negative effects. Finally, we cast the net outwardly, showing how the globalisation of design work itself leads to other forms of precariousness.

DESIGN, ART EDUCATION AND AUTONOMY

The difference between art and design is possibly one of the most recurrent classroom discussions to be found among undergraduate design students. To their tutors this often appears to be an undeveloped debate. With the benefit of having experienced the economic practices of design, they are perhaps more seasoned to its everyday nuances and demands that clearly separate it from the world of art. However, a little understanding of their fledglings' own context and experience to date might restore some patience. Two factors conspire to add to the student's confusion in the face of the vexed question of 'is it art or is it design?' at this point in their development.

First, the early stages of design education are laced with a deliberate collapsing of art/design boundaries. In varying measures, this stems from what is often referred to as the 'Bauhaus model' (Findeli 2001; Lerner 2005). Broadly speaking, this works on the basis that the foundations of the creative individual in art and design are established not through learning a series of general rules and aesthetic formulae that are applicable to each of its many specialisms; instead, the student initially engages with a broad base of practical explorations into, for instance, questions of colour, space or form within which both artistic and technological issues are enfolded. Thus, for example, learning about the science of colour theory takes place alongside practical engagement with painting, collage or photography. Developed by Walter Gropius and Johannes Itten at the Bauhaus in Germany during the 1920s, this approach dispensed with any initial delineation between art, craft, design and architecture. This way of educating early-stage students subsequently coursed through art and design pedagogy through most of Europe, the USA and Latin America. Here, the details of how art and design might perform differently in an economic and societal frame are not foregrounded. It follows that initial discourse around the differences between art and design circulate around the object and its meaning rather than the specific contexts (commercial, institutional, ideological among others) through which these are played out.

Second, even if the institutional and economic contexts of art and design are considered, to the novice student these may easily appear to be one and the same. On the surface, design's magazines, its books, its TV shows, its museums or its festivals are not too dissimilar to those of art. All of these mediate creative work as that of the work of cultural intermediaries (Bourdieu 1984a). For them, artists or designers are the ones who produce cutting-edge objects, suggest new ways of thinking about or acting in the world, harness novel technologies or systems. Work in related institutions through journalism or curatorship serves to support and show this view. They form part of the 'field of cultural production' (Bourdieu 1984b) that gives legitimacy to the notion that creative labour is about delivering cultural or other innovations. Within this framework, their emphasis on the individuals who do this and on the objects that they produce serves to avoid more sticky questions which might separate specific practices of and within art and design.

Student debate as to the differences between art and design reflects some of the heritage of design pedagogy itself that conspires to cloud notions that design actually engages in the messy world of users, the public, citizenry, commercial acumen or economic systems. There may be good reasons for this, not least that study should allow for the imagination to grow without constant deference to the marketplace. Alternatively, this view is not without its detractors. One enquiry into design education in the twenty-first century argues that it should place less emphasis on individual creative autonomy and more on learning to collaborate, that it is too focused around objects without understanding the systems in which they operate, that students should learn more about the 'real world' of business and the management of design (e.g. Design Skills Advisory Panel 2007).

Ultimately, the quandary of the differences between art and design are not difficult to solve. Art rarely has utility – it is not there to serve much practical purpose, it is there to open up the imagination. Design can also open up the imagination, but in addition, it serves a range of quite explicit functions like helping a task to be performed or making a firm more competitive through the quality of its products or services. It works at a different register of economic exchange. Artists are rarely worried about their professional status. Through the twentieth century – thanks to the work of artists like Marcel Duchamp – it became apparent that anything could be labelled as art and that anyone could become an artist. It is clear that art does have institutional apparatuses that control and format what art is promoted and seen (Thornton 2009; Perry 2014). Behind that, who produces the work is entirely open. Meanwhile, there is plenty of historical evidence to show that designers are more concerned about their professional status (Armstrong 2015). This is mostly in relation to their clients rather than the wider public and subsequent sections of this chapter will develop this line.

The main role of this section, though, is not to get bound up in the detail of the different debates as to the position of design in relation to art. Rather, it is to bear witness to these in the first place and to pick out what effect its origins have. In summary, they suggest that the blurring of distinctions between art and design plays a discursive role. First, it pulls any discussion of design – and, indeed, art – to one that revolves more around the meaning of the object rather than design's multiple, economic functions. Artefacts are discussed as to whether they are 'art' or 'design' or both. How cultures of design produce particular understandings, objects and activities that are distinct from the art world does not find such an easy home here. Second, art is the priority point of reference; questions of design's relationship to specialisms such as marketing, advertising, business management or customer experience come later. As such, the design student engages initially with the seemingly free-floating world of artistic creativity, thereby maintaining certain statuses around individual creativity and autonomy for it. This is sometimes vexing for the student who is also trying to think about design as a service. Third, this foregrounding of art in relation to design postpones a discussion of its relationship to other creative industries. It suggests a prior nature of autonomy. But in challenging this assumption, we might find a more nuanced and complex understanding of design and economy unfold.

THE CREATIVE INDUSTRIES AND DESIGN

As design students progress through their studies, they notice that what they are studying is invariably referred to as part of the 'creative industries'. Perhaps their department sits in a Faculty of Creative Industries. Perhaps they have been directed to read some of the academic bibliography on the subject (e.g. Caves 2000; Howkins 2001; Hartley 2005; Hesmondhalgh 2007) or one of the many government or institutional reports available (e.g. European Commission 2010; UNCTAD 2010; Department for Culture, Media and Sport (DCMS) 2014; FIRJAN 2014). They might have heard a businessperson, politician or other advocate on the radio or on TV make the case for supporting creative industries, given their substantial significance in the wider economy.

On the issue of the creative industries and their economic importance, copious statistics are available. Here are three examples:

- Across the 27 European Union member states, it was estimated in 2010 that the cultural and creative industries contributed around 2.6 per cent of the total GDP, providing quality jobs to around 5 million people (European Commission 2010).
- The Brazilian workforce included 892,500 people working in creative professions in 2013, a 90 per cent rise since 2004, which produced 2.3 per cent of national GDP (FIRJAN 2014).
- In the UK, they provided 1.68 million jobs in 2012, 5.6 per cent of the total number of jobs; gross value added of the creative industries was £71.4 billion in 2012, accounting for 5.2 per cent of the UK Economy (DCMS 2014).

The point here is to pay witness to the way that the creative industries have become an important aspect of thinking and policy in political economy across world, pan-national, national, regional and local scales. They have become the object of fine-grain statistical analysis, considerable debate as to what should be included and how their parts can be measured (Bakshi et al. 2013) as well as their wider implications on urban planning and development (Gibson and Stevenson 2004; Cooke and Lazzeretti 2008; Flew 2011), economic policy (Oakley 2004) and social cohesion and wellbeing (Blessi et al. 2016).

The origin of this concept of the creative industries is most often attributed to the UK's Labour administration upon its ascendance to government in 1997. Its policies on creative industries derived, in part, from developments in thinking in the Greater London Council during the 1980s that identified the economic and social benefits of supporting a broad range of cultural activities (Garnham 1990). Here, the term 'cultural industries' was more typically used. Subsequently, the Labour government of 1997 set up its Creative Industries Task Force (CITF) to undertake analysis and evaluation of the sector. Within this, it defined 13 areas of creative professional activity that have been reused or modified since. These are advertising, architecture, the art and antiques market, crafts, design, designer fashion, film, interactive leisure software (electronic games), music, the performing arts, publishing, software and computer services, and TV and radio. At the heart of their definition is that the creative industries includes 'those industries that are based on individual creativity, skill and talent with the potential to create wealth and jobs through developing intellectual property' (CITF 2001: 4).

This denomination is broad and heterogeneous. It includes, as Flew (2011: 12–13) observes, activities that are highly capital intensive (such as film and TV) and ones that are very labour intensive (such as crafts and performing arts). Some of its industries are highly responsive to commercial structures and business cycles (such as advertising and architecture) while others have or pursue greater independence (such as art and crafts). Thus, this creative industries term can be a very blunt instrument, encompassing activities that may be resolutely and obviously opposed to each other in terms of their ethical motivations, working timescales, geographical reach, definitions of professional identity or forms of employment.

Within the creative industries there are, nonetheless, some broad commonalities. First, they are all engaged in 'needs production'. In other words, none of them is absolutely essential to everyday functioning. Believe it or not, we can get along just fine without computer games or antique vases. Second, the creative industries all produce what are termed 'credence goods' (Darby and Karni 1973). These are things that carry costs which are sunk into their development and realisation before it is actually known what demand for or reception of them will be like. Third, their different industries overlap and have some mutual dependency; they draw from each other's skills and resources and often collaborate on single projects. Films use music; publishing employs designers; radio production features the performing arts and so on. Fourth, the creative industries are not subject to professional norms of entry and practice (with, usually, the exception of architecture). They do not have standard examinations, training requirements or required professional association memberships.

How creative or cultural sector jobs are determined and how these are measured and valued has become a source of vigorous debate (Galloway and Dunlop 2007). This has led to the successive emergence of further definitional terms such as 'creative economy' and 'creative intensity'. Table 3.1 provides a summary of the different positions and some of their significance for thinking about design work.

Knowing the ins and outs of the various academic and policy discussions that relate to creative activities provides a foundation from which the specificities of design can be analysed. There are three concerns here. First, closer inspection underlines the issue that while growth in design practice and education coincides with various quantitative and qualitative developments in the commercial marketplace, it also coincides with government policy and academic enquiry regarding the broader role of creative and cultural work. Second, the analysis itself combats a dominant understanding of creative and cultural work that focuses exclusively on its 'frontline' practitioners (e.g. actors, artists and designers working solely in theatres, studios and consultancies etc.) represented in popular media. Instead, we achieve a more varied and complex view which accepts that creative work comes as the result of interplay, collaboration and support between creative people and non-creative people. It is a team effort. Further, creative work takes place in a variety of locations, including ones that are not obviously creative. Third, as different terms and definitions emerge, we can begin to appreciate both the commonalities and the nuances and specificities of different kinds of labour that exist across its industries and institutions.

Design's ubiquity gives it an unusual place in the creative and cultural industries. It overlaps and works with every industry within these. It provides services to industries that have creative expression among their core content in various ways. Theatres engage stage set design, for example, but also graphics for their programmes and websites to give information. Design therefore adds to the content of cultural industries. Furthermore, design, along with architecture and advertising, is notable in that it works both within and without the cultural industries. It collaborates with other cultural practices but the mainstay of its client base is in the non-cultural sphere. An arguable difference that design has with architecture and advertising in these frameworks is that the latter two do not provide content in terms of the shaping of their actual practices, products and services. Architecture services other cultural and creative industries and non-cultural clients to provide buildings in which their work takes place (although it can sometimes be argued that architecture also shapes the symbolic content of organisations). Advertising helps to attract

Table 3.1 Cultural industries, creative industries, creative economy, creative intensity and design

Term Date of origin in government policy Key authors	Definition	Commentary	Status of design
Cultural industries 1980- Lewis 1990; du Gay and Pryke 2002; Power and Allen 2004; Hesmondalgh 2007	Cultural production and consumption that have at their core a symbolic or expressive element.	Origin in (Frankfurt School, 1930s and 1940s) critique of co-option of culture into capitalist production, thereby losing its 'integrity'. Its emergence in policy recognised more positive view on economic and social benefits. It includes activities where innovation and creativity are not central, such as heritage or traditional crafts.	Design works across all cultural industries. It is active in shaping aspects of its contents. However, design's more eplicit client-orientation and commercial ethos might be at odds with some cultural industries' practices. The use of creativity (creative skills and creative people originating in the arts field and in the field of cultural industries) is essential to the performances of design.
Creative industries 1990- Caves 2000; Hartley 2005	Industries based on creative origination of intellectual property (IP).	The term is broad in that in encompasses sometimes contradictory motivations or very different scales and ways of working. It also includes people who are not necessarily undertaking creative tasks within the sector. It is also restrictive in that it implies that 'creativity' is limited to just these industries.	Design works across all creative industries. More often it sells its intellectual property on rather than retaining it (contra, for example, publishing). Activities are not necessarily directed toward artefacts that carry IP; designers may contribute to 'immaterial' elements such as organisational culture or brand management.
Creative economy 2000- Howkins 2001; UNCTAD 2010	Those working in creative jobs in the economy as a whole.	This recognises that there are people working in the creative production of goods and services but not necessarily as part of creative industries organisations (e.g. in-house designers in businesses).	Design tasks may not necessarily be undertaken by employees who would term themselves as designers (e.g. engineers).
Creative intensity 2010- Work Foundation 2007; Bakshi, Freeman and Higgs 2013	Those in the creative industries doing specifically creative things.	The creative economy includes many people in managerial or support roles that are not necessarily or fully creative in themselves. There are many outside the creative economy engaged in creatively intense activities (especially in software). Creative intensity varies greatly between different industries (e.g. 55% in design, 90% in the visual arts).	Recognises the relational, outward-facing qualities of much design practice, e.g. that design studios are not necessarily solely dedicated to designing, but other management and bureaucratic activities as well.

interest in them. But design actually shapes and formats the core offers of other creative and cultural industries and non-cultural activities (KEA European Affairs 2006).

Some further specificities regarding design in the frameworks of creative and cultural industries will be discussed later on in this chapter. In the meantime, a key point here is that in its ubiquity, but also, therefore, in its propensity to couple with such a wide range of actors, both expert and non-expert in terms of creative work, design professionals are cast relationally. By contrast, as Thornton (2009) shows, the visual arts, in their dominant mode, are firmly locked into their own circuits, highly aware and structured through their own field of cultural production. Auction houses, art schools, art fairs, prizes, magazines, studios and biennales are carefully aligned and attuned to each other to reproduce their own logic. Design industries, in all their guises, are much more outward-facing, adjusting to various clients, publics and economic logics. This has profound knock-on effects for the ways through which it operates and constructs its own knowledge-base.

DESIGN KNOWLEDGE IN PRACTICE

Some years ago I took part in a debate that was organised by a design agent, that is, someone who matches the skills and profile of a designer with consultancies or firms offering employment. The theme of the evening's discussion was 'Are Design Graduates Industry Ready?'. The event took place around the time of the annual summer graduate show, when a new batch of students would be released from the clutches of their design schools into the scary world of 'desperately seeking a job'. The premise for this debate was that design education should be in service mode to the design industry. We stumbled through various possibilities of what employers were looking for as the design educationalists present struggled to rationalise how they skilled-up their students. My personal line in this debate was to ask whether 'industry' was, in fact, graduate-ready? It seemed to me that it was an impossible task to clearly state what such a broad and undefined industry might demand; instead, we should equip students to bring new things to it.

A related argument is presented by Wang and Ilhan (2009). Their starting point is to ask whether, in fact, the design profession, like any profession, should necessarily assume that the possession of a distinct body of knowledge should be what defines it. They go on to review the language that is employed in the design profession and in design research, concluding that it is actually very vague and generalistic. Hence, design defining phrases such as '[a] liberal art of technological culture' (Buchanan 1992) are employed that are nonetheless not specific to design. Equally, design knowledge is seen to be both scientifically observable and explicable (Friedman 2003) but also tacitly embedded into its various processes (Cross 2001). More prosaically, they observe that in 2006, of the 48,000 industrial and commercial designers in the USA, only 3,300 were signed-up members of the Industrial Designers Society of America (IDSA). The IDSA does not have any legally enforceable norms for industrial designers but might otherwise stand in for some measure of professional respectability and recognition. Its low proportion of membership, as against total numbers employed in the sector, suggests that adhering to even the most symbolic of professional representation is not regarded as important.

In the absence of professional norms or a precise description that explains what makes design professionally distinctive, Wang and Ilhan (2009) suggest that the latter may be better articulated in terms of how the design profession relates to other knowledge domains. This is a sociological issue rather than an epistemological one, therefore. It is about how designers are constituted socially as a group and how they format themselves in relation to other domains rather than through the solidification of some internal professional definition.

Historically, this different emphasis can be seen in the UK when the Design Business Group merged with the Society of Industrial Artists and Designers in 1986 (which later in the same year was renamed the Chartered Society of Designers). Since its inception in 1930, the latter was largely an inward-looking organisation that emphasised the establishment of professional 'codes of conduct' within the design industry itself in order to gain recognition and respect outside itself while also offering a modicum of professional training on business issues (Armstrong 2015). The affiliated Design Business Group (in 1987 becoming the Design Business Association) reversed this emphasis, providing a set of services aimed at supporting member designers and design consultancies in their dealings with clients. Its foundation suggested a new orientation in how design was thought about. It sought a more dynamic, commercially oriented relationship with potential design clients in promoting the interests of its membership. Thus it compiled and published a directory of design consultancies and their services; it provided client advice on commissioning design; it offered training and mentoring for members to help them deal with the rigours of running a design business (Myerson 1986). Thus, we see here how the designer's preoccupation was predominantly outward-facing towards clients rather than inward towards any homogenising concerns for professional identity.

The evasion of normative procedures and professional identities by the design industry is in no small part the result of its constant adherence to 'following the money' by inventing new specialisms to exploit technological and business opportunities.

CREATIVITY, DESIGN WORK AND PERFORMATIVITY

Designers are Wankers. That's the title of a book by product designer Lee McCormack (2005). It starts from the premise that design students aren't equipped 'with the skills needed to make the transition to design in the real world' (p. 10). This transition involves 'reassessment, adaptation and resignation' (p. 21). In order to successfully make it in world of design work, graduates should embrace this professional world which, when 'studying creativity actively takes you away from it' (p. 23). McCormack's text then takes the reader through a series of useful tips on how, for instance, to relate to clients, present yourself, protect your ideas and get paid.

Aside from a series of interviews with five well-known designers, the rest of McCormack's book draws entirely from the author's personal experience. He is imparting things learnt along the way by trial and error, making the tacit understandings that go on through being a practising designer explicit.

McCormack's book is alive to the troubling juxtaposition of being creative and being commercial and his friendly advice is there to help bridge this gap. It may seem contradictory but, in fact, he is talking about complementary skills. Thus, being good at listening, adopting humility or dropping 'attitude' dovetail with developing a personal style, getting noticed or selling an idea to a venture capitalist. This mixture of discipline and freedom is echoed in graphic designer Adrian Shaughnessy's observation that 'Design studios are a mixture of slave camp and enchanted play-ground' (Shaughnessy 2005: 33).

This relationship of commercial demands and creative autonomy has been explored in broader terms of academic studies of management as well. There is a copious literature to draw from (e.g. Scase and Davis 2000; Jeffcutt and Pratt 2002; Townley and Beech 2010), reflecting inter-est in getting to grips with the relationship of management to creativity. This has coincided with to increased visibility of the creative industries in the wider economy from 2000 onwards. Here, and in the more anecdotal narrative of working in design seen above, the perceived opposition of the two often becomes something of a rhetorical device: it is a starting point to sum up its drama.

What binds these two positions, though? A closer analysis of design suggests that these two sides are both *performed* as part of the necessary, rational activities of its economic work.

Performativity as a concept derives from two sources. First, it is most associated with the work of Judith Butler (1997) in relation to gender. Butler argued that both men and women self-consciously 'act out' prescribed, social norms of masculinity and femininity. This acting out is reinforced by popular representation such as films, magazines or TV. This notion can be trans-ferred to other domains such as being an 'inspirational, good' teacher (Dalton 2004; Burnard and White 2008) or an 'innovative' manager (Thrift 2000). Second, Jean-François Lyotard (1987) related performativity to education and knowledge in a world where fact is not taken as given, but has to be legitimated, or argued for. When, for instance, what makes 'good design' no longer relies on given styles or aims, when it is not always clear to the needs of the client or the end-user or some other demand, then how this is so has to be continually articulated. What delivers value has to be played out in a number of ways. This involves, for Lyotard (1987: 39), an element of 'language games' where terms are not fixed but employed for their linguistic appeal. Specialist words, for instance, or ways of explaining things are created to give particular weight to business practices, to make them appear up to the minute or the result of considered analysis.

Lyotard paid particular attention to the commoditisation of knowledge (1987: 5). When, under the conditions of advanced capitalism, what constitutes knowledge is multifarious, relative and in need of explication it also becomes an item of economic value to be bought and sold. Hence, designers normally sell intellectual property. But this intellectual property as a commodity is not necessarily generalisable to all situations. Rather, it is something that is traded to specific users of it, such as a manufacturer, a retail chain or a public service provider. The more generalisable bit is the particular service that each designer or design consultancy can provide to their specific intended market specialism. These conditions have a number of effects on the ways by which designers work and present themselves.

The knowledge economy of design is performed both within the design space between design workers and outwardly with clients and potential clients.

THE DESIGNER IN THE DESIGN STUDIO

Design graduates may have been used to messy studios, where models, drawings, printouts or sketch books pile up, but this doesn't seem so evident in their first professional design job.

They may be used to long hours, but not to accounting for what happens in them. They may be used to showing their work to others, but not to promote the way they work as having value over other ways.

Professional design studios are often surprisingly ordered, clean environments. Rows of work-stations, composed of chair, desk and computer, almost make them look like any other office space. Here they process projects according to 'occupational formulae' (Negus 2002): previous work is recycled; design magazines and books are plundered for ideas; photos are sourced from image libraries such as Shutterstock. The 'look and feel' of the finished piece, in graphic design for instance, will probably have already been determined through meetings between the studio's account manager and the client where other details such as production requirements, budgets and what 'raw material' the client can provide, such as images they can supply will have been discussed (Dorland 2009). Design work can be much more *routine* than studying design, where students are developing their personal approaches and learning their creative styles through varied projects. Instead, in the professional context, it may sometimes be questioned the extent to which they might be labelled as 'cultural intermediaries', given the bureaucratised, repetitive and risk-minimising processes they often engage in (Moor 2012).

This may be surprising for clients as well. After all, ultimately the design studio is selling creativity in some form or other to their clients. And yet, there seems little material evidence of this in a traditional sense, were they to visit the design studio. Anecdote tells us that design studios have been known to 'jazz up' their studios, for example by putting more drawings on walls or piling up models, in anticipation of client visits. Creativity is performed for client benefit and reassurance, even where a long-term client relationship already exists. When projects are presented to clients – more normally at clients' offices than at the design studio – this is more frequently done by the studio head and/or by someone with presentational flair. This person may not be the person who has carried out the majority of work on a project, but someone who is able to connect with and excite the client (Julier 2010).

At the same time, workflow and tracking procedures for projects are invariably employed. In small studios this might come down to simple 'to do' lists. But in larger studios or with more complex projects, computer-based time-sheets and workflow systems – supported by programs such as Oracle Workflow, co.efficient or HighOrbit – help to allocate, quantify, cost and monitor the distribution of tasks within the design firm. This can also help to back-track if something goes wrong in order to pinpoint where and how this happened. Tracking is more usually a 'below the line' issue for design studios which isn't shared publicly with clients, although a simplified version is instructive for them as they can see and appreciate what they are paying for in terms of time and organisational input. As one design company head put it, 'We want to give [a] good insight into how we systematically work to achieve solutions for our clients. If we explain in an easy-to-approach manner how we work, it will be easy for the client to buy design from us' (Törmikoski 2009: 248). Here, internal procedures become presentational supports in the micro-economic interactions of designers and their clients.

To find that a studio uses tracking procedures may be reassuring for the designer who has recently joined the profession. They provide the impression that things are stable, that clearly defined tasks are assigned and that the completion of tasks is set up in timeframes. The reality is that while design work may be structured into billable units of time, designers often find themselves providing input outside these (e.g. working late, outside the workflow framework).

Further, the dividing up of design tasks among separate, identified staff in order to systemise the process has the added effect of multiplying and fragmenting the number of audiences to the work. Dorland (2009) uses the concept of 'product image' to explain how creative work often involves not just thinking about satisfying clients or end-users, but also fulfilling internal demands. Thus the junior designer will also be thinking about how what they produce will get passed the approval of, say, the studio manager. A design project is broken down into the fulfilment of a series of materialisations such as briefing documents, sketches, models, prototypes, mock-ups, proposals, client presentations or proofs, each of which has different expectations and audiences. Design work therefore becomes a precarious set of negotiations to get through the studio hierarchy. The designer's performance in this environment is therefore also measured against these, which become a cumulative set of evidence to allow, or not, their career progression.

The designer is therefore locked into a set of procedures that control and mediate their success. On the surface this may not be apparent. Indeed, the design studio is far more easy and relaxed than perhaps all this talk of measurement and tracking implies. Reflecting on spaces where creative labour takes place, Dzidowski (2014: 44) refers first to Weber's notion of the 'iron cage' of bureaucratic systems of the early twentieth century where office employees were arranged into neat, disciplined rows and undertook clearly defined, specific tasks that added up to a larger, highly rationalised system (Weber 1978). Then in the later twentieth century comes the 'glass cage' where the workplace is so seductively configured that the employee is flattered by the gloriousness of the environment they find themselves in (Gabriel 2003). In the creative world symbolised by Google – with its gyms and playful corners (translated into sofas or table football in smaller organisations) – there is the 'gilded cage' that is marked by an 'illusion of self-indulgence'. This is where licence is given, at least symbolically, to see the workplace as somewhere of chance encounter, flights of fancy or a space to let the imagination relax and run wild, but in a way that is always turned into productivity. Within this, living and working in the hope of the 'big break' – a brilliant technical innovation or a design that captures widespread notice – keeps the designer in their place.

DESIGN WORK AND ECONOMIC FLUCTUATIONS

Meanwhile, productivity is only something necessary if there is something to be productive for. A review of the larger context suggests that the relationship of the commercial success of design industries to wider, macro-trends in the economy is uneven. It doesn't necessarily follow that the design industry thrives in periods of growth and vice versa. Instead, the design industry expands and contracts, changes its emphases and practices in asymmetric ways. This may have the effect of putting many designers, particularly junior ones, constantly on the back foot as they have to deal with unexpected slack periods, redundancies or rises in work demands.

One of the most frequently told stories from design history is how American designers such as Raymond Loewy, Walter Dorwin Teague and Henry Dreyfuss flourished during the economic depression of the 1930s (Votolato 1998; Miekle 2005). The narrative goes that these designers helped American companies such as General Electric to reposition their products towards a consumer market through their re-styling but also through a more integrated approach to corporate identity. Thus, extending from these stories, it is taken that design is a tool that works as an enabler for business development in times of economic challenges.

Figures do not exist to investigate whether or not this holds truth for the wider American design industry of the 1930s – it rests on a qualitative turn in design that is focused on just a few designers. More recently, available statistical data, in the UK and elsewhere (Grodach and Seman 2013; Rozentale and Lavanga 2014), allows us to speculate more thoroughly on the relationship of design and wider economic performance.

Following the economic crisis of 2008, the UK economy in terms of GDP growth went into its deepest recession since the 1930s. Overall, until 2013 its economy may best be described as 'flat' (Hardie and Perry 2013). And yet, over the same period, the creative industries, and design in particular, were in significant growth. In terms of gross value added, design grew by 8 per cent between 2009 and 2012. Between 2011 and 2012 there was a 10.8 per cent growth of employment in design within the creative economy as a whole and a 16.2 per cent increase within the creative industries (DCMS 2014). During the same period, the UK economy as a whole dropped into recession three times.

We may also contrast these statistics with a reverse situation between 2001 and 2007. This was a period of relative stable growth in the overall economy. Turnover in the design industry dropped from £6.7bn in 2001 to £3.1bn in 2004 (British Design Innovation (BDI) 2004, 2005). Roughly speaking, over the same period employment figures in design varied but overall remained the same. This means that designers' fee income was therefore dropping in the context of overall economic growth.

A number of factors explain this growth of design services against a slower national economy. These include: that the UK design industry is very export oriented (Design Council 1998, 2003, 2015) and so it can weather domestic economic slump; that the UK creative economy experienced growth more generally as against other sectors, particularly and notably manufacturing and financial services – overall growth in the creative industries as a whole was three times the national economy (Montgomery 2015); that there was also growth in other high-value creative industries such as film, TV, information technology services and software with which design services are closely entwined (DCMS 2014).

The design industry and the creative and cultural industries in general carry both strengths and weaknesses in the same economic contexts. One weakness is that they are largely highly dependent on high levels of consumer spending, but also, as a heavily client-oriented sector, they are affected negatively by business downturns elsewhere. Scott (2007: 1466) notes how the cultural economy is 'intimately dependent on the expansion of final markets'. Other observers (Rantisi 2004; Neff et al. 2005; Hesmondhalgh 2007) suggest that – given its fragmented, precarious workforce and low capitalisation – the cultural economy is highly susceptible to economic fluctuations. However, it is precisely these conditions that, according to Pratt (2009), facilitate their flexibility and, therefore, their survival. With low start-up costs they are more open to risk and are therefore able to move towards new products or ideas with relative ease.

Similarly, design does not always thrive in high-cost places with booming economies. For example, Grodach and Seman (2013: 22) note how in the USA, designers working in particular centres where there is a strong cultural economy – such as Boston, Minneapolis, Seattle and San Diego – have experienced strong growth rates. These are not necessarily the 'frontline' cities of the cultural economy (such as San Francisco, Miami and Portland) but relatively well-off places where, nonetheless, business and living costs tend to be lower.

> There is no neat correlation between general national economic performance and the fortunes of the design industry.

To summarise, a simplistic view would say that there is less demand for design services in periods of growth because there isn't the need for repositioning products or redesigning services in ways that reduces costs, for example. But we also have to factor in issues of supply of design over demand, varying business and living costs that affect the ability of designers to continue in business or not, the impact of technologies on cutting costs or the greater propensity of designers to put up with working longer hours to make up for dropping per-job revenue. The next section pursues the question of precariousness in design work further.

PRECARIOUS LABOUR IN DESIGN

It has long been observed that design is generally a long-hours, low-turnover profession (e.g. Business Ratio Plus 1998). But more recent surveys reinforce this view even further. In a survey of 576 people working in design in the UK in 2013, 85.6 per cent said that 'clients expect more work for less money', around two-thirds of respondents agree that 'agencies are using more free-lancers' (68.1 per cent) and about two-fifths (42.5 per cent) agree that 'agencies are using more unpaid interns' (Design Industry Voices 2013).

These are worrying statistics, particularly for the junior designer setting out to forge a career. They underline a generally held view that design work offers little job security, involving flexible employment patterns and constant downward pressure on project budgets by clients. The extent to which junior designers fall into the category of the precariat is debatable.

'The precariat' is a broadly deployed term used to describe workers who are in insecure labour, who are in expectation of this situation and are often over-qualified for the jobs they are doing. As such they may be qualified in professions but they don't necessarily anticipate that they will find their way into long-term positions and they may be working beneath their capacities. Within this, precarious working involves constantly having to learn new technical, commercial, social and communication skills as they move from organisation to organisation, adapting to their specific structures and processes. In terms of design, this characterises working life for many graduates as they get taken on with short fixed-term contracts, requiring them to familiarise themselves repeatedly with changing working procedures and giving them the impression that they are always having to start from scratch. The term 'precariat' derives from a contraction of the words 'precarious' and 'proletariat' and in doing this, the originator of the term, Guy Standing, recognises this category to constitute an identifiable class on its own (Standing 2011, 2014).

An alternative view is that precarious work in design provides junior designers with opportunities to build experience in a number of organisations and broaden their skills, perhaps before establishing themselves as freelance designers or setting up their own studios. The rise of internships in design is clearly directed at this notion, providing short-term opportunities for graduates to build their experience while practically working for free.

This ambiguity has been captured by the establishment of *Intern* magazine in 2013, a biannual print publication aimed at providing and showcasing the work of interns in the creative industries while acting as a platform for debate around the negative issues this form of work carries. Within its pages, the question of profile-building through internships that enhance the CV and demonstrate experience of having worked with recognisable 'names' is clear. One such 'name', who herself had undertaken internships prior to becoming a partner with renowned graphic designer Stefan Sagmeister, stated it as follows: 'Our [interns] are unpaid. We pay for their lunches. I think it's on a situational basis whether people are comfortable with that, and can handle that. But I think internships in general are just a fantastic opportunity for people to learn and *get close to people they really admire and respect*' [my italics] (Walsh, quoted in Quito 2014). Being 'comfortable with that' would include having sufficient finance already to cover ordinary living costs while undertaking that internship, then.

The economic costs of internships to participants are significant. Elzenbaumer (2013) illustrates an example, alighting on internships that were offered by graphic designer Bruce Mau. These existed as part of his 'Massive Change' project that sought to address the future of design, in particular in the context of global environmental and social challenges between 2002 and 2005 (Mau 2004). The project was commissioned by the Vancouver Art Gallery. Participants were expected to put in 40+ hours a week unpaid on the project (thus would be unable to work a part-time job in addition to cover living costs, would be expected to lease an Apple iBook at an approximate annual cost of $1,600 (Cdn.) and pay fees on the associated study programme accredited by George Brown College).

The instances of the 'precarious' design employee or the intern may be read as being driven by decades of pressure to drive design costs down. Alternatively, they may be interpreted as a plugging of the gap between the education of design students and their training in commerce that was identified by McCormack (2005) near the beginning of this chapter. However, we might also view these in a wider context of changes in labour relations since the 1980s and the symbolic role of design. This is the topic of the next section.

FLEXIBLE ACCUMULATION AND THE SYMBOLIC ROLE OF DESIGN WORK

'Flexible accumulation' is a term that was employed by David Harvey to describe developments both in labour and in finance (Harvey 1989a). In labour this refers to the loosening of the places and scales on which production takes place, but also the regulatory frameworks that had previously defended these. Thus production is no longer rooted to traditional locations, but instead found where it is cheapest. Relatedly, the deregulation of financial systems has allowed for its quick and easy flow across borders, thereby facilitating the globalisation of trade and manufacture. The network within which money is moved in pursuit of sources of value is larger and more varied. In both these cases, labour and capital, economic power is achieved through complex and multiple channels.

This view onto flexible accumulation has had its detractors. Another side to it has been that much of this system has developed in the informal economy outside regulatory frameworks:

health and safety requirements may be absent, and conditions where worker protection, through, for example, trade union membership and support may not exist (Murray 1987; Hadjimichalis 2006). Equally, a reverse side to the view that flexibilisation is emancipatory is that this also celebrates the pliability and casualisation of the workforce (Pollert 1988). Flexible accumulation can also be found in sweatshop conditions.

Creative industries work has always been casualised: it presents few professional opportunities to establish a 'job for life'. The emphasis in the creative industries – particularly observable in design – on flexible working conditions, project-based employment structuring, multi-skilling, entrepreneurialship and individualism fits the labour regimes of neoliberalism since the 1980s. Creative workers therefore take on a symbolic role in the wider neoliberal economy (McRobbie 2004). As Ross argues, 'the kind of development embraced by policymakers seems guaranteed merely to elevate this traditionally unstable work profile into an inspirational model for youth looking to make an adventure out of their entry into the contingent labor force. If the creative industries become the ones to follow, all kinds of jobs, in short, may well look more and more like musicians' gigs: nice work if you can get it' (2009: 17).

A more positive spin may be given on this development by looking at the world of freelance work in certain creative sectors. The design industry in particular has seen an ongoing rise in the proportion of professionals engaged in freelance work (BDI 2005; Design Council 2015). At one level, this may be read as part and parcel of the rise of precarious labour: freelancers may not just be working alone, but, for example, may frequently be hired into design companies on a project-by-project basis. On another, there may be other factors at play. Research on professionals working in creative digital activities shows that many freelancers prefer the flexibility that working alone affords. It allows them to move between clients or other digital companies they service, expanding their knowledge and experience as they go along; it provides a wider set of social contacts through work; and providing things go well it also permits relative autonomy on working hours (Sapsed et al. 2015).

NETWORK SOCIALITY AND ECONOMIC GEOGRAPHIES OF DESIGN

Regulatory frameworks and industry structures give clear points of entry and expectation for workers. If these are not enforced in law they at least can become bargaining points for pay and conditions. They exist in conditions of stability and coherence and are supported by what might be viewed as 'old' social infrastructures such as social housing and social welfare that are more or less fixed assets. By contrast, the new economy is redolent with the features of 'new' social – social media, social networking – that are more ephemeral and fluid (Bauman 2000; Marres 2014).

In the second version, social life is created through and supported by processes of networking. In this, the sense of belonging is maintained through the interchange of information. This can be quantified, for example, through the number of LinkedIn referrals, Facebook 'likes', Twitter re-tweets or through the number of business cards collected at an event. Network sociality, as Wittel (2001) has termed it, involves potentiality in that it engages the accumulation of social capital. Being part of a network involves building up relationships with others in the hope and expectation that these will render something of benefit at some other stage. It is a source of future value.

This notion is particularly active in the design industries. McRobbie (2002) identifies being visible and available amidst other designers as vital to getting work. Hanging out in bars after work in order to maintain this – something that privileges younger people without families – is part of such requirements: something that automatically blurs the distinctions between work and leisure.

This is taken a step further when planning policy is fashioned to provide spaces that encourage network sociality among the creative industries. The identification and development of so-called creative quarters within cities are deliberate attempts to provide a soft environment within which designers, digital media professionals, artists and other such workers can develop their businesses. While not explicitly using the term 'network sociality', the assumption is that these clusters would provide a location where horizontal connections between creative practitioners can be developed. Additionally, with their galleries, restaurants and bars they would also foster the 24-hour lifestyle where art is life and life is art (Frith and Horne 1987; Wood 1999).

But these also have a semiotic role (Koskinen 2005) in terms of city promotion and suggest economic wellbeing. Locations such as Manchester's Northern Quarter are fostered and promoted because they provide a showcase for the notion of an entrepreneurial city (Julier 2005, 2014: ch. 10). Just as the creative worker signals wider transformations in labour, so the creative quarter indicates that a city includes entrepreneurial and innovative employment.

This notion of creative quarters reflects a wider approach to economic development policy, in which cognate resources are focused into a location. Haughton et al. (2014) call this 'agglomeration boosterism'. Here, already dynamic local industries are assisted to grow as opposed to putting aid into struggling areas in order to rebalance national and regional economies. The former is therefore a quicker fix as it involves building on an upward trajectory of what is already there; the latter involves turning an economy around, usually involving greater investment in new human and physical infrastructures. The effect of this is to produce uneven economic geographies. Spaces outside and between such agglomerations are destined to become economic wastelands. The agglomerations themselves triumph, but also run the risk of overheating: property prices rise to outstrip the abilities of citizens or businesses to afford being located there; too many sectoral workers flood into these centres meaning that supply can outstrip demand and cause a downward pressure on wages.

The effect of this can be seen at the small scale of creative quarters where, classically, professionals were originally attracted by low business costs but as they flourish, so these go up, forcing them back out (Zukin 1989; Mommaas 2004). But this also takes place on a wider level where cities become strong draws for creative practitioners but end up as victims of their success. Such has been the case in London. With over 435,300 occupied in the creative industries as a whole in 2010 (Freeman 2011) and 46,000 designers working there (Design Council 2010a), the city has achieved recognisable status as an international capital in these sectors. But at a national level this has the effect of draining talent from other regions. London and the South East of England has accounted for nearly half of the nation's design businesses (BDI 2005).

To draw in the theme of sociality and performativity that runs through this chapter, it is as well to note that while copious studies focus on the benefits of spatial clustering of creative industries, this may not always be for the usual cited reasons. Invariably, these benefits are presented as existing for the intra-sector networks that result. Creative businesses can capitalise on their proximity so that collaborations can be built between individual units that encourages overall levels of innovation. In turn this has led to the widespread application of urban planning policies to produce these (Bagwell 2008; Chang 2009; Foord 2009). An alternative reading is that design businesses seek proximity to potential clients, hence being close to corporate head offices, often found in regional or national capitals or to transport hubs. The designer's knowledge and business networks are more multilayered and nuanced than simply being around other creative types (Reimer et al. 2008; Sunley et al. 2008). Meanwhile, conversely again, while 'the buzz' of being in a creative quarter may be attractive to designers (Drake 2003), it is also attractive to clients seeking, if only more in symbolic terms, the feeling of alighting on that ambience.

THE UBER DESIGN PRECARIAT AND PLATFORM CAPITALISM

So far this chapter has viewed design work as being relatively geographically concentrated. This is taken in terms of the studio culture, the social networks between designers and the apparent 'clustering' of designers for reasons either of competitive advantage, symbolic capital or, merely, 'the buzz'. In addition, we may read it as the effect of layers of economic reasons or globally circulating policy orthodoxies. Different scales of territories are at play here. But what happens if design work is deterritorialised? What if a design task can be undertaken anywhere and, almost, by anyone? What kind of labour emerges and, indeed, how does this happen?

The global rise of the ride-sharing company Uber from 2011 has come to signify the fine line between the flexibility and the exploitation that can emerge in platform capitalism. This is where digital systems – like Uber or Airbnb – connect customers and services, passengers with drivers, guests with hosts. Schmidt (2015: 25) argues that in platform capitalism there are always three groups of stakeholders: there are the providers of these who own the software, control the rules and the communication and take the fee; there are the clients who profit from the cheap supply of a service; and there are the sellers or 'crowds' who provide the service.

In 2008, three crowdsourcing platforms for logo design were launched. These were 99designs (with over 850,000 registered designers by 2014), DesignCrowd (with over 440,000 designers by 2014) and crowdSPRING (incorporating graphic design and naming with over 160,000 designers and writers by 2014) (Schmidt 2015: 168). Similar platforms such as 12designer, MycroBurst and designenlassen (the English version being designonclick) followed. The general idea of these platforms is that potential clients can place design briefs on these platforms and allow designers to pitch for the work, supplying costs and design proposals. It is like the free-pitching method where, traditionally, a client will invite several design consultancies or freelancers to enter into unpaid competition in order to capture a job. The obvious difference is that this internet system allows the client to spread the net globally and drive down the remuneration for work as they tap into low-wage economies and a much wider labour marketplace. For the platform owners, the rewards can be high: with a 40 per cent commission, 99designs were taking US$1.3m per month from an overall US$3.3m of turnover in late 2014 and early 2015 (Schmidt 2015: 179).

For a very few designers at the other end of these platforms, there can be good rewards, both financially and in terms of their profile that is publicised on them. Most of these platforms have a ranking system that shows the relative success of members. In Ecuador, Xavier Iturralde reportedly made 34,577 euros over four years via the platform jovoto, with an average earning of 110 euros per design idea. For many, it means very low remuneration – Grace Oris in the Philippines reported earning as little as US$4 per day on 99Designs for her logo design work (Schmidt 2015: 208 and 197).

This also involves constant cycles of hope and disappointment as designers plug away in the expectation of eventually getting 'the big break' and landing a good client. It is therefore not necessarily about a full-time occupation for these designers but something undertaken in addition to the day job, so to speak. This example is perhaps not exclusive to this form of platform capitalism that hinges on the blurring of distinctions between labour and leisure. It is something where partipants labour on for small rewards in anticipation of it eventually leading somewhere. Kuehn and Corrigan (2013) call this 'hope labour'.

Needless to say, these platforms can only service specific sectors of the design industry, such as logo design, particularly for small businesses. Larger, more complex branding schemes that require fine-grain understanding of a corporation's internal structure and culture, its audiences and strategies demand close and long-term relationships between designer and client that cannot be replicated online. Nonetheless, some of these platforms try to emulate some of the social world of design elsewhere. Hence, meet-ups of participants are encouraged and spaces on their websites are organised as places for information exchange and, moreover, giving the feeling that they are part of something.

The large numbers of hopeful designers who are signed up to the platforms belie the fact that only a small minority are consistently active on them. For most, participation in platforms is an extra to the day job, almost constituting an occasional hobby more than a serious source of income. This underlines the blurring of work and play that often goes on in digital labour (Scholz 2012) or, otherwise, in 'immaterial labour' (Lazzarato 1996). The extent to which they represent a threat to the sociality, performativity or straightforward commercial practices of mainstream design is debatable.

CONCLUSION

In this chapter I have given two axes. One is longitudinal and temporal and focuses on the twists and turns of moving from design education to early career. I have steered clear of the more senior, established end of the design career, not least because this is already much more represented through design media. These tend to focus on the big success stories. We hear little of the designers who continue working the long hours for relatively low financial reward or those, indeed, who after a decade or so leave design altogether to do something else.

My focus has therefore been on the struggles for recognition, both internally in design and externally with clients. This gives way to a process of sociality where designers are constantly networking to maintain a profile but also to pick up on trends and movements around them. Overall, I have attempted to draw out the precarious qualities of design work and how these are produced and how designers respond. At the same time, the blurred distinctions between work and play, bureaucracy and autonomy come into view. These qualities fit in with wider developments in labour through contemporary capitalism, in particular, as part of systems of flexible accumulation, albeit that it is highly nuanced and variable in the design context.

The second axis in this chapter have been latitudinal and spatial. We have reviewed the various ways by which policy and academia have attempted to create taxonomies relating to creative work and how design fits into this. The overriding conclusion is that not one single model successfully accounts for design. Nonetheless, this analysis has shaped certain policy orthodoxies that are serially reproduced in different locations, as much concerning received understanding of design work as how this feeds into spatial planning issues. This chapter has also looked at the finer detail of labour in the design studio. Here, questions of individual autonomy and creativity overlap with concerns regarding the bureaucratic management of labour and design projects. Again, a measure of performativity is at work here, where designers act out 'being creative' as a necessary selling-point for their clients. Design work appears to emphasise tight, social interactions between designers and with clients, which affects decisions as to locating design businesses.

At the same time, just as in many other fields of service provision, platform capitalism has found its way into some design work. This adds a further dimension to the precarious quality of design work but it also underlines its unevenness and volatility in the context of globalisation. The next chapter focuses on global trade and mobilities to pursue these themes.

GLOBAL TRADE AND MOBILITIES

The notion of globalisation often suggests an increasingly homogenised world. Global trade has indeed grown exponentially as barriers to the movement of finance and goods have been relaxed and transportation has been made easier. Chapter 4 shows how, as a result, the geographies of design have also become more varied. An example here is in the fashion industry where design and production can either be separated or concentrated, depending on the relationship of local conditions to global factors. Beyond trade, we also consider the movement of people between countries and how design facilitates mobilities.

Sometimes, globalisation involves the flattening out of cultural data. The homogenous design of word-processing programs, jeans, banking facilities or fast food outlets suggests an increasing world of sameness. Global infrastructures facilitate the flows and movements of goods, finance, services and people, producing increased possibilities for value creation. This is where we can talk about 'extensities' – serially reproduced goods, services and systems.

But extensities are also dependent on intensities. In straightforward design terms intensities may be such things as prototypes or brand guidelines that lead to extensities; that is, their mass, serial reproduction, either as direct facsimiles or through various applications in different formats or registers. There are also spatial intensities that produce more design outcomes. These may be cities that are renowned for their fashion industries or global corporate design headquarters. Or we might even think of processes of urbanisation as producing concentrations of both consumer and producers that feed into global processes of trade. Fashion production has become increasingly dependent on migration to cities as a labour source and as a market, for example. Paradoxically, it seems that the deployment of sameness is also dependent on the concentration of difference. Globalisation produces relocalisations and vice versa.

This chapter focuses on the processes that *make* globalisation, the relationships of local and global economic activities and how design is active in this making. We can look at this in terms of macro-economic shifts, particularly those facilitated by waves of deregulation since the 1980s. Or we might analyse it from the perspective of more detailed business decisions concerning the availability of creative and productive labour, transport costs or the availability of materials. And we can also take into account localised governmental policies that privilege particular design economies in locations. It is a multilayered and uneven world of design out there.

In the first section, the scale of global trade that has developed since the 1980s, but speeded up through the new economy of the 1990s, is discussed and reviewed. This is placed in the context of the bigger picture of legislative change that has contributed to the deregulation of markets and the formation of global economies of design. The central part of this chapter, however, is concerned with constructing an alternative account to conceptions of globalisation that involve mass standardisation, frictionless movement and the death of distance. Instead, I show that the geography of design and production is more variegated and subject to many factors in its arrangement and distribution. While this mostly focuses on the design, manufacture and distribution of goods, the latter part of this chapter discusses the movement of people in two ways. One is in how mobilities can creative particular, intensive design agglomerations. The other is on how particular designed systems are widely deployed, in part to absorb mobilities. Half-way through this chapter, as a disuptive insertion, I provide an account of more 'activist' responses to the environmental and human costs of globalisation.

GLOBAL TRADE

The general trends in global trade since the 1980s have worked in two complementary vectors. One has been in the massification and standardisation of overall infrastructures that facilitate the production, movement and reception of merchandise. This includes the harmonisation of technical and legal structures but also the standardisation of things such as communication and transport protocols. The other has been in a move to more complex and detailed trade relationships. These have made the grounds of competition progressively more intense, within which design has assumed an increasing central role.

The evidence for the exponential growth in global trade is incontrovertible. This is easily demonstrated statistically. World merchandise exports rose in value from US$2.03 trillion in 1980 to US$18.26 trillion in 2011 – a 7.3 per cent annual growth. In volume terms, world merchandise trade quadrupled through the same period (World Trade Organisation (WTO) 2013: 55). Since 1985, world trade has grown nearly twice as fast as GDP output – economies have grown more on the basis of exportation and importation than on internal trade.

To put this in more everyday terms, it is not an exaggeration to say that practically every garment we wear, every electrodomestic item we use or every brand logo we look at is the product of global networks of production and trade. Very few of these broadcast the details of what it takes to bring them to market. In 2001, two journalists traced the origins of each material, process and component of a pair of Lee Cooper LC10 jeans, bought in the UK. They observed: 'on the inside label … it doesn't say where they come from, which is perhaps just as well, for what would you put, if you really knew? "Made in Tunisia, Italy, Germany, France, Northern Ireland, Pakistan, Turkey, Japan, Korea, Namibia, Benin, Australia, Hungary"?' (Abrams and Astill 2001).

Three broad reasons may be given for this growth in global trade and the increased complexity of supply chains. First, the end of the Cold War (1989–91) opened up trade with Central and Eastern European countries while reducing military expenditures to boost investment in other areas. Second, the internet and the digital economy has facilitated connections to worldwide markets, production bases and systems of financial exchange as well as provided faster and more accurate ways of tracking inventory and distribution. Third, large developing countries such as China, India and Indonesia have undergone economic reforms that have led to their catch-up and entry into global trade (WTO 2013: 57).

These technological and geopolitical trends have been enhanced by a progressive deregulation but standardisation of transport systems and trade barriers since the 1980s. For example, in the USA the Ocean Shipping Act of 1984 instigated a global process of addressing shipping company monopolies and promoting free market competition between them (Buderi 1986). In turn this would push transportation costs down and open up new shipping routes. At the same time, one must take into account the gradual standardisation of shipping technologies in the process, for example through containerisation.

The shipping container first came into usage in Canada and the USA in the early 1950s. Their size was initially constrained by train and truck dimensions. By the late 1950s, the standard size was 2.4m x 2.6m x 6.1m or 12.2m. Since they were mostly in operation in the USA, it was this size that was adopted in the late 1960s as the global standard through the International Organisation for Standardisation (ISO). Ultimately, then, these steel boxes provide a uniform volume for carrying merchandise, making calculation on costs easy; they also promise swift and low-cost interchange between shipping, rail and trucks. Of global trade these days, 90 per cent of goods moved by ship do so in containers. In this way, global trade penetrates into national and local infrastructures, the latter adapting to accommodate and facilitate the former (Heins 2015). Thus, for example, rail bridges have had to be raised to accommodate 'double-stacking' of containers; inland ports where containers accumulate or are interchanges between transport infrastructures develop (Cidell 2012).

The container is a standardised design in itself that facilitates the movement of mass produced design objects; it also conspires in the redesigning of locations and infrastructures.

If containerisation gives the impression of a world of massification of and sameness in its objects, then this view misses the complexity and intensity of the qualities of global trade. It is important to note, first, that goods have occupied an increasing proportion of global trade. From 1900 to 2000, manufactures grew from 40 per cent to 75 per cent of world trade, the sharpest rise of which has taken place since 1980 (WTO 2013: 54). But this rise is also marked by greater diversity in the goods being traded and in the territories that are doing the trading. Between 1990 and 2011, exports in merchandise from countries of the global South to other countries in this category rose from 8 per cent to 24 per cent of the world total (WTO 2013: 65).

The evidence of China's impact on the world in terms of manufacture, trade and design since 2000 is incontrovertible. Between 1980 and 2011, China's share of the value of exports went from 1 per cent to 11 per cent, making it the world's largest exporter (WTO 2013: 5). As an indication of the growth of its knowledge base, the number of higher education institutions in China grew from 1,022 to 2,262 between 2000 and 2010 (Shepherd 2010). By 2011, design courses in China were producing over 300,000 design graduates per year. Government policy has led to over 200 'creative clusters' or 'creative industries parks' across the country (Murphy and Hall 2011). China's shift from manufacturing and exportation of goods into the global knowledge and creative economy is inexorable. It's not all China, however. The figures still leave, for example, 89 per cent of exports elsewhere in the world. What is happening in other countries is clearly affected by China's rise, but each has other design stories to tell as well.

THE NEW ECONOMY, GLOBALISATION AND THE 'SECOND UNBUNDLING'

Thinking around the New Economy that emerged in the 1990s privileged flexible approaches to production and distribution networks and was based on fine-grain information to deliver 'better, faster, cheaper' by whatever means and through whatever geographical constellation necessary. The world is seen as a resource that needs organising to allow this process.

There is a danger here that when talking about globalisation one is playing into a certain discourse that emphasises sameness (e.g. Friedman 2006). Certainly, to travel through the world's airports and shopping malls or to spend time in theme parks and hotel chains suggests an endless serial reproduction of brands, brand experiences and branded products. So much seems to be the same wherever you go. Things in 'liquid modernity', it is argued, are increasingly detached and deterritorialised (Bauman 2000). A plethora of semi-academic texts have appeared and been avidly read in business schools to support this orthodoxy. Coyle's *The Weightless World* (1999), Kelly's *New Rules for the New Economy* (1999), Cairncross's *The Death of Distance* (2001) and Reich's *The Future of Success* (2002) all promote a vision of a globalised economy where location doesn't matter as much as the rapid satiating of desire. Kasarda and Lindsay's text entitled *Aerotropolis: The Way We'll Live Next* (2011) argues for a world where industrial complexes are planned around mega-airports to allow for even swifter movement of goods to their market.

Closer inspection often reveals something more subtle and complex, however. While the growth of international trade and business produces greater requirements for mobilities, deterritorialisations, evenness and standardisation, constant reterritorialisations are also taking place. As Hannam et al. (2006: 3) put it, 'There are interdependent systems of "immobile" material worlds and especially some exceptionally immobile platforms, transmitters, roads, garages, stations, aerials, airports, docks, factories through which mobilisations of locality are performed and re-arrangements of place and scale materialised.' To this list one might add design studios, design schools, design associations, workshops, hardware shops, warehouses and many other places that make up localised design cultures.

While some goods, businesspeople, finance, designers and architects are whizzing around the world, so there are objects and practices that produce friction against these movements. Further, rather than think in terms of 'either global' 'or local', it is more productive to talk in terms of various hybridities of these. This results in a layering-up of practices and orientations. Lived experience involves layers of local and global goods, media, social relationships, varying technological engagements and so on that involve disjunctures and differences as an ordinary part of everyday life (Appadurai 1990). Cultural experience within globalisation is mixed (Nederveen Pieterse 1995). Equally, design and production are subject to multiple geographical orientations and levels in their relationships. We should therefore be considering complex interweavings of global networks and local capabilities rather than in broad-brush terms.

A way of advancing this is in terms of what has been called 'the second unbundling' (Baldwin 2011a, 2011b). The 'first unbundling' was in the nineteenth century with the decline of transport costs, industrialisation of the West and the dominance of global trade in primary materials and agricultural products. These allowed production to be distanced from consumption but also assumed that tasks involved in making products remain in one place. In the second unbundling, competition is such that tasks are undertaken in different places and become an important basis of trade. To be more precise about this, Baldwin (2011a: 5) calls the trade–investment–services nexus as being 'an intertwining of: 1) trade in goods, 2) international investment in production facilities, training, technology and long-term business relationships, and 3) the use of infrastructure services to coordinate the dispersed production, especially services such as telecoms, internet, express parcel delivery, air cargo, trade-related finance, customs clearance services'.

This way of thinking about global business is useful because it does two things. First, it accepts that the arrangement and distribution of different activities that go together to design and produce goods and services is predicated on multifarious sets of calculations and decisions. Second, it draws attention to the entwining of static issues – such as available know-how, resources or facilities – with infrastructural realities such as communication networks or cross-border business relationships. The next section takes fast fashion design and manufacture to explore these issues.

FAST FASHION AND DELOCALISATION

Fast fashion is often associated with sweatshop factory conditions (Siegle and Burke 2014), unsustainable production and distribution methods (Fletcher et al. 2012), serial violations of intellectual property rights (Scafidi 2006) and a key element in the insatiable drives of consumerism (Schor 2004) and throwaway culture (Morgan and Birtwistle 2009). It is fast because it is configured to move through design, production, distribution, consumption and disposal as rapidly as possible. Its low cost makes it the kind of commodity that is subject to quick changes in design that respond to high, catwalk fashion trends that are mediated through popular culture and retail information on buying habits. Designs of garments are sold in limited numbers. Short-batch production of these garments favours small workshop-based manufacture in low-wage locations such as East Asia. Exponents of fast fashion include the brands Zara, H&M, Mango, New Look and Top Shop.

Clearly, fast fashion opens onto several related debates regarding design, contemporary culture and economic practices. But I want to focus this section mostly on questions of the arrangement and distribution of fast fashion networks, particularly in the context of issues deriving from 'the second unbundling'. This is primarily to show how the economic geography of fast fashion produces a much more varied map than any assumed 'design and consumption in the West, production in the East' model. A more complex analysis reveals how the globalisation of fast fashion produces, in turn, new centres of design activities.

The fashion industry has long been associated with particular cities. The fact that 'fashion capitals' such as London, New York, Paris, Milan and Los Angeles get ranked according to their prowess on the global catwalk (e.g. Global Language Monitor 2015) adds to this giddy excitement. Beyond the hyperbole of fashion capitals that is fed by journalism, Scott (2002: 1304), drawing on his research on Los Angeles and Paris, provides a checklist of factors that, in his view, produce world fashion centres. These are: a flexible manufacturing base; clusters of highly skilled contractors who can produce high-quality, short-run work; an infrastructure of fashion design schools and research institutes; a promotional infrastructure (e.g. media, fashion shows); an evolving, place-specific fashion tradition; connections between fashion and other creative sectors.

This list is important because it provides more complete and tangible reckonings on what is required to support fashion industries than the mere anecdotalism provided through the pages of fashion magazines. However, Gilbert (2013: 24–5) observes that fashion capitals are being eroded by fast fashion systems. The ability of places in China, India, Morocco and Turkey to turn out high-quality fashion goods has, arguably, replaced these fashion capitals. The result of this is that traditional fashion capitals are 'hollowed out': they exist more in terms of symbolic production – as places where fashion journalism, famous designers and fashion shows predominate – than in the actual production of garments (Reinach 2005).

There has been extensive deregulation and liberalisation of global constraints on clothing and textile trading. This includes, for example, the ending, in 2005, of the Multi-Fibre Arrangement (MFA) that dominated the geography of production since the 1970s (Glasmeier et al. 1993). Prior to the MFA, quotas had been imposed on the amount of textiles and clothing that developing countries could export to developed countries. The ending of the MFA led to fears that China would then overwhelm the global marketplace (Pickles and Smith 2011). As it happens, the outcome has been a much more varied global picture where new localities have become established as specialist centres.

In the 1990s, Benetton was frequently cited as the chief example of lean production: the company focused on core assets of design and strategy while manufacturing tasks were outsourced (e.g. Harrison 1994). By the 2000s, Zara had taken over this role (Sull and Turconi 2008). Benetton's design centre in Treviso, Northern Italy, assumed a two to three month lead between the conception of a design and its appearance in the shops. For Zara, centred in La Coruña, north-western Spain, this would be just two weeks. This is partly to do with the bureaucratic organisation of its headquarters and how this in turn necessitates a particular business model around it. Within Zara's La Coruña offices, around 200 designers are located amidst its market specialists, procurement and production planners so that the viability of designs can been rapidly checked against manufacturing costs and availability in its production networks (Ferdows et al. 2005). These enhanced design capabilities are costly, needing a large design staff, trendspotters and rapid prototyping capabilities. These costs have to be offset by various means, but principally by avoiding markdown through sales: all garments have to be sold at premium price, which means that they are produced and sold in short runs (Cachon and Swinney 2011).

The rapidity of Zara's design and supply chain is also to do with proximity. For Zara, China and other East-Asian manufacturing possibilities are basically too far away from Western markets. Shipping from there would take too long for Zara's model of rapid response and replacement. It therefore produces most of its clothing in more costly European and North African factories (Cachon and Swinney 2011). Other factors that come into the mix in deciding where to locate production include responsiveness to changes in size, colours and fabrics, quality and handling reliability (Pickles and Smith 2011) as well as currency exchange advantages and governmental incentives. Thus it isn't merely a case of garment production automatically going to the most low-wage locations, more likely to be found in East Asia. The trade–investment–services nexus of Baldwin's (2011a) 'second unbundling' produces a more varied geography of design and production relationships.

FULL-PACKAGE SUPPLY AND THE RELOCALISATION OF DESIGN IN TURKEY

In assuring high-level quality in production along with short turnaround time, brands increasingly turn to 'full-package' supply. This is where elements of product design, packaging, labelling and logistics are handled by their suppliers rather than being generated or coordinated by the core brands themselves. This is particularly prevalent in Turkey.

Turkey's strength in full-package supply of clothing, in part, grew from long-standing international associations, particularly with Germany. The German department store Karstadt set up links with Turkish suppliers in the 1990s; retailers such as Hertie, Kaufhof and Printemps followed on as buyers (rather than contractors), as did brands such as H&M and Mexx. Such enduring relationships have meant that Turkish suppliers have had time to develop their own capabilities in providing full-package supply rather than simply being garment makers. This, combined with preferential trade agreements with the rest of Europe and strong governmental support in Turkey, has meant that while producers could not offer low labour costs as compared with lower-labour cost countries such as China or Vietnam, overall price, technical capabilities, speed of response and quality gave them competitive advantage (Neidik and Gereffi 2006).

This trend starts with buyers gradually handing over more and more design responsibility to suppliers. Buyers may have 'trend meetings' where heads of buying offices of a retail brand from different countries meet to discuss trends in different locations. This information is then given to suppliers so that they themselves can develop interpretations on this. In other words, a broad design brief is passed on. But suppliers also begin to source international market information in terms of 'moods' and 'themes' through magazines, the internet and trade fair photos. As they build finer-grain understandings of these, so their design input and, indeed, confidence grows. Knowing the production capabilities that were available while having access to global market information, Turkish clothing designers were gradually able to make proposals to their buyers. They could develop fabrics, interpret fashion ideas into designs, run them up and show them to visiting buyers of fast fashion brands from Europe and the USA. These could subsequently be modified and then moved to market (Tokatli and Kizilgün 2009).

From here it is short step for Turkish companies to be designing their own products and brands, sometimes working in a mixed economy as supplier to other brands while also market-ing their own (Tokatli et al. 2008). For example, Marks and Spencer's fast fashion label, Per Una, was designed and manufactured in Denizli, Western Turkey. Erak is a company that had been a full-package supplier to many European and American brands before launching its own brand of 'Mavi' jeans (Tokatli and Kizilgün 2004). Indeed, in cultivating its domestic market in Turkey during the 1990s, the Mavi brand featured in a series of advertising campaigns that showed that it could compete with global brands with equally high-quality merchandise. The ads featured an actor playing an American CEO who is sent into a panic while comparing his own company's products with those by Mavi, as his assistant was saying that they also have their American jeans manufactured in Turkey. The ads ended with the Turkish emblem of the star and crescent on the sky. What one CEO said in one of the TV ads – 'Don't say it's the same product, George!' (*Aynı malı deme Corç!*) – became something of a catch phrase in Turkey (Kaygan 2016). By 2015, Mavi had retail outlets in Canada, Germany, Russia and Turkey, becoming an international brand.

The stronger entry of China into the global fast fashion supply chains from 2005 also spurred on Turkish producers to compete further in designing and producing more distinctive and close-to-market garments. In the same year, Turkey had become the world's second big-gest exporter of clothing, with a net export value of US$12.7 billion as against China's US$70 billion (Tokatli and Kizilgün 2009: 146). The deregulation of international markets does not necessarily suck manufacturing out of economies like Turkey or Morocco. Instead, it has the effect of pushing them to become more actively engaged in design as a way, also, of protecting their productive capacities.

The Turkish instance provides a compelling case of the complexity that surrounds global trade processes and the role of design therein. Rather than regard the fast fashion industry as being wholly about brands retaining core capacities and outsourcing to the cheapest labour market, there are a number of considerations that have to be taken into account. Fast fashion requires continual supply, ensuring that the right garments arrive on the right day. Quality and adherence to strict temporal rhythms can outweigh production costs in calculating where to source supply. In turn, suppliers are not static and neutral. Where there is support and capacity, they may develop their own design strengths and distribution networks. In effect, what we have here is a constant

4.1   Mavi jeans store, Rize, Turkey (Photos: Harun Kaygan)

process of delocalisation where outsourcing distributes production and distribution. This may gradually lead also to a *re*localisation as suppliers build their own networks and capabilities to design and produce their own goods. However, in turn, this may result in another cycle of delocalisation as they themselves build global trade networks and outlets.

This example demonstrates the instabilities and dynamics that are at play in the globalisation of trade and the clustering of economic capabilities, including design. Whether through careful economic planning on the part of governments, through market dominance or a combination of these, just as one place may hot up in its ability to design and produce goods so others, including its hinterland, cool down (Haughton et al. 2014). To give Harvey (2010: 148) the last word in this section, 'the uneven geographical development that results is as infinitely varied as it is volatile'.

GLOBAL RELOCALISATION: SLOW CITIES, TRANSITION TOWNS AND MAKERSPACES

Some activists and designers have responded to this volatility by attempting to refocus design cultures away from globalising systems of finance and resources. All around the world, groups and individuals in villages, towns and cities have driven campaigns to relocalise economic processes and everyday lives. Motivations for this differ widely, including: a cultural resistance to the bland standardisation of consumption by globalisation (found in the Slow City movement); preparation for the challenges that a post-carbon world may produce (as led by the Transition Towns movement); or the decentralising opportunities afforded through technological advances in manufacture (such as by 3D printing and the establishment of so-called makerspaces).

The Slow City movement originated in Greve-in-Chianti in Italy in 1999. The mayor of this small town organised a meeting with three other municipalities to define 54 rules as to what would make a *città lente* – slow city. The concept built on the Slow Food movement which began in 1986 as a reaction to the opening of a McDonald's restaurant in the centre of Italy. It has been dedicated to maintaining the viability of local restaurants and food production. The denomination of 'slow city' only applies to localities of less than 50,000 inhabitants and is awarded by a committee representing the membership organisation (Knox and Meyer 2013). By 2015, there were 201 such slow cities in 30 countries (CittaSlow 2015).

The Slow City movement emphasises local distinctiveness in urban development. The overarching principles include the design of high-quality environments, free of pollution and that are calmer in their overall, convivial atmosphere, of preserving local aesthetics in the built environment and fostering local crafts, produce and food networks. It therefore involves the strengthening of localised design cultures, ensuring a tighter indigenous fit between and promotion of creative practices, resources and networks for production and everyday consumer practices.

As such, the Slow City presents an alternative urban regime to the 'corporate-centred city'. The mainstream, neoliberal conception of the city is largely driven by and organised around an economic growth agenda. This is mainly based on industrial and corporate interests, which, for example, are homogeneously celebrated and signified through the office block as a symbol of this (Grubbauer 2014). This is a replicable model that is more attuned to other such cities than to its own, local cultural grain. Contrastingly, slow cities draw from localised assets of production networks, material resources and visual styles, emphasising grassroots decision-making and more idiosyncratic economic activities (Mayer and Knox 2006: 325). In terms of urban design, an emphasis is placed on nodal points – such as public squares or street markets – that 'collect' people together (Parkins and Craig 2006: 81).

The Transition Towns network shares many of the aspirations of the Slow City movement in terms of such things as strengthening local food networks and communitarian, grassroots decision-making. However, its chief motivation springs from a perceived need to build resilience in the face of Peak Oil. 'Peak Oil' means the point at which we pass the maximum global rate of crude oil extraction. The exact year that this has happened or will happen globally is debatable depending as it does on new discoveries of oil sources. Globally, it is expected to be in the first decades of the twenty-first century, but several oil-producing countries have long passed this individually (Hirsch et al. 2005; Bardi 2009). The net effect of this is a sizeable increase in the cost per barrel of oil that has taken place since the 1980s. While it peaked to $147 per barrel in 2007, it then dropped to $50 shortly after (North 2010); this kind of volatility in price – which has been happening since the 1970s – has been a root cause of many economic recessions.

The Transition Towns movement focuses on building resilience in the face, first, of overall oil depletion and, second, against such price volatility. Resilience is therefore about lowering the dependency of places on external factors that may start with oil but also extends to other oil-dependent commodities. This is mostly done through the relocalisation of production, services and other supports to everyday living.

As an approach, Transition Towns is rather less prescriptive than the Slow City movement, providing guidelines rather than rules for qualification. Its 12 steps are designed to lead to an Energy Descent Action Plan while engendering an inclusive, grassroots participation in the process (Hopkins 2008). As of 2015, there were 472 official Transition Towns initiatives (those that meet criteria designed to maintain the movement's identity) globally, with another 702 'muller' ones (those 'mulling over' or contemplating whether to adopt an initiative) (Transition Network 2015). Material outputs from these communities include: the creation of local currencies to encourage hiring of services and the buying of goods from the locality; the adoption of low energy input, permaculture design principles for food growing; the (re)establishment of repair workshops and training in associated skills.

Given their enthusiasms for relocalisation, one might expect the Slow City or the Transition Towns movements to engage with new manufacturing opportunities afforded by 3D printing, a technology that has developed gradually since 1977, but has gained increased global prominence from about 2000 (Birtchnell et al. 2013). Otherwise known as 'additive manufacturing', 3D printing allows for a number of new possibilities: first, it distributes manufacturing so that objects can be printed closer to their consumer base, rather than being shipped; second, it provides for mass customisation so that consumers can specify their own variations of a basic form; third, it can facilitate rapid prototyping so that design ideas can be tested more easily than with traditional fabrication methods. As a result, 3D printing has the potential to relocalise making while returning the work of designers closer, in temporal and spatial terms, to the manufactured output (Birtchnell and Urry 2012).

The rise of 3D printing may be read alongside other worldwide developments such as the development of the Maker Movement from about 2005. The Maker Movement invariably involves combinations of traditional craft practices such as metalwork or calligraphy with digital tools, including 3D printing, to create new products and applications. Although differing in styles and ideological motivations in different countries, it is typified by practices of tinkering with and hacking into products and technologies, and the open sharing of innovations and technical knowledge. Thus it combines shared workshop facilities – makerspaces or Fab Labs – with the global sharing of information via the internet. By 2015, there were 97 makerspaces across the UK (Sleigh et al. 2015: 4). An important functional aspect of these in the UK has been to provide social meeting points for like-minded creative people. Meanwhile, by contrast, following the 2015 visit of China's Premier Li to the Chaihuo makerspace in Shenzhen, makerspaces became an important element of national economic planning for encouraging creativity and design (Saunders 2016).

The Maker Movement and 3D printing have been interpreted as part of a wide-scale turn away from mass manufacture towards localised systems that are more responsive to varying desires and needs of individuals and communities (Anderson 2006). As such it is prone to hyperbole among its advocates, where they are assumed to lead to a 'new industrial revolution' (Marsh 2012; Tien 2012). Novels such as Cory Doctorow's *Makers* (2009) explore the designerly, social and economic possibilities that are made available here. Often, however, there appears to be little distance between speculations based on observation and those that are fabricated for fictional purposes (Birtchnell and Urry 2013).

Where something of the Maker Movement and hacker culture ethos does form more sustained and impactful industrial economic practices is in the *shanzhai* phenomenon in China (Li 2014), which is discussed in detail in Chapter 7. But while *shanzhai* draws on localised design and production networks and ongoing tinkering, its marketplace is far from localised, it being heavily oriented towards domestic trade and exports directed at the global South. Another way to think of makerspaces is as sites of 'microproductivity' where very focused design innovations take place that draw on the intensive coming together of designers and makers (Hartley et al. 2015: 103–06).

In the meantime, however, beyond a shared enthusiasm for relocalising economic and design practices, it is important to note how the Slow City movement, Transition Towns and maker-spaces are all rhizomatic. They each have their respective baseline requirements of varying prescriptiveness, but these are intended to be rolled out on a worldwide basis, not least through internet-based sharing. As such, they link relocalisation to global political and environmental concerns. By operating out of close-knit, communal practices that emphasise strong social and economic links in a locality, they become intensities. By providing reproducable and report-able frameworks, these can be replicated and so they are also extensities.

Makerspaces – and indeed the Slow City and Transition Town movements – have undergone impressive growth as concepts since the mid-2000s. However, while providing interesting and occasionally influential counterpoints to dominant paradigms of trade and mobilities, they remain relatively insubstantial in terms of their numbers. The remaining sections of this chapter explore global mobilities, how these produce particular design intensities and how design facilitates fur-ther movement of people.

Globalisation involves not just the movement of goods, but of people and information. This also involves the circulation of ideas, techniques, policies and aspirations as well as their concentration, reproduction or contestation. Design is active in the infrastructures that facilitate these processes, creating possibilities for capital accumulation and circulation. It can also conspire to produce fric-tions that slow things down or reconstitute the geographies of economic and social practices.

MOBILITIES

Alongside the movement of things and ideas, the sociological study of mobilities includes, as one should expect, the movement of people. Work in this academic specialism emerged in the 2000s to claim a 'new mobilities paradigm' (Sheller and Urry 2006; Urry 2007). This does not present mobilities as a new concept, although heightened speed and intensity of mobilities *is* a contemporary phenomenon. Neither is it a statement of global borderlessness. Rather, it defies the notion that what is 'normal' in life is about 'stability, meaning, and place' while contesting 'distance, change and placelessness' to be 'abnormal' (Hannam et al. 2006: 208).

Undoubtedly, mobilities have become more intensified and widespread in recent years. We have already seen evidence of the growth of global trade, but this is matched by growth in the international movement of people. Legal international arrivals to countries grew from 25 mil-lion in 1950 to 534 million in 1995, and 803 million in 2005; between 2005–2007 this figure grew by a further 100 million (Dubois et al. 2011: 1031). People are travelling further and more frequently. To give another example, total distance travelled by citizens in Great Britain rose fourfold between 1950 and 2007 (Office for National Statistics 2010: 170).

Mobilities research opens out the locations and networks that are valid and worthy of consid-eration, drawing attention to both how movement between places happens and what it means, and how localities and everyday practices are transformed by these. It is about connections, but in itself connects scholarly traditions. Cresswell (2010: 2–3) notes how it: brings together the social sciences and the humanities in that it marries geographical investigation of spatial effects with the affective domain of how movement and pausing are experienced; links different scales of moving, attending to rapid, long-distance travel such as flight as well as short-distance, slower practices such as walking; reviews the interconnectivity of devices and human movement (such as mobile digital technologies); considers mobilities to have differentiated politics (such as travelling 'Business' or 'Economy' class); is also about immobility or stillness; requires the researcher also to be mobile.

How does design facilitate or, even, format various types of mobility? How does it allow mobilities to happen or shape their experience? And how does design engage distinct economies of mobility?

In the following sections I propose two opposing directions in which mobilities take place in order to draw out specific ways that design functions in their different economies. The first reviews two ways by which mobilities *into* a locality affect their design cultures. The second explores how certain formats of design are serially reproduced and are active in encouraging or assisting mobilities while also formatting the economic grounds within which those mobilities take place.

MIGRATION AND DESIGN INTENSITIES

It is an unassailable fact that migration has increased since the 1980s. The number of cross-border migrants rose globally from 155.5m in 1990 to 213.9m in 2010, a rise of 38 per cent. This still represents only 3.1 per cent of the world population (WTO 2013: 123–4). However, this has deep influences on the population make-up and skill bases, both of source and host countries, which is also reflected in design.

Beyond the statistics, however, it is important to note that there are different types of migrant labour. For the purposes of this section, we shall focus on high-skilled and low-skilled labour of migrants. To add nuance to this, the composition of migrants is often, overall, more skilled than natives (Docquier et al. 2009). In the short term, the wages of these skilled migrants will drop, but they will create a net positive effect on host economies (WTO 2013: 128). Studies generally show that host economies benefit from immigration, both from low- and high-skilled arrivals (e.g. Peri 2012; Constant 2014).

An example of the benefits of this mix to a design economy is to be found in Los Angeles. Mexican migration of relatively low-skilled labour to California was an important factor in the rapid growth of apparel, textiles and food products industries there (Hanson and Slaughter 2002). Equally, the Los Angeles apparel industries benefitted from Korean immigrants who were highly skilled in the apparel industries. They came from Brazil and Argentina in the late 1980s and 1990s, driven by currency crises, inflation and political and social instability there. Gradually, they connected to clothing brands, such as Forever 21 and Urban Outfitters, and to their own international production networks. These included fabric and trim sources, sample-makers and sewers in Brazil, Vietnam and China. Second-generation offspring of these Korean immigrants then went to university, learning about branding, logos and merchandising skills which were then introduced back into family businesses. Thus, while also drawing on the lower-wage input of Mexican and Asian workers in the garment district of Los Angeles, these Korean family businesses became increasingly design-led, developing and consolidating the apparel industry of the city (Moon 2014).

While we might associate the notion of outsourcing with the growth of fast fashion, we can also consider *in*sourcing as a stimulus. The movement of skilled migrants into design-intensive locations provides new skill-sets and international knowledge networks. Aside from the example of Korean migrants to Los Angeles, a similar impact of Chinese migrants to the Prato area of Italy in stimulating a fast fashion has taken place.

In a more self-consciously strategic way, corporate global design centres are created precisely to draw in talented and cosmopolitan creative practitioners. Formerly a supplier to Motorola, the Taiwanese manufacturer BenQ moved into its own-brand electronic products in the late 1990s. It established its own Lifestyle Design Centre in Taipei in 2002, where over 50 international designers were recruited to extend its global reach (Bryson and Rusten 2010). The location of global design centres for Ford, River Island, Sony and Nokia in London since 2000 evidences a presumption that design studios may be physically distanced from both their productive infrastructure and their consumer bases. However, in addition, design and prototyping centres are developed in locations where new products can be fashioned and tested in the context of a 'global city'. Part of their reasoning for locating in London was that, as a cosmopolitan city, it provides both a consumer testbed and stimulus for designers. By 2006, 30.5 per cent of the population of London (2.23 million) was foreign-born (Gordon et al. 2007: 13). As a global city, it is assumed, it can model a global marketplace.

The example of the Los Angeles garment industry and the impact of Korean immigrants on it demonstrates a cumulative process where design know-how gradually gets imbricated into business practices. This is where family and business networks that are brought to the city are built on and hooked into pre-existing design-led companies. Meanwhile, the establishment of corporate design centres is a more self-conscious strategic attempt to leverage the cosmopolitan capital of designers working there and, more generally, that of the host location. Either way, mobilities can result in intensified design nodes that in turn feed into extensive, global trade.

MIGRATION, MCDONALDIZATION AND DESIGN EXTENSITIES

The last section was concerned mostly with high-skilled, mobile subjects. However, many migrants are not high-wage earners and occupy low-skilled menial jobs. In the UK, for example, 2 million migrants have occupied 16 per cent of low-skilled employment (Migration Advisory Committee 2014: 2). Their employment typically includes work in agriculture, construction, factories, services such as cleaning or hospitality that does not necessarily require post-16 qualifications. This section reviews the possibility that certain systems are configured and designed in order to provide a frame for or, even, exploit this sector. This is in the serial reproduction of highly planned and designed systems.

Historically, it is argued that the development of flow-assembly systems in manufacture – otherwise called 'Fordism' – was partly related to considerations of immigrant labour (Batchelor 1994). By breaking down assembly tasks to simple actions that required little training, the Fordist production line provided an easy entry point to immigrant workers, particularly with reduced language skills in the host nation.

We might also align mass manufacture with mass entertainment and consumption in this context. The alienated labourer working on the factory line portrayed by Charlie Chaplin in the 1936 film *Modern Times* could easily be the follow-on character from his 1917 *The Immigrant*. In his novel, *In the Skin of the Lion* (2012 [1987]: 43), Michael Ondaatje reflects on how silent movies themselves provided accessible entertainment to a polyglot, immigrant audience in America. He was referring specifically to a scene in *Modern Times*. It is also interesting to note that Chaplin chose to make the film as a silent movie so late ('talkies' were, by the 1930s, well established). It seems that Chaplin knew his mass audience. Similarly, Walsh (2012) places mass immigration to Canada and Australia in the post-Second World War period alongside the promotion of the idea of mass markets in goods. A standardised, largely homogenous consumer culture provides a stabilising, common ground for migrants, easing their assimilation into the host nation.

A more contemporary example where something of this dynamic takes place is in the so-called 'McDonaldization' thesis put forward by the sociologist George Ritzer (2000). In many respects McDonaldization is an extension of Fordism. The latter relies on the breakdown of tasks to make them easily manageable and understandable; it involves specialist equipment to perform these tasks; it draws on the scientific management of time – tasks and outputs are rendered calculable to draw out maximum efficiency. McDonaldization is oriented more towards service delivery than manufacture, however. Its systems may be found not only in fast food outlets, but in the configuration of telephone call centres, public-facing bank operations, amusement parks and hotel chains, for example. As opposed to the Fordist system of manufacture where operatives undertake just one, repeated task, in McDonaldization they may carry out several scripted tasks that are more algorithmically organised. Workers follow a menu of commands, responding to customer preferences.

Ritzer (2000: 12–13). summarizes McDonaldization to be about efficiency, calculability and predictability both for the employee and the consumer. Its systems are predesigned to 'guide' them through a series of decisions and actions; each 'episode' in the process is carefully planned, weighing up the relationships of input and time; the range of products and services will be identical across the brand.

From the point of view of certain sectors in migration, this McDonaldization concept may be interpreted to neatly fit mobile populations and their work needs. Migrants invariably take on work that lies below their habitual skill levels (Migration Advisory Committee 2014). Just as the large-scale Fordist factories and its associated mass cultural formats provided a 'home' for migrants in the early and mid-twentieth century, so we might view McDonaldized systems as their late-twentieth and twenty-first century counterparts.

To focus back onto fast food, Eric Schlosser (2002) has pointed out that English was the second language in at least one-sixth of North American restaurant workers and about one-third of these didn't speak any English at all. Responding in part to the high proportion of migrant labour in this sector, Burger King, McDonald's and Tricon Global Restaurants (who also owned Taco Bell, Pizza Hut and KFC) collectively advocated the simplification of the design of kitchen equipment. This would ensure minimum training and allow workers to slot into jobs quickly. In this respect, the graphics of outlets involved photographs rather than text to communicate more easily to migrant workers (Schlosser 2002: 70–72).

Annual turnover of 3.5 million employees in the fast food industry in the USA has been around 300 to 400 per cent and therefore a system that involved 'zero training' has been the fast food industry's ideal (Schlosser 2002: 73). From an employment point of view, the growth of McDonaldized systems may be aligned with many other factors in addition to increased migration. Systems that are designed to allow workers to 'learn the ropes' and introduce them quickly into the workplace with minimum need for training also support the prevalence of zero-hours contracts, flexible hours and irregular employment more generally.

Ultimately, we may view McDonaldized systems as extensities. First, these are often found among recognisably global brands that have relatively standardised systems of product and management. Second, this standardisation allows for easy entry points on the part of both clients and workers, in particular migrants with limited host country language skills and who are willing to undertake low-skilled, menial work that is relatively easy to learn.

Arguably, this model of extensities has consumer appeals too. In the context of an analysis of Polish migrants in the UK, Horolets (2015) suggests that the McDonaldized format provides a measure of security for mobile individuals. Extending from Augé's notion of 'non-places' (Augé 1995) that are relatively easy to navigate and understand for first-time users, places like airports, motels or theme parks have a special appeal to dislocated people. They provide easily digestible environments for migrants, it is argued (Horolets 2015: 7).

It could also be that the interchange of consumerist subject positions and the reproduction of McDonaldized formats in working environments constitutes a certain disciplining into neoliberal object environments. These reinforce modes of flexibility and calculability that are the core of contemporary capitalism.

MOBILE OBJECT ENVIRONMENTS

Mobilities can also involve the easy movement of entire object environments as well. One example of this is easyHotel. Launched in London in 2005, this franchise was created for relatively small hotels of between 50 and 75 rooms. The franchising benefits are that franchisees get the brand and brand name, website and booking system, training, design and specifications manual (further discussion of the design of franchises is developed in Chapter 6). Internet booking and self check-in contribute to keeping costs down. Being part of the wider 'easy' brand (as in easyJet, easyMoney, easyGym etc.) gives recognisability as well as a tie-in from its other services. As a result of this, day rates for rooms in London can be half the price of a standard budget hotel room.

The easyHotel design offered 'durable long lasting materials which are almost free of maintenance costs' and allowed for an increase in the rooms on offer (easyHotel 2014). This was facilitated by the design of a pre-fabricated modular hotel room that could be retro-fitted or installed into new buildings. In 2001, Joel Saunders Architect in New York developed concept work for this where 'Waterproof fibreglass, painted in the company's signature orange, is used in wet and high traffic areas, while soft surfaces – mattresses and cushions – wrapped in durable vinyl', meaning that 'the entire room can be wiped clean with only a damp cloth' (Saunders 2016). So-called 'pod hotels', in which pre-fabricated room units provide a homogenised offer and very low-maintenance costs, were inspired by first-class airline cabins and Japan's 'capsule hotels' (Victorino et al. 2009).

Generally, the hotel industry is of a fairly conservative nature. It is also capital intensive in that investments require payback horizons of 25 years (Allegro and de Graaf 2008). However,

4.2 EasyHotel, London (Photos: Guy Julier)

the growth of the budget hotel, in which its systems and physical detailing are meticulously designed to keep costs low, forms one side of a growing split in hospitality commerce and elsewhere. Since the mid-1990s, the New Economy has produced access to low-cost brands in products, fashion, leisure and travel. At the other end, exclusive, luxury brands have also grown. In the meantime, the middle range – at least in terms of hospitality – has declined (PriceWaterhouseCoopers 2005).

We could read this as reflecting increased polarisation of wealth that has gathered pace through the neoliberal era. Or we may see it as part of a growing complexity of consumption modalities where savings made in one area (spending on an easyHotel room, for instance) can be allocated to luxury brands (shopping at an Armani store, for example). But we might also interpret this as part and parcel of a global economy of mobilities in which design figures highly to facilitate it. Mobile object environments may be the pre-fabricated pods of an easyHotel, Ibis or a Yotel room. But in the broader context of social practices, these are also 'attached' to other mobile object environments such as luxury brand stores and their serial replication.

Finally, it is important also to consider the workers in all this. The hospitality industry is significantly supported by migrant labour. For example, 25 per cent of employment in Ireland's travel-related sector has been made up of migrants (Baum 2007: 1394). Hotel work involves emotional or aesthetic labour (Hochschild 2003 [1983]; Witz et al. 2003) – service with a smile, looking your best for the customer – using dispositions that are designed to make the client visitor feel at home. Migrant hotel workers, McDowell et al. argue (2007), fit easily into and are, indeed, hired for these roles.

CONCLUSION

This chapter sketches out some broad issues that produce a highly varied set of design economies in the contexts of global trade and mobilities. On the one hand, globalisation provides infrastructures, systems, devices, legal norms and connectivities that facilitate the easy movement of people, ideas and things. Containerisation has led to the integration of worldwide transport networks for goods. Style magazines or websites move trends in taste around the globe. Highly systemised leisure and hospitality chains allow their employees and their clients to move relatively smoothly between locations – to settle in and be at home with ease. These are the extensities.

On the other hand, intensities arise. This is where localised specialisms are consolidated or developed. Motivations for these are varied. They may be straightforwardly in opposition to the environmental and cultural impacts of globalisation where attempts are made to build tighter and stronger local networks of production and consumption. This is expected to produce greater resilience in the face fluctuating global commodity prices and reduce carbon footprints; or it is done to increase stronger local identities and promote better quality of life. While these rest on the importance of locality, they are also part of global networks.

Equally, entrepreneurial activities in some localities lead to the development of tighter networks between designers and producers. Strong examples of this exist in the fast fashion industry. Rather than lead to increased distancing between design and production, the global circulation of fashion trends combined with the need to move product to market rapidly and in quick succession means that the competitive advantage of their co-(re)location is acted on. Economies of design both globalise and localise.

Ultimately, the rise of global trade and mobilities has been afforded by changing technological, legal and financial possibilities. The internet, trade agreements and the easier circulation of money across borders all underpin the New Economy and globalisation. However, this is also to do with people and their readiness to engage in this landscape. Migration creates new localities and global connections in which design economies may thrive. Infrastructures that support the daily lives and livelihoods of mobile subjects are also designed. While trade and mobilities involve the movement of physical stuff and individuals, these also require people to be able and willing to engage in their processes and implications.

FINANCIALISATION AND ASSETS

Financialisation involves using money to make money. However, investment has to go *somewhere*. Chapter 5 investigates two scenarios - private homes and shopping centres - to show how design is used to create assets. Home decoration and improvements are used to add value to properties in order to make them more attractive to potential buyers. Retail spaces are designed to increase shopping visits and keep rental earnings up. This then provides a dependable return for property developers and their investors. We see how design operates to produce spaces that are in the service of finance.

The idea of financialisation often suggests invisible flows of money through the electronic networks that make up global stock exchange systems or the currency markets. But financialisation also involves investment *in* things. Design often makes these flows material. The things to which finance gets attached are not static as if the inflow of cash is just there to keep them alive like a money-bound, life-support system. They are not unchanged by that investment. Indeed, they are invariably configured *for* investment and investors as well as to produce return. The point of this chapter is to explore how some things are designed in order to achieve investment and with an eye on future value.

Office blocks, shopping malls, car parks, apartment blocks and hotels are all the objects of financial investment. Property developers handle the interface between investors, architects and designers, city planning authorities and the public in order to maximise return on investment. This is chiefly done in two ways: through selling the property on to other owners once it is developed or refurbished or through annual return on rental. Vast swathes of our towns and cities are produced through this. Few elements of public life are not touched by this. But financialisation also finds its way into our private lives. Homes are where we eat, sleep, spend time with our friends and families. For home owners they are usually the biggest investment they make in the course of their lives and therefore represent a means of financial security and, possibly, gain. They are assets, and design is employed *within* them to make those assets work most efficiently.

In Chapter 1, I identified financialisation as something that has come into ascendancy in contemporary capitalism. To repeat, financialisation may be typified by strategies to maintain or enhance the value of shares, brands, real estate or capital flows. This chapter is chiefly concerned with real estate and the exchanges that go on between such tangible assets and expectations of return on investment. To put this somewhat simplistically, within this, there is the actual economic performance of an entity – whether, for instance, it is achieving good sales through a defined period which will enhance preparedness of investors to support it. And there is the image that an entity portrays – whether it appears to be in robust health or not – which will also affect shareholders' enthusiasms or, for that matter, the entity's ability to raise other forms of financial support such as loans.

It is no coincidence that during the 1980s in the USA and UK, while there was a significant growth in companies floating on the stock exchange, so there was growth in the sector of graphic design for company reports. Producing a clean, sober image or marking out the uniqueness of a corporation is something done for consumers. It is also done for shareholders and the annual report, designed and produced ahead of the annual general meeting of a corporation is an important device in this process. It is noticeable that even in 1987, graphic design consultancies in the UK engaged in more work for clients in the financial services sector than in consumer products manufacture (McAlhone 1987: 22).

Design can be used to influence investor relations in other ways, too. For example, investors in mobile phone producers look to the quality of or innovation in more easily known features such as appearance, attractiveness or usability as opposed to their more complicated technical capabilities such attainable bandwidth. In turn, Aspara (2010, 2012) shows that these more accessible or understandable details may be emphasised through the product development process in the service of securing favourable evaluations on the part of investors. The roll out of a new design, its timing and how the event itself is designed are carefully managed to capture the imaginations of consumers and journalists, but, most importantly, to keep investors happy and also to attract new ones.

The rise of design in contemporary capitalism goes hand-in-hand with the rise to dominance of financialisation over economies, government policies, corporate practices and, even, everyday personal choices and actions. Design is intimately bound up in formatting and communicating assets whether these be through the regeneration of part of a city to attract inward investment, the fashioning of corporate literature or homeowners undertaking makeovers prior to selling. In turn, assets provide opportunities to leverage further capital. As Sassen (2003) remarks, financial services are able to liquefy the value of real estate, thereby releasing ever more capital into global flows. From the point of view of this book, what does this make buildings other than bricks and mortar, concrete, steel and glass? If, from the 1980s, the American motor industry consistently made more money through dealing in loans to consumers – secured against the automobiles they had bought – then what does this make the car? Indeed, this instance is illustrative of a general trend in US corporate profits. From the mid-1990s onwards, finance-derived profits there far outstripped manufacturing across the board (Harvey 2010: 22). Between 1980 and 2007, global financial flows grew faster than any other type of flow (Manyika et al. 2014: 4).

French economist Thomas Piketty (2014) provides a long view on the strength of capital and its effects. The broad thesis is that, historically, the return on capital has been consistently higher than the overall rate of economic growth. This is the capital:income ratio, a ratio that is between 4:1 and 7:1 in developed capitalist countries. The value of capital is typically much greater than the value of the total annual economic income of these countries. The only time that this disparity has narrowed has been during the mid-twentieth century, but since the 1980s, the gap has widened again. The effect of this is growing income inequality in capitalist states: capital produces more capital for those who have it; for those who don't have it, it is their labour that has to create that wealth for others. Piketty adopts a broad brush in his approach to capital, putting together residential and corporately owned real estate together with commodity, stocks, shares and other assets. But to look closer at the kinds of capital we are talking about, it is clear – even from Piketty's own statistics – that in most countries, real estate takes a growing lead in its value as a percentage of national income.

The first part of this chapter explores how a certain home aesthetic emerges out of a desire to make them attractive to future buyers. How does the home makeover function for that asset? The second part investigates how shopping centres are designed as 'deep wells of finance'. This is both in attracting investors and in assuring predictable, long-term returns. Through these examples, I want to show how the design of assets makes financialisation and vice versa.

SHOW HOMES: OWNERSHIP AND SPECULATION

Studies of consumption and domestic life invariably focus on the home as a site of individual taste – a place where the sovereign consumer has dominion. It is where people construct their identities through the things they buy and display, a private world of commodity accumulation behind closed doors where the public world does not and cannot encroach and where the 'true' self is expressed (Goffman 1959). Memory, narrative, identity or the aesthetic-self figure as common points of reference in these kinds of studies (e.g. Woodward 2001; Hurdley 2006; Money 2007).

This conception of the home as a private, individual expression of consumer sovereignty might be challenged, though. By thinking of the home as a site of investment, both of money and time, individual taste is tempered by the marketplace. Home decoration and furnishings may be adjusted or even catered to for this reason. A show home or show house is usually furnished and decorated by property developers for prospective purchasers as an example of what other houses on an estate may look like. In this section, I want to take this concept of the 'show home' to explain how the home has been increasingly bound into neoliberal practices around financialisation and how, in turn, this produces a kind of contingency around what it is and how it is treated. By situating the home in the context of wider pressures of the housing market, we can begin to see how design might function differently here.

Since the 1980s, homeownership in the developed West has grown to become a central motivational feature of its economies. In the UK the percentage of households in self-owned properties moved from 57 per cent in 1981 to 71 per cent in 2005 (Communities and Local Government 2009). These figures are roughly similar to the USA over the same period (Garriga et al. 2006). In the UK a boom in ownership took place in the 1950s and 1980s; in both occasions these marked periods of fiscal stability and political encouragement towards homeownership after periods of turbulence. In the USA there was a marked rise in ownership in the period 1995–2005 in the context of a range of new mortgage products being made available (Chambers et al. 2009).

With the exception of Germany, which has a much tighter controlled rental sector, the trend in government policies of European, North American and Australasian countries has been to promote individual homeownership over the past 40 years. In 1987, British prime minister Margaret Thatcher advocated a 'home-owning democracy'; in 2004, George W. Bush declared his mission to create, in the USA, an 'ownership society'; in 2006, Nicolas Sarkozy affirmed that France should become 'a nation of homeowners' (Rossi 2013: 1070). Despite the financial crisis of 2008, government policies in these countries have continued to push in this direction while other models, such as co-housing, continue to be difficult to progress (Chatterton 2014). Equally, in Latin America, cuts in state expenditure on public housing through the 1990s and 2000s meant that the deficit in dwelling units passed from 38 million to 52 million in this period (Rolnik 2013: 1061). Housing for low-income families thus takes the form of *favelas* or massive private housing schemes on urban peripheries.

Furthermore, the cost of housing as a proportion of household budgets has increased dramatically since the 1980s as demand for affordable housing – in particular due to falls in the amount of social housing being made available – has outstripped supply (Lawson and Milligan 2007). House prices in Australia, France, Ireland, the Netherlands, New Zealand, Spain, the UK and the USA hit record levels in relation to incomes in 2005 (*The Economist* 2005). The UK housing charity Shelter put this into context by calculating what the costs of ordinary food items would be if they had kept pace with housing since 1971. The price of the average of home in the UK had gone up over 43 times by 2011 (Shelter 2013). If this rate was applied to other commodities, a bunch of eight bananas would cost £8.47, half a dozen eggs would come out at £5.01 and a chicken would set you back £51.18! Of course, property values vary greatly. In 2014, US$50,000 would buy 0.9 square metres in Monaco, 1.5 in London, 4.4 in Tokyo, 20.2 in Budapest and 60.2 in Cairo (Space Caviar 2014: 154).

As we have seen with the debt foreclosures, house repossession and the dramatic fall in the housing market since 2008, the trend towards greater, more secure private ownership of homes is far from stable. While the 1990s saw a steady rise in the percentage of homeownership as against rental in the UK and the USA, there has been a sharp drop since 2000 as the differential between incomes and house prices has grown, particularly for the under-40s (PriceWaterhouseCoopers 2015).

Rather than provide the 'home for life', ownership enters citizens into the vicissitudes of the neoliberal marketplace, therefore. These fluctuations include the rise of flexible working and portfolio careers within a move to service-dominated economies, higher divorce rates and attendant break-ups of the traditional family units and longer life expectancy that demands leverage on the value of the home as a pension plan. Just as there are housing ladders through which people can build capital as they move up from apartment or starter home, to family home, to house and garden, so there are housing snakes that compel them to start over again.

In this situation, gaining maximum value at any stage of one's 'career' as a house owner is important. Homeownership is about providing a roof over one's and others' heads and a locus for self-expression; but it is also bound up in global financial flows. Financial systems are able to liquefy the value of real estate, thus turning capital assets into cash through equity release. Houses therefore become a source of future value. If the stock market is, at base, concerned with looking for places to invest where value is expected to rise, so homeownership is driven by the same priority. Indeed, in the UK these two came together with the creation of endowment mortgages from the late-1980s. Here, the life assurance company would take on the loan from a mortgage lender of a home and invest this in the stock market while the mortgagee would pay the interest on the loan to the life assurance company. With a booming stock exchange at the time, the expectation was that the return on this would be significantly greater than the loan. In such conditions, and more generally then, the home and its owner are closely implicated into systems of financialisation.

The home is, of course, a place where people express themselves through furnishings, decoration, fixtures, layout or modifications; but it is many other things too. It occupies a key role in the fashioning of the self, not just in terms of aesthetic identity or memory, but in terms of what it means to be a 'rational' participant in neoliberal society. There is a biopolitics at work here (Rossi 2013). Social relations – what it is to be a member of society and how to achieve this membership effectively and happily – are bound up in notions of accumulation and reproduction of particular norms. Ideas about what the home should or could be are contingent upon other forms and practices outside it. The next section opens out how design is sometimes active in this process.

MAKEOVERS

Design can give homeowners and sellers the edge on this process of accumulation. Just as the steep growth in homeownership in the 1950s led to a rise in do-it-yourself (DIY), so the same thing happened from the 1980s. This is best evidenced by the concomitant development of DIY superstores in the UK, such as Homebase, B&Q and Wickes, since the 1980s or the spread of the Bauhaus chain across Europe. Along with housing ownership has come a rise of enthusiasm for personal care and improvement of the home.

Rosenberg (2011) provides a compelling argument that connects home improvement, domestic taste and the property market in the context of neoliberalism. The turn towards home improvement may be read in terms of neoliberal conceptions of self-improvement. How one furnishes the home, cooks and gardens has intrinsic pleasures, but they are also about how one constructs an identity and self-presentation. Lifestyle is multilayered in its motivations (Featherstone 1991; Chaney 1996; Bell and Hollows 2005). It is also something that is governed from afar. The state or some other single source is not telling neoliberal citizens how to live. Instead, 'experts' are distributed across such institutions as universities, schools, health and the media and they relay 'advice' on how lifestyles are carried out (Ouellette and Hay 2009). In this respect, a plethora of home improvement and domestic property websites and TV programmes that came into being from the 1990s are worthy of attention.

In 1996, *Changing Rooms* hit the British TV airwaves. The programme ran through 15 series during eight years and was franchised to the USA, New Zealand and Australia. Its 30-minute format showed householders swapping houses for each to re-vamp a room under the tutelage of 'expert' interior decorators. Its emphasis, therefore, was on taste and home improvement in equal measures, revealing, on the one hand, tensions or coincidences between people's individual styles and, on the other, the sheer *speed* with which changes could be made.

This idea of speed – of rapid makeover – was subsequently adopted in the garden redesign show *Ground Force* (1997–2005), which saw expert gardeners, assisted by family and friends, transform a garden over two days. Again, the emphasis was on quick solutions with copious use of decking and other hard-landscaping tricks and with the installation of mature plants and ready-to-lay turf. Again, versions of the show also went out in the USA, New Zealand and Australia. Even stronger reference to this fast economy of home improvement was made in the UK with programmes such as *DIY SOS* (from 1999) and *60 Minute Makeover* (since 2004).

5.1   Covers of *House Doctor, Property Ladder: Sarah Beeny's Design for Profit* and *Adding Value to Your Home* (Photo: Guy Julier)

Explicit reference to any attendant rise in value of the home was not made in these programmes. However, a parallel set of shows were concerned with buying and selling property. They often highlighted the necessary home improvements required to add to value. These included, in the UK, *Property Ladder* (2004–09), *Property Snakes and Ladders* (from 2009) and *Help! My House is Falling Down* (from 2010), all presented by the property developer Sarah Beeny, as well as *Homes Under the Hammer*. *Property Ladder* – a version of which also went out in the USA – that saw individuals buy and sell homes within a limited timeframe, making (often cosmetic) changes in order to maximise accumulated equity. At the end of each show, real estate valuers would assess the property to confirm whether or not a target had been met. Following the banking crisis of 2008, Beeny also presented *Village SOS*, which focused on how householders might take collective action to improve their neighbourhood, introducing a timely communitarian spin (Marshall 2011).

If these practices of speed and home improvement leading to advances in equity were made most explicit, then this was in the Australian programme *Auction Squad*. Here a team of designers, builders, landscape architects and gardeners undertook a property renovation in just a day prior to its going to auction. Light structural work was carried out – such as removing stub walls or treating dry rot – but also detailed decision-making was made on plants or interior colour schemes. In terms of the home decoration that was prescribed, Rosenberg (2011), drawing from Grimshaw (2004), identifies the prevalent use of what he terms 'soft-modernism'. This is typified by subdued colours such as off-whites and caramels, colours that are regarded as 'sleek and modern' rather than carrying the harshness of modernist monochromes.

This soft-modernism is prevalent in other home-lifestyle media, including the design magazine *Wallpaper**. But it also finds its way into the housing market as a way of selling the idea of 'contemporary yet comfortable'. Equally, one might read IKEA's 'democratic design' within the same framework (Rosenberg 2005). The IKEA paradigm allows for rapid furnishing of the home that facilitates smaller-scale expressions of self-identity. Its furniture is relatively neutral while storage, picture frames and wall-hangings provide platforms for more personal touches to be added in. These are tactics of balancing personal taste with a concern for future buyers. Rosenberg (2005: 16) puts this more pointedly, stating that 'The depersonalization process thus fractures the relationship between the dweller's identity and the house and contents. This is the aim of all makeover – to create something new that can be exchanged in the neo-liberal economy.'

The home itself is a design culture in the way that its space is arranged, thought about and filled out by its inhabitants. Householders are playing the roles of designers, producers and consumers at the same time. In the scenarios described by the TV makeover and property programmes this is taken up a level. Professional designers show their thought processes, all be they highly simplified – this *is* TV after all! They are joined by other specialists such as real estate agents, property developers, architects, carpenters and gardeners. Householders collaborate both as producers and consumers in these transformations. In

5.2   *Wallpaper** magazine covers and 'Space' sections (Photos: Guy Julier)

their exchanges a discourse emerges regarding the relationships of taste and value – be that environmental, social or economic. Here, then, design culture spins upwards and outwards to take on board neoliberal ethics, the marketplace and finance. In this way, the home ceases to be a bounded locus and, instead, is constructed relationally to a set of external fields and future possibilities.

> Design is often tied into economic possibility. It produces sources of future value. It can also *point towards* value *in potentia*, drawing attention to something's competitive strength in the marketplace that is yet to be realised.

Given many of the cultural traditions within which the home resides, the connection to finance and conceiving of it as an asset are not so explicit. We have to dig around a bit and think about how some homeowners' thinking might be influenced by such things as TV programmes and magazines. Larger-scale, more complex forms of real estate, such as retail developments or office blocks, are more overt in what drives their investment patterns and how this influences their appearance and use. The next sections expand on this.

CLONE TOWNS

In 2005, the city of Exeter was labelled as having Britain's blandest high street. In its 'clone town survey' the New Economics Foundation (2005) reviewed the retail offer of 150 villages, towns or city areas around Britain. Their definition of a 'clone town' was where the 'individuality of its high street shops [was] replaced by a monochrome strip of global and national chains'. More emotionally, they termed this as where local character had been crushed 'under the march of the glass, steel, and concrete blandness of chain stores built for the demands of inflexible business models' (2005: 1– 2).

I spent my youth in a sleepy rural town near Exeter. In the 1970s, global outlets like Gap, Zara and River Island didn't exist. Nevertheless, Exeter's High Street offer of national chains such as WH Smith and Woolworths still provided enough excitement to warrant an hour's bus journey to the city. It wasn't the city's majestic medieval cathedral or its fourth division football team that drew my friends and me: it was a day's wandering around its shops, occasionally consummating the visit with a purchase. Since then, and, indeed, since 2005, things have layered up in Exeter. In 2007, a new 'shopping quarter' was opened in the High Street. With over 60 stores spread through 39,000 square metres of retail space, Princesshay seemingly added a new dimension to this city centre at a cost of £78m (Gardner 2007). Proposals for its expansion were put forward in 2014. It seems that there is an insatiable appetite for more of the same but a bit newer.

To return to their report, the New Economics Foundation (2005: 3–4), a UK thinktank on economic innovation, made a series of recommendations to avoid the continual cloning of clone towns. These included: a guarantee of fair market access to small, local and independent retailers; ensuring local procurement of goods and services; stronger controls on planning and tenancy processes. These recommendations were largely repeated in 2011 by a similar, but more high-profile report on the high street by the British retail consultant Mary Portas (Portas 2011). But none of their proposals really got to the background economic issues that reproduce town centres as they are. So I want to re-pose their question and add another. What makes this sameness of high streets? And what gives them diversity?

In the next two sections I want to tell something of the story of Princesshay and another shopping centre, Trinity Leeds, in more detail, examining the connections between capital investment, design and the layers of interest that are involved in their production. Within this, I draw attention to the interplay between the management of risk and invention. This process varies between national economies; for example, different countries have their distinct planning laws that offer varying protection to independent businesses in city centres. They might also have different systems of capital investment. However, while my account below is localised to the UK, many of the driving stakeholders are multinational firms which are involved in global flows of capital. Their logic in terms of assets and their treatment is reproduced around much of the world. The narrative I give is densely packed with references to the various actors involved in order to give a sense of its complexity.

'COMPELLING EXPERIENCES': RETAIL DEVELOPMENTS AND PROPERTY COMPANIES

The land on which Princesshay was built is owned by Exeter City Council. In other words, its freeholder is the local government. For Princesshay, the lease was 50 per cent owned by Land Securities, the largest commercial property company in the UK. Land Securities became a Real Estate Investment Trust (REIT) in 2007. A REIT is a category that originated in the USA but has come into being in many other countries since the mid-2000s. It signifies a company that owns or invests in real estate, paying an annual dividend to their shareholders. Broadly speaking, company law in most countries favours regular income streams and long-term appreciation for their investors. Land Securities owns and manages over 2.5m square metres of commercial property in the UK (Land Securities 2015). The other 50 per cent of the Princesshay lease was held by the Crown Estate, a semi-independent company that manages the property portfolio of the reigning British monarch.

Land Securities engaged three separate architecture firms for the design of its parts. Chapman Taylor, which specialises in retail architecture, worked on its central core and glazed arcade; Panter Hudspith, with experience in historic contexts, dealt with the area nearer the city's cathedral; Wilkinson Eyre concentrated on its northern end that incorporated car-parking, 122 residential units and an underground servicing yard (Gardner 2007). Landscape architecture and urban design was undertaken by Livingston Eyre Associates. The logic in using a mix of architecture firms was mostly that this allowed for a more sympathetic meshing of this development with its varied and historical surroundings and avoided appearing as a 'shopping mall bloc', as had previously been proposed by BDG-McColl. Coherence of the overall palette of colours and materials had been agreed through a masterplan that was formulated by the City Council, architects, Land Securities and English Heritage (Exeter City Council 2008).

5.3 Princesshay Shopping Quarter, Exeter (Photos: Guy Julier)

5.4   Trinity Leeds, shopping centre, Leeds (Photos: Guy Julier)

In 2014, Land Securities sold its 50 per cent of Princesshay development to another property company, TIAA Henderson Real Estate for £127.9m. At the same time it bought TIAA Henderson Real Estate's 50 per cent stake in another shopping centre, Buchanan Galleries in Glasgow, for £137.5m. This gave Land Securities full ownership of the Buchanan Galleries lease. Previously, its stake in the latter had rendered rental income for Land Securities of £7.5m annually (Land Securities 2014).

Meanwhile, Chapman Taylor Architects feature in another Land Securities venture. Trinity Leeds is a 93,000 square metre shopping centre for 120 stores. Opened in March 2013 it featured, as a centrepiece, a glass dome designed by SKM Anthony Hunts. Notwithstanding the flourish of this architectural feature, for its investors, trust in the scheme rests on the fine-tuning of a number of design and other issues that are critical to its success.

On Thursday, 11 April 2013, just after its opening, Land Securities conducted an investor presentation of Trinity Leeds. With an hour-long PowerPoint presentation by the company's Director of Investor Relations, its Head of Retail Development, Portfolio Director and its Leasing Director, followed by a tour of the development and lunch, these provided a fascinating glimpse into the relationships between investment and design issues. Asset managers present included representatives from Morgan Stanley, AMP Capital, Investec, Deutsche Alternative Asset Management, JP Morgan Cazenove and Kempen & Co (Land Securities 2013a). These companies largely deal on a global scale with investments from organisations such as insurance companies, pension funds, investment banks as well as private individuals.

Summarising from a transcript of the presentation (Land Securities 2013b), the key issues in its early weeks for the Trinity Leeds investors were:

- *Population growth and urbanisation*: The population of Leeds was expected to grow by 12 per cent to 840,000 by 2021.
- *Demographics*: The 'preferred' Trinity Leeds shoppers that were shopping there; following the ACORN market research taxonomy, these were 'Educated Urbanites', 'Wealthy Achievers' and 'Secure Families'.
- *Spending and dwell*: This was averaging £60 per visit with a shopper spending an average of approximately 96 minutes there.

The presentation of this data illustrates both the wider picture of population change and the more detailed information of consumer habits that are of interest. Property developers often carry out fine-grain tracking of shoppers to monitor footfall on the shopping centre's various parts. At the Princesshay development there was some contention surrounding this as real-time location data of the mobile phones of shoppers had been used for this purpose, raising privacy concerns (*Express and Echo* 2012). Alternatively, an array of research companies, such as Savills, PMA and Edison Investment Research, carry out this data collection and analysis, feeding it into property companies.

For investors, their interest is in future value. This is rendered in two ways: through the payment of rent by tenants of the development's units; and through the rise in value of the overall development – its equity, in other words. Each, quite obviously, is dependent on the success, judged by turnover and footfall, of its tenants. To put this from the point of view of Land Security's perspective on Trinity Leeds, its Head of Retail Development stated to its investors:

> In a world where physical shopping is seen by some people as an unnecessary activity, as developers, we've got to create compelling experiences that will delight our guests, the shoppers; and that will then encourage them to come back, come back again and keep coming back, and through that we will drive rental growth. (Land Securities 2013a)

What makes 'compelling experiences'? Aside from the general architecture of the development, this is achieved at two levels of design. One is in the overall planning of these spaces, the other has to do with the complex and sometimes messy practices of retail design.

THE PLANNING AND DESIGN OF RETAIL SPACES

In the overall orchestration of their retail, hospitality and leisure offer, developments depend on particular well-known brands that provide the 'big draw'. These are the larger destinations for shoppers and are called 'anchor stores'. In the UK, this includes established brands such as John Lewis, Marks and Spencer or Debenhams. These may already be in the town and so a development will leverage this asset by co-locating alongside them (as was the case of Trinity Leeds). The notion is that shoppers are drawn into these tried-and-tested stores and then extend their expedition into other parts of the development. Their dependability, size and significance also help to ensure financial stability for it.

Making retail developments 'compelling experiences' also requires detailed design work at a second level of their units, ensuring that they provide extra pizzazz. This is partly to do with ensuring the right mix of outlets, including food, but it also depends on their design competitivity – how they will stand out amidst the cacophony of brands in the space. This is where we have to look to further layers of creative practices.

This pizzazz may be achieved in part by allowing token independent shops as part of the development. These add variety and contest the accusation that property companies produce bland uniformity. Land Securities assigned 14 units to independent shops at Princesshay for this reason (Land Securities 2007). These may act culturally to add diversity and surprise to retail developments. Ultimately the chains will dominate for it is they who are usually more able to pay prime rental, are more dependable in terms of demonstrating and maintaining turnover and whose design language and palette are more easily understood by the property companies.

Prominently placed at both the Princesshay and Trinity Leeds are flagship stores Topshop-Topman. These are almagams of the men's and women's shops which are more often in separate units. As of 2015, there were 250 Topman stores in the UK, with a further 154 in 31 other countries (Topman 2015); in 2013 Topshop included 319 stores in the UK and 137 franchises in 37 countries (Hsu 2013). Topman and Topshop are part of the Arcadia Group whose other clothing operations include Burton, Dorothy Perkins, Evans, Miss Selfridge, Outfit and Wallis. The Arcadia Group has had several in-house design positions, including: creative directors for its different parts; fashion design (with its women's, men's and children's specialisms); trends research; brand development; retail design and visual merchandising. Overseeing this has been a Head of Design, with a 15-strong department, who has held weekly update meetings with its Group Chief Executive (Ryan 2012).

Alongside the in-house design functions of such groups as Arcadia, a halo of design consultancies and freelancers feed specialist skills into them, retail designers, either in-house or outside, take care of mid-term store design, which may change every few years. Meanwhile, expert visual merchandising studios deal with product presentation (such as window dressing) that will change with the roll-out of the new season's clothing. In London, for example, Blacks VM and StudioXAG have both done visual merchandising design, fabrication and installation for Topman. They involve strong creative input with high production values and an emphasis on spectacular, theatrical presentation.

Retail design has a sharp, direct but complex relationship with its clients and its publics. Kent and Stone (2006) usefully summarise, in Table 5.1, its qualities by contrast with product design.

Table 5.1 A comparison of product and retail design characteristics (Kent and Stone 2006)

Product design	Retail design
Long concept development phase	Short concept development phase
Anticipates problems and resolves them in advance	Deals with problems as they occur (snagging)
Discrete stages and finite concept life	Evolutionary phases and continuous 'tweaking'
Controlled prototyping and evaluation behind closed doors	'Pilot' store designs evaluated in full view of customers (and competitors!)
Supplier relationships based on shared risk, trust and mutual benefit	Supplier relationships based on contractual obligation and adversarial conflict

Particular creative input, often using freelancers or external consultancies, is undertaken for flagship stores. These occupy prominent positions (such as London's Oxford Street) and carry the largest range of goods, sell exclusive ranges and host new product launches. Aside from their role in promoting popularity and loyalty for consumers, they also work to promote the brand for investors and the wider public. Direct sales from these are therefore of secondary importance.

The success of chains within retail developments works for them but also for their landlords. The job of the retail designer involves several clients. They have to achieve sign-off from the brand and/or group it belongs to. The retail development may be managed by a separate, specialist company or directly by the property company (or companies) that own the site and will require convincing. Occasionally the landowner may place restrictions or guidelines on design issues. And finally, anchor stores for developments may also have some influence. Much of the designers' time may be taken up in shepherding projects past different gatekeepers (May 2015).

Property development, where it happens and what is put in place, is driven by global investment capital, as we shall see in more detail in the next section. However, it is erroneous to assume that one single interest – such as pension funds – shapes this. Rather, a varied network of interests are at work here (Bryson 1997). This is, nonetheless, motivated by a desire for stable, steady turnover for investors, property developers and tenants alike. To summarise thus far and also help with thinking about the next section, the ecosystem of retail developments, with all their actors, institutions and interests is outlined in Figure 5.1.

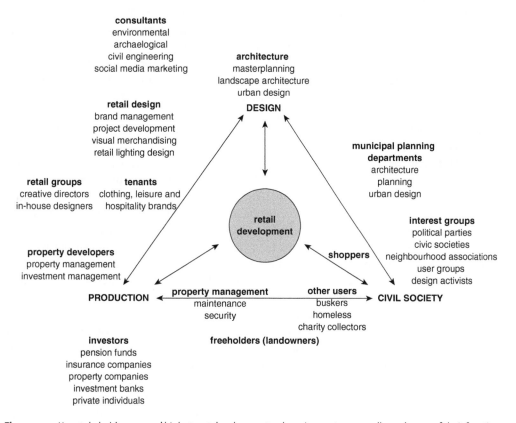

Figure 5.1   Key stakeholders around high street developments, shopping centres or malls, and some of their functions

RENTAL, INVESTMENT AND RETAIL BRANDS

The structure for return on investment has a direct relationship back to the overall design of shopping centres and of their individual units. Rental is paid in two ways. First, there is a base rent on units. In the case of Trinity Leeds, this averaged nearly £115 a month per square metre in 2013 (Land Securities 2013b). A second source of revenue is through turnover rent. In this case, the tenant only pays 70–80 per cent of the full base rental value; after that, they pay a percentage of their annual turnover to the landlord, usually up to an agreed amount. This is negotiated on a case-by-case basis and requires transparency by the tenant in terms of showing their turnover. For the landlord, this indicates that they benefit more immediately from tenants' success rather than when there is a rent review. It also means that they get feedback on tenants' performance in a development. For the tenant, this system spreads risk and, additionally, it means that it is in the landlord's interest not to introduce damaging competition to the development.

Such arrangements have had profound impacts on the way that retail, particularly of clothing, is carried out. We saw in Chapter 4 how the development of fashion networks of production and distribution have accelerated the movement of these goods around the world and how it has pushed costs down. These factors have combined with financial pressures at the retail point. During the 1990s, mergers of independents into retail brands and then retail brands into groups – such as the Arcadia Group – allowed for the internationalisation of distribution networks. This permitted greater economies of scale but also exerted greater pressure from investors on retail brands for minimum amounts of return on investment. At the same time, the fixed costs of retail unit rental increased substantially as property companies sought greater monopoly control over these (Cietta 2008).

This has meant that the retail brands themselves have had to push sales volumes up to keep abreast with these rising demands. In turn, this leads to de-specialisation. While the volume of individual designs on display in clothing stores has not increased greatly, many brands build on a more 'total look', catering for a reasonably wide age range (e.g. from kids to middle-age parents, in the case of Gap) and variety of clothing types (e.g. smart and casual). Their aim is to shift more product by tapping into wider demand (Cietta 2008). This is how they are able to pay their bills and keep their own investors happy. In terms of retail design, creative pressure is on ensuring emotional attachment to the brand through fixing the right ambience. Consumer repeat visits are imperative in order to fill out the various functions required of a personal wardrobe from the same brand. This is achieved through lighting, surface textures, circulation, product presentation and so on, but also through associated features such as the brand's website, advertising and promotional events.

In view of the property company and its investors' will to maximise return, then equity, base rent and turnover rent all mean that maintaining footfall and consumer spending is paramount. Therefore, the design and orchestration of the development as a whole interlinks with the importance of design of its respective units to help maintain these as spectacular, changing spaces, while the overall concept is reproduced and redeployed from one urban centre to another.

Trawl through the annual reports of property developers or interviews with their key executives and you fill find, time and again, references to the need for good architecture and design. They also make reassuring statements about continually expanding opportunities – both locally and globally – for these (e.g. Colliers International 2014; Land Securities 2015). In these, they are addressing their investors, be they insurance companies, pension funds or individuals. Investing in retail developments has a particular attraction for these.

In addition, insurance companies and pension funds, mutual funds, investment banks, commercial trusts, endowment funds and hedge funds are also known as 'institutional investors'. This means that, collectively, they invest other people's money rather than money they have themselves. Apart from hedge funds, which deal more aggressively in risk, the others are largely looking to an assured, steady growth of their investments over time. They all have mixed portfolios, investing, for example, in bonds, venture capital funds, commodities, infrastructure and real estate. Of these, real estate normally provides long-term return that is relatively 'illiquid' (meaning that cashing in an investment is not so immediate and quick a process as with, say, stocks and shares). Insurance companies and pension funds require a certain amount of liquidity to pay customer claims on them (Insurance Europe and Oliver Wyman 2013). Otherwise, they are looking to low-risk investment and predictable returns that, so long as they are doing their job well enough, retail assets can provide.

Pensions can involve 40 years, or even more, of investment on the part of the employees and their employers. In turn, pension funds invest these payments, looking to long-term stability. Pension fund assets in the UK, for example, hit an all-time high of £1.7 trillion in 2012; they had grown by 5 per cent during that year and had more than doubled since 2002. This was a trend seen in most developed economies (Towers Watson 2013). These pension funds may be held and managed by employers themselves or accumulated and managed by commercial firms. In Europe, over 90 per cent of them invest in real estate, with 75 per cent doing so in the USA (Andonov et al. 2013). This may be done directly, by actually buying and managing buildings or, often, through property companies like Land Securities, who act as real estate investment trusts. Retail developments, but also offices and industrial properties, are of interest here.

From 2000, investment law in many countries gradually freed up the amounts that institutional investors could put into properties abroad by raising or abolishing limits. Capital could flow globally from national pension funds to retail developments elsewhere. Thus, to give an example, in 2012, the Canada Pension Plan Investment Board that manages the Canadian public pension, announced that it planned to partner with the Nordic property company Citycon to buy Kista Galleria, one of the largest shopping centres in Stockholm, for US$700m (Flood 2013). A growing and ageing population in Europe and the USA has seen to the doubling or even trebling of the assets of insurance companies and pension funds since the 1980s (City of London Corporation 2011). This results in more institutions competing to find or create sources of return on investment. Real estate provides an increasingly attractive investment for institutional investors (Insurance Europe and Oliver Wyman 2013).

Shopping centres, malls and high streets are deep wells of financial intensity. They provide reasonably discreet concentrations of control, predictability and calculability. Shopper tracking, footfall measurement and turnover monitoring provide data from which property managers or companies can respond to consumer demand in terms of the overall design and orchestration of the space. It can also identify the strong and weak spots among tenants, incentivising or coercing them to up their game. In turn, this may lead to increased retail design input on their part to attract customers. Brands, such as Gap or Marks and Spencer, concentrate their financial resources on their core business of retail rather than getting involved in property development. Risk is therefore spread between the key actors: the investors, the landlord (being the property developer and manager) and tenants.

Ultimately, known brands have the infrastructure and capital to be a safe bet for the owners of and investors in retail developments. Introducing, for example, independent stores disrupts this predictability and therefore the relatively low risk of investment over long periods that they are seeking. This is to the extent that in downturns of the economy, they would sometimes rather leave units empty than allow newcomers to use them. Property developers and investors will only invest in prime areas.

Nevertheless, there is still a cycle of increased consumer demand, construction, occupancy, more construction, overheating, oversupply, ceasing of developments, stabilisation of rents, disappearance of surplus and return of demand that follows wider economic cycles. There are time lapses between rises of demand for retail space and supply of units. Thus there are instabilities with periods of under- or over-supply of units (Bryson et al. 2004: 184). Overall, it is more profitable, however, to maintain the status quo of filling these units with the same national or global brands and the same city centre activities (shopping, eating and drinking) everywhere rather than let them be occupied by independent shops. While in times of recession there may be some relaxation here, generally the aim is to ensure occupancy by the higher rent-paying and more recognisable brands.

These are some of the reasons why so many modern town centres and retail developments are so utterly dull.

By considering design as an asset, it may not just be the end-users of products, services and environments that are the priorities in contemporary capitalism. Sometimes, it is the agents of capital itself that are more influential in their shaping.

THE SPATIAL FIX

Let us step back from the dense minutiae of retail developments at this point and flesh out a broader picture of how global investment capital functions to produce spaces like them. The commercial jargon of finance underlines its complexity, which sometimes feels intentionally difficult to grasp. The further it is out of our reach, the more that the finance sector gets to write its own rules it seems (Lanchester 2015: xiv). Ultimately, though, capital has to go somewhere as investment and be taken from somewhere as profit. It is dependent on real places, but it also transforms them.

Here, therefore, I want to push the role that capital, its circulation and its allocation, plays in making particular forms of design. Harvey's concept of the 'spatial fix' (Harvey 2001) is useful here and is a term that has been frequently discussed in the context of neoliberal arrangements (e.g. Herod 1997; Schoenberger 2004; Arrighi 2006; Jessop 2006).

Investment banks, pension funds, insurance companies, mutual trusts and other investors build up surplus capital. As money is paid into them through, for example, insurance premiums or pension contributions, so these institutions have to find places to put the money where it will then accumulate profit. When there is too much capital for economies to cope with it – when there is more money than can be usefully invested – we get 'over-accumulation'. Harvey (2010: 148) has argued that there are just two ways by which this process of capital allocation can be done: one is through developing new products and technologies; the other is to expand geographically. This can be done through shifting production offshore or in developing new markets.

The latter has been highly visible in economies that have sat on the periphery of Western capitalism or that are transitioning to market economies. Places such as Spain, Portugal and Greece in the 1980s, Eastern Europe in the 1990s and South-East Asia in the 2000s all saw leaps in foreign investment of surplus capital, materialised, for example, through new shopping malls and hotels. Alternatively, investment might take place closer to home, as we have seen in the cases of Exeter and Leeds, where population increase and consolidation of favoured market segments, the existence or development of transport infrastructure to access these spaces and, for example, incentives by municipalities (such as relaxation of planning constraints or the provision of other infrastructural facilities) are offered (Bryson 1997).

The spatial fix therefore works in two ways. It is a 'fix' in that it provides a solution to a problem. *Spaces* are produced as places where money can go as investment. It is also where capital is *fixed*, where it is allocated into immobile assets. What was liquid is now solid.

This process invariably involves 'accumulation by dispossession' (Harvey 2003: 149). Jessop (2006: 151) sees this leveraging of under-exploited resources as part of a broader process of expropriation of the commons. Spaces have to be 'fixed' in order to provide mechanisms to make money. They have to be commodified. A riverside, where people go fishing, sunbathe or walk, does not turn much of a profit except, perhaps, through angling licences or the odd ice-cream stand. A waterfront development, replete with chain restaurants and prime-value apartments, does so much more efficiently for investors. Thus, the dispossession that takes place in this is in the turning over of what was previously a common resource to the interests of capital. Invariably, this involves the literal privatisation of these spaces (Minton 2012). The dispossession therefore works at two levels: one is in the general sense of common spaces coming under private control; the other is that access to these privileges only those who can afford it.

Urbanisation may be read as the result of population growth and migration. But we may also understand it as a process of rationalisation, a way of ordering and fixing surplus capital. There is a tendency to represent speculation through currency dealing, stock and commodity broking or asset trading as if it were somehow dislocated from the material friction of the everyday world. In fact, the opposite is the case. The relationship between these two is neatly summed up by Harvey in the following, often-quoted words, taken from *The Urban Experience*:

> Capital flow presupposes tight temporal and spatial coordination in the midst of increasing separation and fragmentation. It is impossible to imagine such a material process without the production of some kind of urbanization as a 'rational landscape' within which the accumulation of capital can proceed. Capital accumulation and the production of urbanization go hand in hand. (Harvey 1989b: 22)

And design is deeply implicated into this production of space.

CONCLUSION

This chapter has chiefly been concerned with how capital is turned into design with a view to its subsequent production of further capital. In other words, it has considered the ongoing relationship of design and financialisation. A considerable amount of scholarship exists which looks at such processes in terms of the built environment and the public realm, particularly in relation to gentrification processes and property development (e.g. Moreno 2008; Lees et al. 2013; MacLaren 2014). However, when considering design we have to look in finer detail at what is happening in terms of the arrangement and features of spaces.

The claim of the link between financialisation and property is not exclusive to private homes or shopping centres. We could also be talking about office blocks, hotels or, sometimes, university student residences. These are also part of the system of institutional investment that looks to long-term assets that provide a relatively predictable return, so long as the overall circumstances of political economy remains the same. In terms of the home, there has been a particular construction of neoliberal ownership that is mediated through popular TV shows that are arranged around the drama of the makeover. In this, the chief aims are rapid renovation within tight time and budgetary constraints with a view to maximising value. In turn, a certain aesthetic of 'soft-modernism' is forced.

The development and management of shopping centres works in different temporal frames. Here the aim is for highly calculated processes that take in a range of data regarding market conditions. This guides their sizing, orchestration, timing of opening and financial relationships with tenants. While a spectacular, attractive overall scheme has to be produced, at the same time, individual shops are subject to rapid turnover in their design. This is controlled in relation to the demands of a number of actors, including the leaseholder, the freeholder, the development's management organisation and also the respective shop's brand. Mediating these relationships through the design is mostly the job of the retail designer.

Ultimately, the specific example of the shopping centre stands for a wider process of urbanisation. This is where the needs of capital to produce new markets and market opportunities contributes to the creation of zones, built forms and consumer practices. These are reproduced on global levels, themselves reproducing the global flows of capital. In broad terms, design functions in two ways in such cases. One is straightforwardly in fashioning attractive spaces for investors, brands and consumers that produce rent. The other is in signalling future value. In either case – and indeed in the case of private homes as well – design is being used to enhance the value of the overall package. This is in the value of the building but also in potential investors' or buyers' enthusiasm to put their money into them. Finance is at work in the materialising of these spaces, just as architects and designers are in fashioning them and builders and shopfitters are in their construction. Their materialisation is vital to the production of further finance.

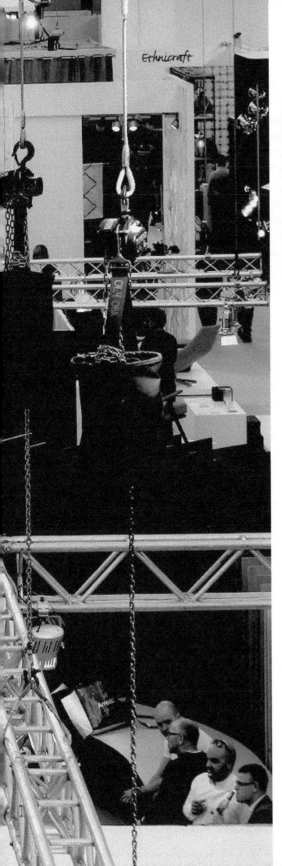

6

INTELLECTUAL PROPERTY

The economic value of design is in the shaping of new forms, mechanisms, symbols, services and systems. The originality of these is located in their intellectual property, which designers usually sell on to their clients. This intellectual property can be legally protected against copying through patents, trademark and design registration. Chapter 6 explores the roles that intellectual property plays in design. On the one hand, it can be used by companies to strategically defend market share against competitors. Meanwhile, only a minority of designers actually pursue the registration of their own work. We see how, particularly in fashion and furniture design, trade fairs set the pace of innovations, leaving intellectual property concerns behind.

Intellectual property (IP) can be a very dull topic. It is redolent with its legal terms (e.g. patents, registered design, trademarks, copyright, trade secrets), institutions (e.g. World Intellectual Property Organisation or the Hague System for the International Registration of Industrial Designs) and its agreements (e.g. the Patent Cooperation Treaty or the International Trademark System Patent Cooperation Treaty). In the global context of the many ways by which IP is treated in design, these have to be learnt and understood. It's hard work.

But it's also a captivating topic. And when you look at individual cases of IP, it becomes utterly compelling. These tell us as much about differing cultural and intellectual practices of places as about their legal systems. The creative industries are very much built on unashamed borrowing, quoting, cutting and pasting, improvising on, extending from and so on. Its open culture of sharing may seem at odds with the privatising impulses of IP. How this nexus is dealt with provides for fascinating entry points into understanding the cultural norms of different economies of design.

We have seen in Chapter 5 how urbanisation acts within processes of asset production and how design operates within this to produce value. In this chapter, we see how design functions to produce assets through intellectual property (IP). A key definition of the creative industries is their ability, through the work of individual creativity and talent, to produce IP (Creative Industries Task Force (CITF) 2001) and therefore it stands that we must regard this as central to design as well. IP is an asset that derives direct profit through licensing, royalties or its sale. Indirectly it functions to maintain monopolies over specific products and services and can be employed defensively to ward off competition from other firms. Like real estate, it can be used as an asset to generate rent, but it can also be used strategically in corporate positioning against rivals.

The rise of the importance of IP in relation to design is part and parcel of shifts in political economy during the past 30 years. IP has grown in sheer volume terms, as demonstrated by the number of patent and design registrations, the increase in governmental support in promoting these in many nations and moves to regularise and standardise approaches across the globe. This has worked both to protect intellectual property rights (IPR), especially for those countries whose economies depend more on these, such as the USA and in Europe. It has also been employed to stimulate global trade and investment.

Thus, IP has evolved through a mixture of regulation and deregulation: regulation as protection and as a framework for commerce to create scarcities out of abundances; but deregulation because it hinges so much on the opening up of trade systems and the breaking down, for instance, of tariff controls on importation and exportation. Effectively, it takes part in much of the transfer of power in trade from state to corporations.

All this said, many designers have an ambivalent relationship to IP, as we shall in the next and penultimate sections of this chapter. In the middle sections, we shall see how the IP in designs is wielded most vigorously to create corporate monopolies and defend their profit-making capacities. This may be in terms of a tight, intensive business model or in maintaining control over its wider network, as in the case of franchising. Here, design is highly embedded into the production of value at the heart of corporations. There are other contexts, however, where IP is less easy to police. This is explored in relation to furniture and fashion design, in particular via the scenario of trade fairs and how these affect the rhythms of design.

THE POLITICAL ECONOMY OF IP REGISTRATION

Since 1995, worldwide patent applications have grown exponentially, growing from 3.9 per cent per year to 9 per cent by 2013 when there were 2,567,900 applications. Of these, 81 per cent were filed in just five patent offices: China, the USA, Japan, the Republic of Korea and the European Patent Office (EPO). Across these dates, trademark registration has risen from just below 2m to just below 5m per year, with greatest concentration in the offices of China, the USA, the European Union, France and the Russian Federation. Registration of industrial designs have similarly risen from less than 200,000 in 1995 to nearly 1m in 2013, this time with 53 per cent in the office of China followed by the European Union, South Korea, Germany and Turkey (World Intellectual Property Organisation (WIPO) 2014).

Each nation has its particularities that are influenced by factors such as government policies in promoting IPR, trade balance of exportation and importation, or industrial strengths and weaknesses. However, two overall global trends are clear here: one is the unarguable rise in IP applications since the 1990s; the other is in its high concentration, with the USA maintaining its strength in patents and China asserting its dominance in all IP application fields. The USA is the country with, by far and away, the highest receipts from external royalty payments on IP (in other words, through selling IPR to other countries), followed by Japan, Germany and the UK (Johnson 2015: 7). After this, though, it is notable how countries such as Turkey, Ukraine, Iran, Morocco and Mexico have increased IPR activity markedly. Large and economically powerful countries dominate and continue to grow in IPR, but mid-sized, middle-income countries are also increasingly active. Table 6.1 sets out the different forms of IP protection and summarises some of the ways that these are applied.

In broad terms we may attribute this growth of IPR activity to being, quite simply, the result of rising standards of living and consumption growth – the more expendable income there is, the more consumers will spend on differentiated goods and services. This demand will be met by broader supply – differentiation of goods and services leads to increased employment of IPR to protect market share. Allied to this, the growth of global trade (not least supported by developments in information technologies and shipping) means that producers will protect their innovations in more countries. Hence, there has been a rise in IP applications.

We can't take IP to be an invention of the recent past, however. Indeed, law to protect inventions can be traced to back to ancient Greece, with important consolidations taking place in fifteenth-century Venice, seventeenth-century England and eighteenth-century America. Varying lengths of protection under fluctuating conditions have been applied ever since. What we have seen since the 1980s, though, has been the intensification of IPR activity alongside its greater global harmonisation through cross-nation agreements as to its processes and enforcement. All this points to a number of qualitative changes in economic, but also ideological, practices, within which design is deeply and multifariously implicated. Summarised, these are shown in Table 6.2.

From Table 6.2 we may concern ourselves in more detail with the third and fourth economic practices. These involve considering the codification of knowledge and the relationship of intensities to extensities. The question of the turn to knowledge economies and the privatisation of knowledge has been dealt with in part by earlier chapters. Another way of viewing these

Table 6.1 Summary of different forms of intellectual property protection

Type	Indicative definition	System of registration	Common duration
Patent	Protects a broad range of inventions, including but not limited to: processes, machines, articles of manufacture and compositions of matter; and in the US, new, original and ornamental designs for articles of manufacture (similar to 'Registered design' below) and biotech inventions.	National European Union WIPO Patent Cooperation Treaty in 94 contracting parties.	20 years but requires annual renewal.
Registered (industrial) design	Protects 'the appearance of the whole or a part of a product resulting from the features of, in particular, the lines, contours, colours, shape, texture or materials of the product or its ornamentation' (UK IPO 1949 Act).	National European Union WIPO Hague System for the International Registration of Industrial Designs in 62 countries.	25 years but requires 5 yearly renewal.
Trademark	A distinctive word, name, symbol or colour that is used in trade with goods to indicate the source of the goods and to distinguish them from the goods of others.	National European Union International Trademark System Patent Cooperation Treaty in 145 contracting states.	In perpetuity as long as it is used but subject to renewal to demonstrate use.
Copyright	Copyright is a form of protection provided to the authors of 'original works of authorship' including literary, dramatic, musical, artistic, and certain other intellectual works, both published and unpublished. This includes computer programs.	Can be made without registration although some countries provide optional system of registration.	Life of author + 50 or 70 years.
Trade secrets	Information that is not publicly known but has commercial value by giving advantage over competitors. It must be protected by reasonable steps taken to keep information secret.	On a peer-to-peer basis, for example by issuing non-disclosure agreements among employees or contractees.	Unlimited so long as it is commercially valuable.

Table 6.2 Economic practices and their effects on design and IPR

Economic practices	Indicative features in design
The promotion of knowledge and informational economies over, in particular, extractive, agricultural or manufacturing sectors	• Government promotion of design education and running down of trade or vocational training • Geographical separation of design and innovation capabilities from manufacturing base • Clustering approaches to spatial planning of cities to produce creative or knowledge hubs
The transformation of knowledge as a global public good into a privatised, commodity state and thus the repositioning of this from abundance to scarcity	• Student fees are levied for design education and/or it expands in the private sector • Governments and institutions promote IP awareness among designers • Design consultancies explain and then copyright or trademark differentiating aspects of their specific approaches to protect their 'uniqueness' • Prevalence of 'non-disclosure agreements' between designers and clients
The creation and use of systems of valorisation and codification of knowledge assets through their articulation into quantifiable forms	• Rise of measurement systems for creative industries activity and brand value • Codification of design tasks to help in the management and calculation of value of knowledge work
Increased emphasis placed on the creation of intensities or, otherwise, singularities that produce extensities	• Increased emphasis on producing 'parent' design outcomes such as brand guidelines, masterplans, design guidelines, software architecture, franchising guidelines • Establishment of corporate 'design centres' as knowledge 'hot houses'

issues of knowledge codification and intensities is to explore how these operate as part of the competition of monopolies that drives some of the constitution and distribution of neoliberal economic practices.

THE COMPETITION OF MONOPOLIES

The notion of a monopoly implies an owned resource that is unassailable, producing monopolisation that cuts out competition. This, however, draws from its more restrictive sense of being about single sellers of goods or services. Instead, I use it here to indicate 'firms with sufficient market power to influence the price, output, and investment of an industry – thus exercising "monopoly power" – and to limit new competitors entering the industry' (Foster and McChesney 2012: 66).

Historically, twentieth-century economics up to the mid-1970s is often referred to – particularly in Marxist thought – as the period of 'monopoly capitalism' (e.g. Foster and Szlajfer 1984; Harvey 2010). This is typified by large-scale state or corporate controls over material supplies, price, output, investment and employment. In communist countries until 1989, this involved state bureaucratic regulation of their entire economic structures and workings, including what would be made available for domestic consumption in everyday life. In the capitalist West, control was achieved through an amalgam that included: large-scale vertical integration of material or component supply to manufacture and assembly; the alignment of state economic policies with the needs of manufacturing; the use of economies of scale to create concentrations in research, development and innovation as well as to keep supply costs down; and intra-industrial agreements on wages and prices. This was, to put it briefly, the era of big business, big state and big unions. The challenge here, in these highly controlled and industrially stable conditions, where production costs were relatively low and the profit mark-up was high, was that surpluses of goods and capital would be produced. One important outcome of this was the use of advertising and design to stimulate consumer demand and take up this surplus.

Deregulation spearheaded by Reaganism in the USA and Thatcherism in the UK during the 1980s ushered in a new era of competition. On the one hand, this deemed to break up historical monopolies, particularly on utilities and transport. On the other hand, this resulted in more complex ways by which monopolies or quasi-monopolies were created and defended. After all, it is only rational that businesses should wish for the eradication of competition. Without competition, risk is lowered as market share is reasonably predictable and raises profits as the corporation achieves greater economies of scale. Research and development, marketing and distribution costs for a product or service are more quickly offset when reaching a stable and widespread consumer base.

The key here is in creating and maintaining barriers to entry by would-be competitors in whatever market segment a business is involved in. Shepherd (1997: 210) lists 22 ways by which this is done; these are given in Table 6.3 with indicative roles for design.

Table 6.3   Creating and maintaining barriers to market entry (Shepherd 1997) and design roles

Barrier	Example	Examples where design is employed
(1) capital requirements	A large firm may have access to cheaper loans because of its greater size and security.	
(2) economies of scale	Newcomers are unable to provide sufficient volume of supply to make their offer cheap enough to be attractive to consumers.	
(3) absolute cost advantages	An established firm may have preferential terms on the cost of materials or may be better located in relation to workforce and skills.	
(4) product differentiation	Strong product and brand recognition may be already established, requiring the marketing and advertising campaign of competitors to be expensive in order to gain visibility.	Strong use of advertising and branding, product design and service design.
(5) sunk costs	If a firm wants to leave a market, some costs (e.g. in machinery or advertising) are not recoverable. This pushes the risks of return on investment entry up.	
(6) research and development intensity	In order to enter a market, research and development commitments may be high.	The creation of corporate design centres in cities that are key to global markets.

Barrier	Example	Examples where design is employed
(7) asset specificity	Assets, such as particular skills or access to specific materials, may not be flexible and only applicable to particular products or services. This restricts the flexibility of newcomers to use these in other ways if they initially fail.	Keeping external designers on a retainer – meaning that their expertise in particular products or services is exclusive to a company.
(8) vertical integration	Ownership of two or more levels (e.g. component manufacture and assembly) is expensive.	
(9) diversification by conglomerates	A diverse firm can deploy assets at specific points to fend off specific competition.	
(10) switching costs in complex systems	Consumers of new products or services will have to 'learn' them or be trained in them — learning a competitor's alternative offer may create additional costs.	Designing supporting platforms that are specific to the product or service that makes it difficult and costly to swap to a competitor.
(11) special risks and uncertainties	New entrants may not know the marketplace well, making them a risk to lenders.	
(12) information asymmetries	Acquiring information and skills for working in a marketplace can be costly.	
(13) formal barriers set up by government or industry groups	Governments create legal barriers or industry-wide groups set rules that work to the advantage of existing firms.	Health and safety standards on products that local designers can work with more easily.
(14) pre-emptive action by incumbents	Established firms may ramp up their market share through reducing prices or introducing more product variations in order to 'suck up' market capacity and make it even harder for others to enter that marketplace.	Design of several variations of the same product.
(15) excess capacity	By demonstrating readiness to produce more if demand rises, this shows competitors that should gaps in the market appear, these can be easily and quickly taken up before rivals are able to get there.	
(16) selling expenses, including advertising	Enhancing greater demand, through advertising or marketing, can also help in ensuring that competitors are unable to find potential entry points.	
(17) segmenting of the market	By supplying more specific goods to particular market segments (e.g. age or gender profiles), through product variation or packaging, potential entry points are closed down.	More product design variation within a brand.
(18) patents	Patents give control over inventions, but they may also be used as 'sleeping patents' — ones that a firm doesn't actually use but competitors may wish to but cannot except under licence.	
(19) exclusive control over strategic resources	A firm may have the entire access to a vital material or people with specific skills.	Use of designers with particular understanding of specific technology – e.g. a software application.

(Continued)

Table 6.3 (Continued)

Barrier	Example	Examples where design is employed
(20) taking actions that raise rivals' costs	A firm may give incentives to new customers, perhaps drawing on its own infrastructure, such as extended warranty.	
(21) high product differentiation	A firm, or a small number of firms working in collaboration, may, though offering a wide range of brands with in a product type, saturate the market offer.	Again, more product design variation.
(22) secrecy about competitive conditions	A firm may be able to control access to knowledge about market and other conditions.	Use of exclusive trade secrets agreements when contracting design consultants.

Obviously, the more of these conditions a corporation can control, the more it can protect itself from market entry by competitors. As a result, this favours the consolidation of larger corporations or the creation of conglomerates who have more human and financial reach, first, in its ability to work strategically towards these and, second, to hold power over other forces to this advantage, such as through their influence over policy making across territories or tying up suppliers in exclusive contracts. Competition and monopoly are therefore entwined. And this leads to successive concentrations of economic power as larger corporations neutralise competitors and dominate markets and production systems.

It is a truism to say that we live in an age of seemingly boundless consumer choice, of a proliferation of brands, goods and services that are available in the capitalist marketplace. However, behind this lies a reality that the majority of these exists due less exclusively to their quality in design terms – their attractiveness, value for money, functional efficiency or durability – and more to the constellation of factors that harness differentiation while, by multiple means, denying the possibility for competitors to enter into that very particular market sector. We must therefore regard IP and design knowledge as working together in various ways.

> By being legally protected, a piece of IP is turned into a scarcity in that it has singular ownership. Put otherwise, it allows for the monopoly over an invention or a design.

In the following sections, three different formats through which design knowledge and IP play out are analysed. These do not provide a complete, global picture. Rather, their variance illustrates just some of the key factors through which design is performed.

1-CLICK BUT MANY PATENTS: GLOBAL CORPORATIONS

Between 1997 and 2014, the American multinational e-commerce company Amazon (founded 1994) went from 1.5 million active customer accounts to around 270 million (Statista 2015). We might attribute this exponential rise to many factors, not least Amazon's voracious business model of aiming for very low margins on goods while edging out competitors to achieve high market coverage. But if we were to pinpoint just one design feature at work on its

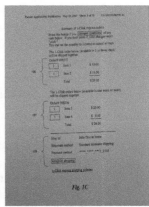

6.1   Parts of Amazon's US Patent application US 2007/0106570 A1 for 1-click system (Photos: Guy Julier)

webpages that takes away the friction of shopping, speeding up the move from consideration to consummation through purchase, then this would be its '1-click' process. The system is also one of the most controversial of Amazon's exclusive claims to IP.

Amazon's '1-click' system allows its online shoppers to purchase goods without having to provide credit card or shipping information. By exploiting information that is stored by cookies on the customer's computer, Amazon is able to fill this in for them, thus removing the tedious process of their having to do this themselves every time they make a purchase. Needless to say, by speeding things up and creating a more seamless shopping process, Amazon's '1-click' system brings it one step closer to the immediacy of offline shopping. While these things are impossible to accurately calculate, one blogger has estimated that this provided Amazon with an additional US$2.4 billion in annual revenue (Arsenault 2012).

A patent for Amazon's '1-click' system was filed in the USA in 1997 (US 1997/0928951) and granted in 1999. Amazon went on to license this patent to Apple in 2000 for its online store. From 1999 to 2002 it also undertook a high-profile litigation against its rival Barnes&Noble.com for patent infringement of its '1-click' system. However, Amazon was not so successful in Europe. Their patent application to the European Patent Office (EPO) went through a litany of acceptances and rejections between 1998 and 2013. In 2011 the EPO's objections were that the '1-click' system 'does not involve inventive step' and was viewed that it merely 'amounts solely to the presentation of administrative information' rather than 'any technical problem'. More detailed feedback included an argument that '1-click' was a misnomer as purchasing sometimes required several clicks and that it isn't altogether clear where that 1-click actually takes place (Boards of Appeal of the European Patent Office 2011).

This European denial of patent protection highlights the different cultural norms that affect IP approaches. By and large, American IP law may appear to work comparatively more in the favour of the patent applicant. Table 6.1 reveals, for instance, that patent law in the USA also includes ornament and biotech. The judgement shows how rulings and categories are based on varying interpretations across different jurisdictions. By contrast, for example, typefaces are not protected by copyright law in the USA but it is by patent law (Lipton 2009). In other words, in the USA what might protect a digital font is the coding behind it rather than its artistic element.

Diagrammatically, the '1-click' system is presented as a straightforward series of algorithms in its patent applications. Patent applications have to be understandable to the lay reader, but at the same time, the algorithmic diagram simplifies the technical level employed. This can then push it towards the possibility that it is perceived as a general idea rather than specific invention. However, in the USA, this can also be protected as a 'business method'. This notion was established as a patentable format in 1998 and opened the door for the burgeoning e-commerce market by allowing the computer system as a whole to be recognised as a useful result, rather than the specific coding (FindLaw 2008).

By 2014, Amazon's '1-click' US patent was just one of 1,263 patents it owned in America (Leonard 2014). Each patent is part of a more general approach to building corporate assets by optimising protection of what differentiates the company's business model. Amazon works on very low margins on its sales, relying more on volume and efficiency of procurement and delivery. Many of its assets are quite simple and reproducible and therefore need patent protection. (By contrast, generally and obviously, a complex invention or design, being harder to understand or replicate, is not in so much need of protection.) Amazon's US Patent 8,261,983 is a system for creating customisable packaging for non-standard sized goods. These make shipping of individual items fractionally cheaper. Taken collectively in high-volume shipping, this efficiency gain is of high value to Amazon. IP is being treated within a general engineering design approach.

This means that new ideas are developed incrementally and iteratively. Engineering designers will return to an invention over and over again to make adjustments and improvements. The overall business model is therefore seen as a series of components, each with its problems to be solved. One commentator notes that Amazon's IPR filings 'are reflective of a grind-it-out culture, based on the belief that a systematic series of small gains can add up to something big' (Anders 2013).

Amazon's number of patents is, however, not necessarily high by comparison with some other similar sized corporations. Data from the United States Patent and Trademark Office (USPTO) places the multinational technology and consulting corporation IBM top in 2014, it having registered a staggering 7,534 patents. Apple Inc. registered 2,003 patents in that year (IFIClaims® 2015). Unsurprisingly, the entire top 50 of corporations in a ranking of volume of US patents in 2014 is, in fact, made up of technology-led companies.

Two points are worth noting here. The first is to reiterate that each patent represents a design and/or technology breakthrough in itself, but that these function within an overall business strategy of corporate protection to defend its 'territory'. This may include registering patents that may not be directly usable by the registering company but which stop competitors using the invention. The second point is that while there is a preponderance of technology companies that are highly active in this, the IP they wield is not limited to technology inventions. For example, in 2014, Apple Inc. secured a ruling from the Court of Justice of the European Union to be able to trademark the layout of its Apple flagship stores. It ruled that '*a representation that … depicts the layout of a retail store* by means of an integral collection of lines, curves and shapes, *may constitute a trade mark* provided that it is capable of distinguishing the goods or services of one undertaking from those of other undertakings' (Court of Justice of the European Union 2014, emphasis in the original). In itself, this provides an interesting case of how interior design ideas may be protected. But it also underlines the energetic, 360-degree approach a corporation such as Apple Inc. takes to the protection of its design assets.

IP and, therefore, design in its service, are key weapons in the maintenance of corporate monopolies over their respective commercial territories, reinforcing their armaments, defending their flanks and disabling the agility of their opposition. That I employ a militaristic set of words here is in reflection of much of the language that is used more generally within modern capitalism (Grattan 2002). 'Aggressive takeover', 'sales forces', 'guerrilla marketing', 'target clients' or 'spending time in the trenches' are just some of the common business phrases that suggest a prevailing masculinist mindset (Brands 2014).

Patents, and IP in general, are part of a company's knowledge assets. These also include its human resources, stakeholder relationships, physical infrastructure, culture, and its working routines (Schiuma 2012). Unlike these latter resources, the IP of a company is quantifiable, is clearly explainable (by dint of its needing to be registered) and legally enforceable. This means that it is an asset that can provide direct financial returns through its licensing to other parties.

The more public nature of IP also means that it can contribute to an organisation's reputation. The rankings offered by companies who specialise in IP management and consulting, such as IFIClaims® cited above, can also provide comparative information as to how active a corporation may be in its research and development. IP can therefore be used positively as a way of signalling its overall health, in turn contributing to the maintenance of its share price. One can go so far as to argue that companies can produce 'IP brands'. Information about IP can be spun out in order to support their standing in the marketplace (Berman 2006).

In this section we have seen how IP can undertake two related tasks. The first is, quite simply, in creating and maintaining a monopoly over an innovation, design or a business model. IP is used to defend a corporation's claim to product and/or service form by stopping competitors from adopting these. It is a strongly territorial way of using design in business. The second is more symbolic. It is where IP is used to mark out a company's strength – particularly to investors. Brand image can be supported by quantifying the number of patents filed or designs that are filed in a year. In these ways, IP is a key asset in boosting the perceived and actual value of a corporation.

METADATA IN THE ENTERTAINMENT INDUSTRY

IP may also be key to the organising structures that go beyond the core of a corporation. In this section and the next, which focuses on design and franchising, we see how the asset of IP moves between intensive design processes that configure data and design details to its more extensive deployment. More specifically, I want to show how design is employed in the Hollywood entertainment industries. This is where control over design is maintained in distributed production systems.

Since 1945, in the Hollywood entertainment industries, there has been a gradual movement from the big studios producing all aspects of movies to adopting a more dispersed approach based on widespread subcontracting (from a Fordist to a post-Fordist system, if you like). In particular from the late 1980s the studio system has been superseded by global corporations such as Time Warner orchestrating subcontraction and licensing of production through multiple sites (Silver 2007). A major driver for this change has been in the gradual reassignment of work, particularly in the Silicon Valley digital industries, from defence work to entertainment.

The collapse of the Hollywood studio system in the 1960s ushered in a model where merchants (distributors, financiers and agents) became dominant. In other words, it moved from a 'producer-driven' commodity chain to a 'buyer-driven' one. This, as Hozic (1999: 293) has argued, 'led to the creation of franchise-like media organisations which derive most of their profits from royalties and licensing fees and therefore place enormous emphasis on the purchase, development and maintenance of rights to brand names and characters'. IP and the role of design in formatting products, brand names and characters become centrally important here.

The use of the word 'franchise' in the case of the film industry is a partial misnomer. In terms of the film itself, it is taken to mean 'sequel' in this context. However, at the same time, much of a franchise here is, indeed, *franchised* in that it involves the licensing of the IP to third parties for the design, production, marketing and distribution of the movie-related goods. In some respects, the existence of multiple sequels, combined with a large amount of outsourcing of the creative aspects of making the film itself overlaps with the processes of the selling of its IP through licence agreements.

Prior to the 1970s, the sequel or franchise barely figured among Hollywood blockbuster, big-budget movies. Since 1975, however, they have come to take up 25 per cent of its production among these blockbusters (Silver 2007: 147). From *Star Wars* to *Star Trek*, *Batman* to *Iron Man*, *Planet of the Apes* to *National Lampoon*, the Hollywood system has been firmly oriented to large-scale creations supported by global marketing, massive investment in visual effects and the roll out of product across multiple platforms. Theatrical release, video release, video games, pay TV, merchandise licensing, music soundtracks, novelisation and theme parks all constitute opportunities to make money around Hollywood films (Silver 2007: 261).

In the film industry, the core production to this is known as a 'tentpole' picture or movie. It represents high-level investment with, it is expected, low risk. It has a budget of more than US$100m with secondary products (for instance, DVD, TV, related video games and books, product tie-ins) expected to provide much bigger returns than the theatrical release of the movie itself. This is often viewed as a loss-leader to generate awareness for the former (Sparviero 2013). In order to combat piracy and bad word-of-mouth response, the film is released globally at the same time. Given this global audience (making up 80 per cent of box-office sales beyond the USA), it relies more heavily on visual impact and a simple plot-line rather than complex, involved dialogue. They should also appeal across age-ranges and genders to maximise revenue. As such, the design detailing and processing are core to both the origins (what I call here, 'first-tier design') and how these are then played out in subcontracting their realisation and in licensing such things as merchandise (what I call here, 'second-tier design').

Each of these tentpole movies has its own patina: for instance, its own colour palette, costuming, key props, scenographic language, logos, registers of sound or figures of speech. These are built on in sequels. A multitude of guidelines are created in order to assure continuity between sequels but also between the film and other merchandise. Digitally, this is achieved through the authoring of 'metadata' (Sutton 2009). Here, software packages are authored and distributed that contain the necessary 'kit of parts' for design elements to be combined and recombined, either by freelance designers or small design offices working on a detail of a film or by IP licensees for merchandise.

Corporations such as Time Warner and Sony (who own MGM) thus own IP but also orchestrate the networks through which this knowledge is distributed (Currah 2003). The infrastructure that exists between design or origination and multiple sites of production and distribution is called the

IP pipeline. Sutton (2009: 181) notes that the 'financial power arises less from the IP elements as marketable knowledge, and more from their ability through infrastructure, ICT and film audiences, to recombine the elements in which the IP is invested'. In this way, design is moving in several directions at once. Design concepts may be originated within the corporation, shipped out to freelance designers or small offices for rendering, detailing and refinement, sucked back to the corporation (or the Major) which employs these itself in the movie but also distributes versions of these under licence to franchisees. Metadata, or otherwise first-tier design, are the core currency, but the Major also controls the rates and systems of exchange through which the second-tier design happens.

This is not to say that this design economy works seamlessly and evenly. Transmutations of visual material take place as subcontractees use their own computer programs to process material, compress files or simply go *off-piste* from what is required. The Major has to balance between, mostly, ensuring respect and proper use of the IP and allowing for the possibility of positive innovations that might provide the parent corporation with new material to exploit. The control end may be achieved in part by placing regulations over the software that is sent out, making it difficult to alter and hack. But it may also be undertaken by creating social networks, such as guild committees, that help to police such 'bad' behaviour (Currah 2007).

THE DESIGN OF FRANCHISES

Let us consider design and franchises more widely. Beyond the movie industry, a franchise is where a party is granted access to another's trademark or tradename and also its business processes and systems for goods or services. In exchange, the franchisee pays an initial licensing fee and, usually, a percentage of sales. A key advantage is that the franchisee gets immediate access to a brand name and a business system rather than having to design and develop these themselves. To the consumer, whether or not a business is a franchise is, or at least should be, indistinguishable. For instance, 80 per cent of the McDonald's restaurants worldwide are franchises (Kasperkevic 2015) but their uniformity belies the varied ownership of each one.

A discussion of design in the Hollywood film industry highlights the relationship in design between 'intensities' and 'extensities' that emerges through franchising. In Chapter 5 we considered design intensities and extensities in relation to the spatial clustering and dispersion of design. Here I want to distinguish them in terms of their more temporal aspects. Scott Lash (2010) argues that the neoliberal age has seen a shift to greater emphasis on intensive knowledge (here represented by first-tier design) that gives rise to extensities (second-tier design). Hence, for example, the Majors establish the concept of a movie in terms of its visual patina, key actors and storyline that, in turn, institutes its IP. This is claimed as the intensive, high knowledge-value element which is then translated into extensities in terms of the secondary products. They are singularities that materialise into multiples. Equally, Lash suggests that brands function in similar ways. They start out as *virtual* entities – ideas, positions, words, palettes, strategies – but then they become *actual* products that are consumed in everyday life. As such, brands – and indeed, film concepts and first-tier design – exist *in potentia*. 'Extensities are "beings" while intensities are "becomings"', Lash argues (2010: 5).

In the move from intensities to extensities, it would be wrong to accept that the second-tier design work is either slavish translating or assembling of concepts with little creative work or, alternatively, harbours moments for mischievous subversion beyond the reach of the franchisor. In actualising a brand, a design consultancy may be engaged in complex amounts of interpretation. For example, if a fast food brand is renewed, this of course has to be played out into its implementation through its restaurants. This in itself has to be prototyped through a pilot store. Such is the case of UK-based CADA Design's work for the Domino's pizza takeaway and restaurant franchise. In 2012, Domino's changed its brand identity, dropping the word 'pizza' from it, it having become self-evident that this is what it did. However, a number of other ways by which it related to its consumer base had changed, for example, in its use of social media. Such issues have also to be built through the design of restaurants. Hence, CADA Design developed a store in Basildon, Essex, that made the pizza-making more visible (CADA Design 2013). In this way, by working with a new concept, they developed this into a new interior layout and packaging which could subsequently be rolled out into other Domino's franchises.

6.2 CADA Design work for Domino's pizza franchise, 2012 (Photo: CADA Design)

This kind of downstream work attends to the physical environment of customer contact. It is about surfaces, colours, lighting, spatial distribution and so on. Design in franchising also deals with midstream elements such as equipment. In the case of restaurant franchises, this might include specialist cooking gear. These tie franchisees up in further investment. For example, in the USA McDonald's franchisees reportedly would have to pay US$20,000 for a milkshake machine and US$15,000 for a grill. When they are also paying a franchise royalty between 3 and 5 per cent of profit, 5 per cent for advertising, rent at between 12.5 and 15 per cent and for any remodelling costs, profit margins are small. Wages are not set by McDonald's and these have to be determined by what is left over after these costs by each franchisee (Kasperkevic 2015). Similarly, franchisees of Domino's in France reportedly have had to pay over 40 per cent of their profits to the parent company (Boulard 2013).

Franchise relationships are therefore prone to conflict (Antia et al. 2013). The franchisee benefits from taking on a pre-tested business model and set of design features in exchange for contracting into a long-term arrangement with franchisors, who call the tune in both these aspects. The profit motive exists for both sides: the harder the franchisee works, the more money they will make; the easier the franchisor makes it for the franchisee to work efficiently and happily and to attract customers, the more return they should expect. There are straightforward operational control issues in terms of ensuring proper use of the franchise (Fladmoe-Lindquist and Jacque 1995). These would include ensuring the faithful presentation of the brand, wearing of uniforms and delivery of approved customer care levels and are reflected through copious manuals and design guidelines.

However, it is not surprising, additionally, that the franchisors often make much of the social benefits available to those who take on a franchise. These might include flexible working hours, the possibility of working from home and organised social contact with other franchisees. In this, the upstream management and design of franchise relationships becomes important. Web design consultancy Katatomic in the UK, for example, has produced a web-based management communication tool, a franchise-led management and analysis application, and a voting and feedback system for franchisees for the sandwich franchise operation Subway® (Katatomic 2015). In this, designers like Katatomic are entering into and structuring the social world of work wherein workers also are constructed as consumers of their wider organisation (du Gay 1996).

Franchises are subject to imitation by independent entrepreneurs. Sometimes this is done blatantly and humorously. In the UK, a Leeds sandwich business branded itself as MeccaWay (playing on Subway) and a burger joint presented itself as MahMouhd's (lightly, but very obviously, referencing McDonald's). While franchises enter into litigation to safeguard their trademarks, ultimately these are the most superficial aspects and easiest to copy. Franchises create complex processes and resources that cover all business aspects. Pretenders cannot expect to be able to reproduce these.

6.3   MeccaWay sandwich outlet, Leeds, 2010 (Photo: Guy Julier)

DESIGNERS AND IP

This is not to say that copying is not an issue for designers. Copying in the design industry is rampant, even by their existing or potential clients. A typical scenario might be that a designer supplies designs to a client who subsequently takes details of them and re-uses these in different formats beyond prior agreements (*Design Week* 2002). Or, a potential client invites a consultancy to undertake a 'pitch' – to present speculative designs in competition against other consultancies; the client then takes those ideas and develops them themselves. Such cases are not necessarily specific to design; they are to be found in other creative industries such as, classically, in the 'recycling' of ideas pitched in the film industry (Weisselberg 2009). But avoiding such scenarios, where a designer's work goes unpaid and unacknowledged, requires specific safeguarding actions such as reaching prior agreement on confidentiality and use or creating a 'paper trail' of designs to prove their origins. These can be difficult to undertake where there are time pressures.

There have been attempts by organisations that represent and advocate the economic work of designers to promote more active engagement with IP (e.g. IP Australia 2008; BEDA 2014). This has been driven by several factors: one is that the potential value of their work is not fully exploited for designers when IP is handed over to clients. In the first instance, it is argued, designers who don't hold onto their IP must exist purely from fee income. Second, agreeing to the unconditional full transfer of IPR means that the designers can't exploit inventions and design further for their own advantage; this is left entirely to the client's behest and benefit (BEDA 2014).

Nonetheless, despite this promotion of IPR among designers by their representation organisations, take-up is often low. For example, in 2009 the UK Design Council surveyed 2,200 design businesses. Of these they found that most work on a fixed fee or day rate; 66 per cent did not take any action to protect their IP; only 1 per cent had income from royalties on IPR (Design Council 2010b).

It depends on the sector, though. Engineering and product designers are more embedded into IPR assertion while, broadly speaking, fashion, furniture and graphic designers do not pursue their IPR vigorously. In terms of graphic design, their clients might do this through, for example, trademark registration. But fashion and design-led furniture firms engage with IPR less so. Raustiala and Sprigman (2006: 1691) observe that 'Fashion firms take significant, costly steps to protect the value of their trademarked brands, but they largely appear to accept appropriation of designs as a fact of life. Design copying is occasionally complained about, but it is as often celebrated as "homage" as it is attacked as "piracy."' Similarly, of the design-led furniture sector, Gemser and Wijnberg (2001: 576) found that for some companies having their designs copied by a lower-market oriented firm is considered to be an honour, demonstrating, in fact, that they are market leaders.

So what do those who don't engage with IP do instead? How do they work within, but also create, temporal cycles that weave in and out of IP frameworks? What objects does this produce?

FASHION AND FURNITURE

While many large corporations and franchises attempt to close down any possibility of copying or modifications through the extensive registration of their IP and strict enforcement of guidelines, the world of fashion and design-led furniture is comparatively porous in this regard. This is for two reasons. One reason is that their goods are relatively easy to be copied, given that they are singular designs with low technological complexity: they are not made up of complex assemblages of processes, objects, skills and knowledge as in the case of franchises; they do not involve arrays of patented inventions that fill out technology-driven corporations. The other reason has more to do with the culture of their particular sector of design and their social and creative norms, as we shall see.

This is not to say that fashion and furniture designers and companies are unconcerned about having their work copied. Speaking at the 2013 Salone Internazionale del Mobile di Milano (Milan Furniture Fair), Casper Vissers, CEO of the Dutch company Moooi, stated that new products appearing there in April could be pirated and produced in China by August and in the shops by September. British designer Tom Dixon complained that 'It's becoming a landscape where people feel more confident about copying ... some are overt, [they] come in with iPads or a film-crew.' Copyists go even further, pulling photographs off websites and re-using them or getting furniture dimensions from dealers to reproduce them, Dixon added (Dezeen 2013).

Wherever the furniture is manufactured, a number of loopholes allow unlicensed copies of designs to be retailed. One such loophole is found through the different IP law approaches in distinct countries. For example, in 2012, a report by the Danish Trade Council in London observed that a company called Invertu in Denmark was able to import copies of Danish designs from the UK (Ministry of Foreign Affairs of Denmark 2012). While in Denmark these were protected until 70 years after the death of the author, in the UK protection was only for 25 years from their creation at that time. Another loophole is in giving vague attribution to designers. Thus, we read on some websites of replica furniture firms of 'Eileen Gray style' or 'Florence Knoll style' (e.g. Swivel 2015). In these instances, designs that are widely recognised as 'classic' are being reproduced. These above examples are ones that frequently appear in design history books and decorative arts museums and carry that caché of recognition. At the same time, these companies are able to sell replicas at around between 8 and 15 per cent of the price that the original producers (such as Knoll, Fritz Hansen, Flos or Vitra) charge (Intellectual Property Office 2012: 9).

In 2012, the UK government passed legislation to bring copyright protection of 'authored' designs in line with other European countries by extending this to 70 years after the designer's death. Significantly, this also aligns such authorship with works of art, literature and music publishing. This clearly puts this in the category of 'difficult to originate, easy to copy'. Nonetheless, despite such additions of legal protection, for contemporary designers the copying of new products and, indeed, their indifference to this, creates a different rhythm and set of circumstances for designers. This is also driven by certain norms of self-image and practice among designers and producing companies that we'll consider in the next section.

There are furniture companies – such as the Dutch firm Pastoe and the German company Vitsoe – that provide exceptions to the general rule. Pastoe's designs are intended for longevity, making it worthwhile defending their IP (Scheltens 2015). Another well-known example of this is Vitsoe's 606 Universal Shelving System and the 620 Chair Programme, both designed by Dieter Rams and produced since the early 1960s. These lines are marked by their high quality of manufacture and that their components can be combined and expanded on easily. Their modular systems are utterly unchanging. But in maintaining their space in the marketplace, Vitsoe has had to enter into several plagiarism law suits against other companies. One for the 620 Chair Programme lasted from 1968 to 1973 and resulted in a successful consolidation of its copyright protection in Germany. Meanwhile, the 606 Universal Shelving System has not achieved such protection, making the concept one of the most copied in furniture design. Nonetheless, the pace of design change at Vitsoe is not as relentless as elsewhere. The next section studies how this rhythm is set by international trade fairs and what happens within them.

'NO PHOTOGRAPHY!': TRADE FAIRS AND CYCLES OF DESIGN INNOVATION

International trade fairs provide a useful snapshot of the culture of the furniture design sector and its relationship to design knowledge and IP. These international events have their roots going back, famously, to London's 'Great Exhibition of the Works of Industry of all Nations' of 1851. In

6.4   Views of the 100% Design trade fair, London, 2016 (Photos: Guy Julier)

all sectors there has been a marked rise in trade fairs since the 1980s. For furniture, the largest of these is the Milan Furniture Fair with over 300,000 visitors and 1,300 exhibitors in 2014 (Salone del Mobile 2014). Behind Milan comes Cologne (116,000 visitors in 2006), Helsinki (90,000 in the same year) and Valencia (80,000). But a global circuit of the top 20 also includes London's 100% Design, Shanghai's Furniture China and Moscow's Europe Expo Furniture (Power and Jansson 2008: 439).

For design producers, exhibiting at a trade fair is generally a profitable investment, providing an opportunity for face-to-face contact with buyers and for the sale of design rights and licences. For designers, they also represent places to present their latest work, get media exposure, build contacts and, perhaps, get recruited or commissioned by producing firms. They provide for hard business practice and loose play. During the daytime, stands for companies, designers, professional associations, national or regional design promotion as well as media organisations provide the workplace where deals are negotiated. Exhibitors also tour each other's stands to get information and renew contacts with competitors or suppliers. Seminars and lectures featuring industry experts punctuate the day. At night, dinners, off-site exhibition openings and parties abound where the networking continues (Power and Jansson 2008; Rinallo et al. 2010). Thus, trade fairs provide a heady and intense environment where design knowledge moves reasonably easily between exhibitors while the IP that is embedded in the design objects is safeguarded as much as possible. It is this, after all, that keeps the players in business.

Signs imploring visitors not to take photographs invariably punctuate the trade fair entrance and halls. Despite the 'No Photography!' pictograms, this still seems to happen. Pictures get taken, promotional catalogues are lifted. With relatively few adjustments, knock-off copies of new designs shown at these events can be made. With an acceptance that copying is going to happen in any case, many working at the cutting-edge of design innovations in furniture and lighting are more concerned to use the fair instead to stake their claim as leading originators (Power and Jansson 2008; Rinallo et al. 2010). Getting the attention of design journalists for these is thus more of a priority (Michaëlis 2013). It is through them that wider recognition can be gained and their leading position underlined.

Similarly, companies will adopt strategic behaviours to draw attention to new product concepts by presenting them in a strong fashion. At least when they are copied, it is hoped, imitations are therefore recognised as drawing on *their* IP. Conversely, when a firm copies another's concept,

they will try to give it a particular identity of its own. The new design concept therefore becomes a springboard for competitors to develop their own variations. More blatant plagiarising between exhibitors is rare due to the internal reputation policing that takes place. Information (such as price lists or perceived consumer trends) is freely exchanged between them as friendly, mutual support. However, the informal relationships between firms – particularly those who come from the same geographical area – function to produce communal norms where 'a quiet word in the ear' circumvents the need for expensive litigation, should plagiarism take place. Reputational self-policing also takes place: if a design-led company did copy extensively and noticeably, then its standing as an innovator would be tarnished (Gemser and Wijnberg 2001).

With these internal checks and balances in place, set alongside the inevitability of having new work copied by 'outsider' businesses, the pressure to constantly show new designs is strong. Since the trade fair is considered the most important venue for launching these, it is their annual cycle that structures the business year. If an exhibitor is showing at two fairs, six months apart, they are effectively committing to the design of new products twice a year. In this way, furniture trade fairs (at least at the design-led end) are not dissimilar to fashion fairs with their two season phases (Skov 2006). While back catalogue material is always shown to attract new customers, novelty – shown usually through prototypes – is also required. Tooling up for actual manufacture is traditionally postponed in anticipation of orders. The pace, it seems, is relentless.

There is, at least on the surface, a clear logic to the annual cycle of furniture trade fairs. The Cologne, Paris and Stockholm fairs take place in January and February. This is to signal a 'new year, new look' while also, following the January sales, retailers would know what space and funds they have available for new products. In Europe, though, the annual cycle is really dominated by Milan in April. The New York and Copenhagen fairs would follow to show the latest releases from Milan. Formerly, this timing would allow for the showing of new prototypes to gauge market reaction. Orders would be taken with production pieces then available in September after the summer shutdown (Mair 2015). This anticipates a rise in consumer spending on new furniture in the autumn, when householders spend more time at home.

Dig deeper and we find a complex and moving situation where trade fairs vie with each other for positioning in the calendar. Factors such as internet sales and increased speed of bringing designs to production complicate the annual cycle further. Since 2008, exhibitors at Milan have increasingly shown production pieces rather than prototypes, giving them a faster return on investments. Another scenario is that the internet also allows companies to introduce new products online as teasers before fairs. The fair then works as a reinforcing materialisation of these. Subsequently, orders are made online much later, making it difficult to gauge the actual impact of showing (Michaëlis 2015). With diminishing lead times, therefore, the division between showing prototypes and production pieces is gradually eroded. What matters most is novelty, followed by media attention.

As the internet and shorter lead times begin to complicate the annual cycle, so trade fairs function for other forms of design knowledge and practices. Trade fairs provide crucial scenarios for fostering and building 'buzz' around companies, designers, trends and particular products (Bathelt and Schuldt 2010, 2011; Jansson and Power 2010). In the fashion business, as with design-led furniture, the trade fair not only sets the rhythm of design and innovation activities through the year, it also becomes the window through which these are publicised. Their milieu of networking and building social capital – supported as much by satellite events as by the trade fair itself – acts to augment this expectation of the new.

The social and cultural norms of certain fields of design appear to run counter to strong IPR enforcement.

Furthermore, the fair can also work for designers and producers to test consumer reaction rather than just to boost sales. From the 1980s, Harm Scheltens, director of the Dutch furniture company Pastoe, reintroduced his company to trade fairs in order to understand its audience. He would spend hours watching people visit their stand. 'Where do people go first? What makes them stop, and what do they ignore? What do they find interesting about a piece of furniture? … You can learn an awful lot just from looking and listening' (Staal and Van der Zwaag 2013: 129).

A broader point about the cultural world of designers may be made here that partially answers the question of their apparent indifference to securing their IP through registration of designs or patenting. It seems fair to speculate that many designers appear to be more interested in moving onto the next project than tying themselves up in expensive and slow-moving processes of registration or litigation. For many furniture and fashion designers, trade fairs create a temporal regime to work to. They also reinforce professional norms of differentiation, originality and a project focus that is more interesting to them than the legalistic assertion of IP rights.

CONCLUSION

Global corporations are busy 'hoovering up' IP. Here, design, innovation and legal departments constantly look to ways of creating legal protection for every detail of their organisation and brand. This is in order to defend their monopoly over the particular services or products they produce and, by way of attack, to stop competitors exploiting designs and inventions. Sometimes these seem quite obvious and, to the lay person, barely worth the trouble. But they are worth it if they help to maintain market domination. Every bit helps in the competition of monopolies. IP can also work as an asset for a company through licensing and franchising. Design, here, functions as a form of metadata. It is something that is subject to intense refinement of itself and the communication of its norms. Technical and brand guidelines are important here.

It is also useful to remember that IP can work in favour of the underdog. It doesn't necessarily place all the power in the hands of the big, global corporations. It can allow medium-size companies to lay claim over an invention or design that is at the centre of their business operations. It can buy them time, slowing down the innovation cycle that is driven mostly by a need to stay ahead of the copyists. Other, nuanced arguments about IP can also emerge in relation to globalisation: greater harmonisation of IP regions can provide a more level playing field for designers around the world; IP can facilitate a push back against cultural appropriation and address power imbalances; at the same time, greater flexibility in IP law can allow for cultural difference in recognising the nuances and different conceptions of what originality entails; and, despite claims to IP being of minor concern for some, it is still a source of livelihood for many creative practitioners. In the meantime, the furniture and fashion sectors, in particular, remain largely outside and unconcerned by these possibilities on the whole.

IP is an asset. It underpins the value of a company in terms of its intrinsic strengths – what it knows, what it has to work with and sell. It is also something that can be licensed to other producers or franchised through other providers. Its rise runs parallel with the rise of design and finance in the neoliberal age. However, it is also interesting to explore the spaces between dualistic oppositions of privatisation v. commons, IP v. Open Innovation or scarcity v. abundance. Some of these spaces are explored in the next chapter.

INFORMAL AND ALTERNATIVE ECONOMIES

Design clearly operates in and supports conventional neo-liberal practices. But it is also active at their edges or even outside them. Chapter 7 discusses four examples of design in informal and alternative economies. The first focuses on *shan-zhai* innovations in China that come out of copying and adapting mainstream products. We then consider frugal or *jugaad* innovation in India and whether this movement has the capacity to influence the wider economy. In Argentina, we see how design operates in circumstances of extreme economic crisis and the resulting the political processes of *horizontalidad*. Finally, we visit a timebanking system in the UK that was set up exclusively for creative practitioners as a political response to neoliberalism.

In informal and alternative economies we find a wealth of design and innovation that both feeds off and challenges mainstream capitalism. This can be seen in the objects of design that result. But these come out of wholly distinct approaches to organising design work, valorising intellectual property or the political and social roles that design is assumed to serve. Four such cases are analysed in this chapter.

In the first two, found in China (*shanzhai*) and India (*jugaad*), we see a more fluid approach taken to intellectual property to the extent that design becomes part of a larger system of open innovation. In both these cases, this derives from activities that are mostly undertaken in the informal, non-registered part of the economy. The notion of the definition of the designer as someone who sells intellectual property – as defined in Chapter 3 – is problematic here. Indeed, we can talk of design-like activities, but the designer as a distinct professional actor who sells their skills, knowledge and time in these circumstances is often harder to define. Efforts to absorb these approaches into government economic policies further problematise the imposition of traditional (Western) conceptions of design and the creative industries. In the third and fourth examples, we see how design is mobilised within wider political responses to economic crises. In Argentina we review its connections to so-called *horizontalidad*: attempts to build alternative, grassroots, non-hierarchical and community-focused economic practices. In the UK, we alight on an unusual initiative that provides a parallel framework to the cash-economy for creative professionals to collaborate in. In both these instances, the management of time within design work gets re-ordered while the conceptions of what designing might shift as well.

Three connected issues unfold through this chapter. The first is that open innovation takes place in a much wider set of contexts than orthodox business thinking assumes. In business studies, open innovation is presented as a particular corporate strategy, especially in the digital technology sector (Chesbrough 2003). Here I want to explore how it operates in the more material and visceral contexts of informal and alternative economies. Second, design invariably provides a bridge between informal and formal economies. It is the pivot where questions of intellectual property and the valorisation of creativity are played out and where practices may be seen to weave in and out of different economic modalities. Third, I want to stress how the practices and arrangements that take place within informal and alternative economies express their own distinctive aesthetic sensibilities. These will become clear as we look closer. In the meantime, it is important to establish some working definitions.

DEFINITIONS

The terminology is difficult here. There are overlaps but also distinctions between informal, alternative and mainstream economies. This can cause some confusion. So before we get to the four examples, this section discusses how these are being used here.

The informal economy denotes commercial practices that exist outside the official structures of national governmental legal systems. Thus they are typified as involving non-registered businesses who do not pay tax. In other words, they go unregistered. They work through cash-in-hand transactions between businesses and in payment of employees, but also exist through arrangements of reciprocity in which time, expertise and goods are exchanged without any financial mediation. Being outside governmental legal systems, they also operate outside systems of intellectual property rights, and, thus, design rights enforcement. The informal economy extends to practically all fields of goods and services production and distribution, with, perhaps, the exception of the financial sector. Through much of the world, and in particular the global South, street vendors and traders, small-scale producers, repairers, recyclers, entertainers and many other skilled workers ply their craft outside the formal economy.

Its size and significance is immense. Schneider (2014: 236) puts the value of the informal economies of Latin America, the Caribbean, Sub-Saharan Africa, Europe and Central Asia all around one-third of their GDP. Overall, the informal sector includes many low-value activities, hence employment as a percentage here is much higher. Excluding the agricultural sector (where the figures are even higher), it accounts for three-quarters of employment in Sub-Saharan Africa, over two-thirds in South and South East Asia, half in Latin America, the Middle East and North Africa (Schneider 2014: 240). The OECD (2009) puts the informal sector as 'the norm', not the exception, while Neuwirth (2011) goes further to claim it represent *the* economy through most of the world.

Many informal economy activities also take place *within* rather than outside the formal economy. This is where, for instance, building work or vehicle repair is undertaken through cash-in-hand transactions rather than being declared to the tax authorities. In this case, it is also known as the 'black' or 'shadow' economy. Some activities involve trading in illegal goods or may be undertaken in order to avoid minimum wage or health and safety requirements. Another term to consider is the 'grey economy'. This involves activities that have economic value which is not often recognised and does not include cash exchange. Caring for children and the elderly or undertaking low-grade repair tasks figure here. (The role of the grey economy will be pursued further in Chapter 8.) The informal economy is therefore complex and varied in terms of its activities and relationships to mainstream economies. Some of it may be registerable but is not registered; some of it may be illegal; some of it may have economic value that is not registerable (Schneider and Enste 2013: 8).

Given that the informal economy works outside the usual structures of intellectual property rights, this is also where a degree of open innovation often takes place. Here, free and open exchange of inventions, designs or ideas is found, as we shall see, in the case of *shanzhai* in particular. Nonetheless, in itself, the term 'open innovation' has been aligned with developments in the mainstream economy that took place in the 1990s in relation to digital technology developments in Silicon Valley, USA. In particular, companies like Cisco and Lucent spread their innovation base by investing in independent start-ups and sharing any generated IP. This therefore draws on an external landscape of abundant knowledge (Chesbrough 2003). By contrast to the informal economy, however, this rests on strategically refined commercial thinking in which legal agreements are still forged. In the context of informal economies, open innovation takes place, but not so much as a calculated tactic devised by businesspeople. Rather it is a circumstance born of close social and economic relationships of reciprocity or, even, a concern for common benefit over individual advantage.

Definitions of alternative economies may be viewed in two ways. One is to think of them as self-consciously, often politically motivated differentiations from the mainstream economy. This is where, for instance, cooperatives or Fair Trade companies whose emphasis is on equality or justice may operate. The other is to view the economy as an 'already and intrinsically heterogeneous space' (Healy 2009: 338). Here, the gaps and openings that are created through neoliberalism (and often through its failure) are inhabited by alternative practices. We shall see this in the cases of *horizontalidad* and creative timebanking. As such these alternative economies may in fact be regarded as just part of the variance of an overall condition of neoliberalism.

Ultimately, it is important to view the informal and alternative economies – and the practices of design therein – as working relationally to other economies. Informal and alternative economies weave in and out of mainstream, formal economies. This sometimes makes it difficult to extricate one from another. Putting the cases that are explicated in this chapter under the heading of 'informal' or 'alternative' economies is thus only meant as a starting point for exploring them.

SHANZHAI: A BUSINESS PRACTICE AND A CULTURAL MOVEMENT

A perfect copy of a Ferrari sports car. A copy of an iPhone, but with two SIM card slots. Or even a mobile phone in the shape of a Ferrari. These are just three of the many products that have emerged from *shanzhai* culture. Emanating mostly from the Guandong province of China and, more specifically, the city of Shenzhen, a significant and large-scale industry has risen since 2000 that makes expert copies of well-known products, but also extends on them, creating new combinations that respond to local and global demands.

Shanzhai does not carry specified 'rules' as a business practice. Rather, it is a set of shared understandings that have emerged out of a specific economic and cultural context. Townsend et al. (2011: 19) offer the following summary of the *shanzhai* ethos:

- Do nothing from scratch; build on the best of what others have already done.
- Innovate process ceaselessly at small scales for speed and cost savings.
- Share as much as you can to make it easy for others to see your value and to add value to your process.
- Sell it before you make it.
- Act responsibly within the supply chain to preserve your reputation.

It therefore emphasises iterative prototyping. Nothing is designed from scratch. Technical developments are tried as much in the production process as in the product. Designing takes place very close to its market.

Shenzhen itself is a city of some 12 million inhabitants in China's Guangdong province, close to Hong Kong. Until the 1980s it was a relatively small fishing village. However, in 1980 it became part of China's first Special Economic Zone, giving it more flexibility in regional government policy and greater freedom in its market economy. In terms of global manufacture, it is perhaps best known for its 'Foxconn City' where many Apple, Dell, Hewlett Packard, Nintendo and Sony products are manufactured. Thus, behind *shanzhai* lies a vast resource of components, knowledge and materials in the formal economy that feeds into the informal economy.

The Chinese word *shanzhai* literally means 'the hideout of mountain bandits'. If that sounds like it has a renegade or even anarchic quality to it, then that's precisely the intention (Beebe 2014; Chubb 2015). These 'mountain bandits' of Chinese folklore are taken to be roguish and subversive, operating outside mainstream systems, but also plundering them for the greater good. They are inscribed into the literary imagination by novels such as the fourteenth-century *Shuihu Zhuan* (known in the West by J.H. Jackson's partial translation *The Water Margin* (Nainan 2010)). They live by a moral code of reciprocity and honour while engaging in idiosyncratic and rebellious behaviours. Their ethos of 'robbers as heroes' is thus conceived as something that is in the service of other people's needs and desires.

For a contemporary audience in Taiwan, China and Hong Kong, the *shanzhai* spirit was popularised by at least two TV series and two computer games from 2000 (Hennessey 2012). Thus it is about design and production but it also represents a cultural attitude. The most familiar *shanzhai* product is the mobile phone, although the concept reaches far wider to many cultural forms. There are *shanzhai* coffee bars and restaurants, *shanzhai* TV shows and *shanzhai* novels.

As a cultural movement, *shanzhai* in its contemporary usage mimics but also menaces. It draws from and acknowledges Western forms and technologies, thus paying homage to them. At the same time, by reference to Homi Bhabha's discussion of colonial discourse (1984), Chubb (2015: 263) points out how it is 'disruptive of systems of domination'. The counterfeit mimicry asks 'so what if we copy this stuff?' while the extension of capabilities through the copycat product says 'and, in any case, we can do even better than that'. It speaks to notions of Western entrepreneurialism and invention while offering localised, grassroots challenges to it. As such, the *shanzhai* concept crosses ideological boundaries. In addition to this reading, it has taken shape as a major force in the Chinese design economy to present major challenges to how we conceive design authorship, intellectual property and, even, our sense of modernity, as we shall see later.

THE SCALE AND OPERATIONS OF *SHANZHAI*

Shanzhai largely involves 'below the radar' forms of design and entrepreneurship and therefore it doesn't feature heavily in national economic statistics. Its actual scale is difficult to ascertain. However, a few estimated statistics give a sense of this. There were an estimated 3,000 to 4,000 *shanzhai* businesses working in Shenzhen in 2009 (Wallis and Qui 2012: 114). In the same year, there were some 100,000 people working in *shanzhai* workshops in Shenzhen while *shanzhai* mobile phone share was estimated to be occupying 20 to 30 per cent of the Chinese market (Chubb 2015: 267). Anthropologist Yi-Chieh Jessica Lin states that in 2009, Shenzhen produced 400 million mobile phones in the formal economy, making up 30 per cent of global production. At the same time, she estimated there to have been around 3,000 backstreet 'design houses' that built copycat phones, but had also moved to integrated circuit design, interface or content software and application development (Lin 2011: 21). The Huaqiangbei electronics market in the centre of Shenzhen is an important node in this. Here you will find repair workshops, stands specialising in the sale of smartphone packaging, particular components or casings, sometimes sold by weight rather than number. Others provide bespoke hardware solutions to demand and some assemble either copies or their original designs in front of you.

7.1 Various views of Huaqiangbei electronics market Shenzhen (Photos: Guy Julier)

With brand names such as Hi-Phone, Nokla and Motoloah and referencing in their styling, *shanzhai* phones draw from the visual and linguistic trappings of global corporations (Keane 2013). However, they may also be loaded with TVs, lights and even razors. The referencing is therefore knowing and even taken ironically by consumers. At one level, *shanzhai* cultural forms can be viewed as commentaries on the excesses of Western consumerism.

They also respond to on-the-ground needs. The incorporation of two SIM slots into *shanzhai* phones responds to demand on the part of China's migrant community who move between network coverages – particularly entrepreneurs moving between Hong Kong, Taiwan and Shenzhen – while also allowing division between work and leisure domains of everyday life. They tend to be relatively inexpensive, selling at between 200 and 600 yuan (about US$30 to $90) (Wallis and Qui 2012: 112). Costs are kept down because of minimal marketing and advertising; but these 'bandits' also avoid payment of 17 per cent VAT, network licence fees and sales tax and, crucially, having to pay IP costs.

The Taiwanese firm MediaTek is widely regarded as the godfather of *shanzhai*, at least in terms of mobile phones. Its widespread supply of integrated driver chips to China, following trade liberalisation in 2006, means that *shanzhai* producers can concentrate their efforts on other mobile phone features. These firms work in parallel economies. They may supply companies who make phones for major brands like Apple and Sony, but also engage in night-time production of *shanzhai* phones. Transactions between companies are usually made in cash so as not to provide a trail that reveals their IP infringements. Technical information is shared freely and widely between participants so that innovations are more easily arrived at. Websites such as 52RD.com and PDA.cn provide further fora for information exchange. By March 2009, 52RD.com had 130,000 members and nearly 800,000 postings (Wallis and Qui 2012: 117).

Distribution is made through various routes. For example, *shanzhai* entrepreneurs cooperate with traders from South Asia, the Middle East and Africa who live in Shenzhen and who invariably make large orders for *shanzhai* products (Neuwirth 2011). From 2009 to 2010, overall sales of their mobile handsets increased by 27 million, thanks to exportation to these territories (Chubb 2015: 269). In 2009, 30 per cent of mobile phones marketed in India were *shanzhai* (Lin 2011: 21). Fishing boats and cargo ships circle the East and South East Asian sea in search of locations to sell bulk stocks of *shanzhai* goods (Lin 2011: 35). In China itself, goods are sold through the internet, street stalls and markets as well as through friendship and family networks. Thus a flexible, open ecosystem of design, components supply, production and distribution is achieved, based on informal procedures and relationships.

FROM *SHANZHAI* TO THE MAINSTREAM ECONOMY

This movement between subcontractee of manufacture (Original Equipment Manufacture – OEM) to *shanzhai* copying and development (Original Design Manufacture – ODM) to producing own brand goods (Original Brand Manufacture – OBM) involves a number of repositionings of a company while, at the same time, drawing on the same or similar local infrastructure for components and assembly and, beyond, national and international distribution. Keane (2013: 119) provides a useful summary of the significance of this move that is reproduced in Table 7.1.

Table 7.1 The *shanzhai* and post-*shanzhai* model (Keane 2013: 119)

	Subcontractee (OEM)	*Shanzhai* (ODM)	Own brand (post-*shanzhai*) (OBM)
Products	Software and electronics components, home furnishings	Mobile phones, tablets, low-cost technologies; labour-saving devices, fashion	Higher marketability (formal)
Strategy	Standardised production at low cost: international contractors	Reverse engineering, rapid prototype development, identifying niche markets	Domestic and international collaboration; R&D, sales and distribution partners
Intellectual Property	IP maintained by contractor; fee for services	IP is fluid, usually avoided, informal	IP is shared, formal, public list/joint ventures
Research and Development	Mostly nil	Community knowledge-sharing model; no after sales service	Brand equity; after sales service

For the design entrepreneur, there is a conceptual development that goes along with this. Eric Pan, founder of the Shenzhen-based open-source hardware design and manufacture house Seeed Studio, describes it as being akin to learning a new language. First, you copy words and sentences from your teacher 'such as Apple and Samsung to create a mimic'. These provide the basic skills and infrastructure. Then you learn 'to write a word, a sentence [and] you remember it. From words you can create sentences and grammar, then you can write a whole article' (Pan, quoted in Lindtner 2014: 159).

In this model, creativity is regarded as something that is enmeshed with copying. Originality develops out of this relationship rather than being its prior aim. Within this, there is a DIY ethic in *shanzhai*, working inventively with the materials and technologies to hand and adapting to

7.2   Inside the Seeed offices, Shenzhen (Photos: Guy Julier)

rapid changes in their availability and know-how. As such, *shanzhai* bleeds into open source, open innovation, makerspaces and hacker activities (Seeed Studio established Shenzhen's first makerspace in 2011). Equally, open innovation and open source can work in hybrid ways with mainstream commerce. A Shenzhen example of this is World Peace Industrial (WPI), a Taiwanese electronic sourcing company located in Shenzhen. They develop over 130 circuit boards (*gongban*) a year for smartphones, tablets, smart watches, smart homes and industrial controls. Their design is open-sourced, with the idea that they stimulate the marketplace. This feeds back into the company, for it is they who also trade in the components that are used in them (Lindtner and Greenspan 2014).

These are aligned, not necessarily as reproductions of Western practices. Rather, they have their own, distinct, characteristics that grow out of local industries and cultural understandings (Lindtner and Li 2012; Lindtner 2014). The move from *shanzhai* copying to open innovation in the mainstream economy is sometimes referred to as 'involving makerspaces and incubators', the majority of which receive government or corporate support (Saunders and Kingsley 2016). This has been called *new shanzhai* by one of its chief proponents, David Li, who founded the Shenzhen Open Innovation Lab (Li 2014). It is seen to support the notion of 'democratising innovation' through allowing wider access to its tools and resources (Von Hippel 2005).

In encouraging this development, the Shenzhen Municipal Government provided some 2,000 *shanzhai* entrepreneurs with subsidies for land, rent tax and housing in 2009 (Lin 2011: 21). In 2015, the Shenzhen Muncipal Government called for applications to receive a total of RMB200m of support to set up new makerspaces to work in this ecology. There were over 2,000 applications, of which 30 were successful (Liao and Li 2016). Despite their ambiguous legal status in terms of international intellectual property rights, it appears that *shanzhai* business is not discouraged. Indeed, its development through makerspaces was intended to take the concept several steps further in aligning into the mainstream economy. This opens on to a set of interesting and challenging circumstances for design and the creative industries in China and elsewhere.

Through informal economies and open innovation, design can be engaged in and contribute to the configuration of new economic forms.

CREATIVITY AND POLICY IN CHINA

There is a profound and fascinating challenge concerning the nature of creativity here. The word 'originality' comes from the Greek word *poesis*, that implies something coming from nothing. Likewise, creation myths in much Western folklore and religion (not least seen in Christianity) place the beginnings of the world in the same vain – something that was produced by someone from nothing, or, at least, out of chaos. Keane (2013: 56) shows that in the Western philosophical tradition, 'creativity is inevitably wedded to originality, in particular, the imaginings of the iconoclastic artist'. By contrast, in China, and more generally across the Far East, 'creativity' in this sense of originality and individual authorship does not figure in its philosophical tradition. The word 'to create' was *zuo* in ancient Chinese texts. This means, literally, 'to make' or 'to cultivate'. This confirms a Confucian view that people should model themselves on and reproduce patterns from nature (Keane 2009: 434). Creation is therefore aligned with crafting and reproduction rather than originality. Put bluntly and the other way around, a traditional conception of creativity in China actually reinforces practices of copying.

In China a more recent word denoting 'creativity' in its Western sense of innovation and originality is *chuangyi*. This word emerged in the 1990s through the advertising industries and literally means 'to make new ideas'. Statistical tracking of its usage in Chinese discourse in academic articles shows its exponential take-off from about 2005. In everyday life *chuangyi* embellishes shopping malls, cultural institutions, art zones, new housing developments and media production centres (Keane 2013: 67 and 56). At other times, the English term 'creative industries' is also frequently employed (O'Connor and Xin 2006: 272).

This linguistic turn is indicative of a wider acceptance of Western models and policies of creativity that has taken place since about 2000 by the Chinese government. This is partially motivated by industrial ambitions to move beyond being a mere manufacturing subcontractee to Western corporations. The refrain 'From made in China to created in China' was coined by Liu Shifa, Vice-director of the Market Development section within China's Ministry of Culture in 2004. The general message of a policy shift towards a value-added, knowledge economy was rapidly absorbed into economic planning and the refrain soon became a key branding slogan for China (Keane 2007: 84–6).

There has also been push from outside. Since joining the WTO in 2001, the Chinese government has been under pressure from corporations and governments from the USA and the European Union to adopt a more stringent approach to enforcing and safeguarding intellectual property rights (Montgomery 2010). China's patent and trademark laws first appeared in the 1980s and were revised in the 2000s to align better with WTO demands (Pang 2012: 99). Nevertheless, rampant piracy continues. While investment in intellectual property rights training is high throughout China, enforcement is low. In 2006, 90 per cent of film and music products that were consumed in China were 'pirated' (Montgomery 2010: 108).

Thus, it appears that the importation of Western norms regarding creativity, creative industries and IPR is in direct collision with cultural understandings in China. These Western norms are underpinned by notions of modernity and authorship. The idea of modernity as pinned to cultural creation emerged through the twentieth century in Europe and the USA. It is inscribed into expectations of originality and authorship in artistic practice that is extended into other cultural and technological products. Alongside this, IPR regimes uphold dominant modes of individualism. The very fact that patent law requires the registration of the names as 'inventors' reinforces the idea that innovations come from the minds of identifiable actors, rather than from a wider, anonymous collective.

Meanwhile, China has emphasised collaborative production of ideas and goods and conformity through their reproduction rather than celebrating individual and disruptive action. The planned economy of its communist system has, until the 2000s, stressed the distribution of approved content (Montgomery and Fitzgerald 2006). By entering into global marketplaces, China, at least on paper, has become bound to the Agreement on Trade Related Aspects of Intellectual Property (TRIPs). This could mark an historic shift towards new conceptions of creative practice and individual expression.

In the meantime, a different kind of creativity is at work in the informal economies of *shanzhai*. It could be that 'made in ...' and 'created in ...' are actually so close together in the *shanzhai* context as to be indivisible. The *shanzhai* model and other, similar practices of the informal economy produce a distinct attitudinal disposition and set of economic practices. As such, 'creativity' should be understood in a different way.

In commenting on the establishment of a modern fashion system in China, Montgomery argues that design literacy among Chinese entrepreneurs in this sector was insufficient to 'navigate a tricky landscape of taste' (2010: 87). Understanding and recognising the nuances of what might sell at home or abroad or what might catch the global journalistic eye was something that was, at least during the 2000s, beyond contenders in China.

This view misses two significant points, however. The first is that it is possible that an entirely different form of aesthetic sensibility may be at play in China that has both internal and external appeal and is independent of Western conceptions of what might be fashionable or attractive. The second is that we might take a side-step altogether and reconceive creativity as not necessarily existing within the Western paradigm of individual genius and originality. Instead, creativity within a *shanzhai* mode rests on a number of other features: inventive combination of pre-existing technologies and forms; clever networking between entrepreneurs across production and distribution; openness in sharing discoveries and advances that are derived through making, tinkering, trying out and unanticipated possibilities.

It is perhaps too easy a conclusion to view *shanzhai* as a typically renegade and entrepreneurial activity that straightforwardly and 'naturally' leads on to mainstream, capitalist practices. Undoubtedly, since 2000, China has moved more obviously into Western modes of consumer culture (Gerth 2010). But perhaps design in China takes a different route. Study of Chinese economics, policy, culture and society calls into question easy conclusions as to the 'neoliberalisation' of this huge nation. Neoliberal conceptions of individual property and individualism, free-trade, marketisation and the absence of state intervention require critical reconsideration in the context of China (Nonini 2008; Keith et al. 2014). Systems of social connections that are maintained through gifts and favours (known as *guanxi*); ambiguous, multiple and layered workings of property rights; notions of 'distributed success' as drivers of business and innovation (Li 2016); close relationships between local state and entrepreneurs: all of these produce a complex and nuanced context for economic practices. And as China goes, so goes its design.

JUGAAD AND FRUGAL INNOVATION IN INDIA

Between 2010 and 2012 a flurry of books, reports, articles and exhibitions appeared around the world on the subject of India's *jugaad* phenomenon. The term *jugaad* derives from the Hindi word for an innovative fix and is extended to describe jalopies, the many motorcycles, cars or trucks that are adapted by their owners to take extra passengers and goods. Often featuring enhanced suspension to cope with rutted roads, these hybrid vehicles appear as the epitomes of mend-and-make-do India. This *jugaad* idea is found in the hacking of a wider range of products either to give them secondary uses or, simply, to get them to work in conditions they weren't intended for. The concept of *jugaad*'s origins is therefore in everyday, small-scale innovations made among India's rural and urban poor. But it has also come to represent a wider attitude to 'quick fix' enterprise, synonymous with 'frugal innovation' or, even, 'Indovation'.

Generally, *jugaad* involves one-off problem-solving adaptations that may be copied but are not necessarily upscaled into commercial products. Perhaps the best-known example of a *jugaad* object that has been commercialised is Mansukh Prajapati's design for a ceramic fridge. A village ceramicist, Prajapati drew from the idea of using evaporation to keep water cool in traditional earthenware pots called *matkas* following the 2001 Gugurati earthquake. Through experimenting with different clays, soils and fridge designs, he arrived at a product called the Mitticool in 2005. By 2011, he was selling 50 to 70 units a month (NDTV 2011), rising to 230 per month three years later (Sinha 2014). Retailing at around US$50, it doesn't require an electricity supply and is presented as the 'fridge for the poor'.

The Mitticool story is presented in the opening to the business-school text *Jugaad Innovation*; its authors enthuse about how the idea was 'born out of adverse circumstances', transforming 'scarcity into opportunity' through a 'never-say-die attitude' (Radjou et al. 2012: 3). They go on to show

7.3   Mitticool refrigerator and its originator, Mansukh Prajapati, at work (Photo: Mitticool Clay Creations)

that this entrepreneurial spirit of tinkering is not only to be found in India but also in Brazil (called *gambiarra*), China (*zizhu chuangxin*), Kenya (*jua kali*) and francophone Africa (*système D*) – indeed, across all 'emerging economies' (p. 5). One might add that this also appears in historical moments of scarcity. One notable example was in Poland during Martial Law of the early 1980s where *kombinacya* – making business connections through informal networks – was in full swing as a way of getting round shortages of goods (Crowley 1992). However, it is *jugaad* that has come to signify an innate verve for grassroots innovation that subsequently extends into more mainstream economic practices, in particular the ICT sector, and, it is sometimes argued, accounts for India's startling growth from 2000 (Birtchnell 2011; Rai 2015).

For the Western eye, *jugaad* perhaps serves up a compelling visual feast of clunky, yet ingenious solutions to everyday problems. Exhibitions such as *Jugaad Urbanism: Resourceful Strategies for Indian Cities*, which took place at New York's Architecture Centre in 2011, underscore this. But *jugaad* has also come to function within India's projection of itself to the rest of the world as a serious economic force. At its most basic, it is seen to provide an entrepreneurial route upward for the country's 810 million, bottom-of-the-pyramid citizens, 250 million of whom live below the poverty line (Singh et al. 2012). It is also championed as an approach that finds its way into large-scale manufacture, such as in the case of the Tata Nano low-cost, family car (Bobel 2012).

The dates of this spike of global interest in *jugaad* are significant. The year 2010 was when the effects of the 2008 financial crisis hit hardest in terms of investment around the world. The idea of 'frugal innovation', of achieving high returns that draw ingeniously on scarce resources, might have been a fitting trope for its times. At the same time, GDP growth for India peaked at an astonishing 10.3 per cent in that year (World Bank 2016). Linking frugal innovation via *jugaad* to new possibilities in economic thinking and policy in other countries was fitting for the time. It seems that a reversal of the traditional flow of 'expertise' from West to East was taking place and that India was being utilised to provide answers to the economic crises being felt in Europe and the USA (see, for instance, Bound and Thornton 2012). *Jugaad* may have been seen as a 'meta quick fix' for broken economies as much as a quick fix for everyday objects.

Thus, *jugaad* is distributed symbolically and operationally across a range of contexts. Popular discourse locates it among the impoverished individual while policy discourse upscales it to approaches to more systemic innovation. This shift of discourse is mediated via verbal and visual anecdotes around grassroots inventions and applications that make for compelling stories and pictures. These are then taken into public arenas for design such as exhibitions or business texts and then become the foundation of economic discussion.

THE LIMITS OF *JUGAAD*

Beyond the hyperbole, can a lasting link between *jugaad* and more systemic innovation and, indeed, the commercial use of design be achieved? What are the limits in associating the bottom-up developments in its informal economy with a lasting and professionalised, design-led approach to entrepreneurialism in a global context? If an expectation that India should be a major player in the world economy, is the *jugaad* route appropriate?

At its base, *jugaad* is about fixing immediate needs. This is often done by taking shortcuts with whatever happens to be at hand: a motorcycle is used to power a water pump; an iron becomes a hotplate for cooking; discarded cans are adapted and lashed together to create a canopy that provides shade. Indian industrial designer Sharang Seth regards this as an inversion of 'form follows function'. Objects are re-purposed in *ad hoc* ways, but this re-purposing is limited by the capabilities of those objects. In practice it provides one-off, momentary and localised problem solving rather than an extended engagement between producers and consumers around a particular product or concept in a more generalised sense. The Mitticool example is somewhat an exception to this where someone has gone through an iterative process of developing and testing to upscale from a basic idea to a marketeable product. Seth goes on to align this *jugaad* thinking with internships, arguing that these involve employers hiring someone around a very specific set of tasks, undertaken at low cost. They are 'occupational one-night stands' in his words (Seth 2014).

A second issue with making this connection between *jugaad* and design is that the former exists outside the normal sensibilities of risk and quality control. Birtchnell (2011) sees the risk-taking that takes place in *jugaad* as born of poverty (effectively where there is 'nothing to lose'). Subsequently this is played out in a business vocabulary of overcoming risks as they arise rather than in the planning and design processes. Much of the Tata Nano, launched in 2009 as the cheapest family saloon car in the world (retailing in India at around US$2,000), was designed by assembling and adapting pre-formed components, thus keeping costs down. As such, arguably, it emerges out of a *jugaad* or 'Ghandian innovation' mindset (Prahalad and Mashelkar 2010). At the same time, it is worth noting that this vehicle performed very badly in German vehicle-safety tests (Oltermann and McClanahan 2014). When reviewing the final result against other standards of risk and user wellbeing to which designers are normally required to adhere, efforts made through frugal innovation may be disputed.

In wider terms, *jugaad* may be taken to either exist as just part of a pathway to more systemic innovation or to suppress this progression. Its ethic of 'mend and make do' may maintain daily functioning and even give poor people incremental access to new openings. Alternatively, it may also continue to reinforce the acceptance of low expectations of performance and safety standards. Its 'quick fix' approach may provide short-term solutions to everyday challenges while actually perpetuating the routine practices that are part of the causes of poverty in the first place.

India is a country of startling and uplifting levels of creativity. It is also a country of shocking levels of inequality. India's informal sector accounts for 90 per cent of its labour where wages and productivity are very low. Female illiteracy sits at around 27 per cent (Drèze and Sen 2013: 23 and 5). India's child healthcare levels are worse than in Sub-Saharan Africa and Bangladesh (p. 144). This is while, between 1991 and 2001, the Indian economy trebled in size. The natural comparator to India would be China, a country also with well over 1 billion citizens that has also undergone rapid economic growth in the past two decades. However, China has gone much further in raising life expectancy, expanding general education and securing healthcare for all its people.

Creative problem solving may thrive in the contexts of informal economies, unbound by restrictions such as the health and safety requirements of the mainstream sector. By considering how concepts such as *jugaad* play into the more normative context of mainstream enterprise we see its limits and, indeed, the edges of design. Perhaps a larger conclusion may be drawn about economies of design themselves and how they are reliant on mainstream structures and supports. A further question arises as to how reliant design and innovation are on the stability and wellbeing that a state is prepared to produce through its policies that address inequalities. In other words, a poor, illiterate and unhealthy population is unlikely to provide much of a context where design may prosper. Systemic innovation may require systemic change before it can happen.

HORIZONTALIDAD: ECONOMIC CRISIS AND SELF-ORGANISATION

The examples of informal economies and design that have been given so far exist firmly among entrepreneurial or quasi-entrepreneurial activities. *Shanzhai* differentiates from the mainstream norms of contemporary capitalism in that it is founded on the open sharing of technical information and is highly reliant on social networks for its functioning. *Jugaad* involves re-purposing through the hacking and adapting of objects or components and is, by and large, a response to immediate needs. *Shanzhai* could be said to derive a design approach in response to abundance (of technological resources, ideas, manufacture and assembly bases as well as market opportunity). *Jugaad* is a response to scarcity (of capital, materials, production opportunities, transportation and much more). In either case, design occupies a different status than that largely experienced in the West. It is less recognisable as a distinct, professionalised pursuit. Rather, it is embedded within informal and semi-formal networks of entrepreneurial activities. Nonetheless, these activities – and design therein – are the product of given economic, social and political realities. While they may be active in changing these, this is not their primary roles. They are, in essence, reactive.

What economies of design emerge where processes of political and social change feature more self-consciously? This section takes the context of *horizontalidad*, or horizontalism, as practised in Argentina, to explore this question. In doing so, it slips away from more obviously informal economic arrangements to consider design as part of alternative economies. This trajectory is picked up in the penultimate section as well, where we consider timebanking.

Argentina has played a varied and sometimes confrontational role in the face of contemporary, global capitalism. Its political and economic history is marked by periods of repressive, right-wing dictatorship (e.g. the *junta* of 1976–83), economic crisis (1983–89 and 1999–2002) and headlong embracing of neoliberal policies (1989–95 and again from 2015). Throughout this history, Argentina has suffered recurrent hyperinflation and national debt problems.

The country's worst economic depression began to unfold in 1995 but properly took hold 1998–2002, when the economy shrank by around 20 per cent (Weisbrot and Sandoval 2007: 2). In order to avoid bank savings haemorrhaging from the country, the government imposed a *corralito* on them in December 2001 and throughout most of 2002. This involved very tight controls on bank withdrawals and deprived the middle-class of their savings while inhibiting the cash-based informal economy, on which many of the poor were dependent. By mid-2002, over half of the population was living in poverty as compared to 22 per cent in 1994 (Levitsky and Murillo 2003: 155). December 2001 saw widespread protests and rioting against the government, which led to the resignation of two presidents in as many weeks.

In this turmoil, grassroots neighbourhood assemblies began to take shape across Argentina. With the paralysis of the mainstream economy, people gathered in street meetings to find ways of supporting one another and began to form barter networks and people's kitchens, taking over buildings, including abandoned banks, and converting them into community centres (Sitrin 2006: 10). From this an alternative economy was consolidated. Barter networks were formed across the country with 'nodes', often set in church halls, disused factories or car parks where foodstuffs, clothing or even services such as haircuts could be exchanged via locally established credit notes. The largest such node, in the city of Mendoza, involved 36,000 participants (North 2005: 228).

The types of self-organisation that were developed via the neighbourhood assemblies and the barter systems began to coalesce into a description of a political process called, in Spanish, *horizontalidad*. First and foremost, this concept expresses a desire to do away with vertically arranged, hierarchical structures of governance so that equality becomes everyone's responsibility. Furthermore, *horizontalidad* is conceived as a network structure so that divergent opinions and actions can be accommodated through multiple hubs, as opposed to seeking unity within a geographical area. Finally, differing opinions within a group are not voted on; rather, they are brought together through the collaborative re-writing of proposals to include these, while leaving possibilities for varying courses of resulting action (Maeckelbergh 2013).

Versions of *horizontalidad* are to be found elsewhere. For example, it had been developed among the Zapatistas of Chiapas in Mexico from the 1990s; it has also been fundamental to the 15-M movement that arose in Spain in response to the austerity measures following the 2008 financial crisis. Importantly, *horizontalidad* is taken to be a tool in addition to being an end in itself; it is a process of self-organisation and open democracy that radically alters the workings of power. It can also provide openings that reconceive the economic processes of design practices, as the next section explains.

ACTIVIST DESIGN AND ECONOMIC CRISIS IN ARGENTINA

A distinctive feature of urban life during this 1998–2002 period of economic depression in Argentina was the growth of *cartoneros* working the streets. These included men, women and children, often from poor *barrios*, scavenging for discarded cardboard and other recyclable material that they then sold on to recycling centres. In 1998 there were an estimated 10,000 living by this means in Buenos Aires; this had risen to 40,000 by 2002 (Whitson 2011: 1404). Another 2002 estimate put this figure for the Buenos Aires metropolitan area at 100,000 (Chronopoulos 2006: 168).

The economic depression precipitated the emigration of many architects and designers from Argentina. Others, such as Miki Friedenbach and Laura Leavy, remained to engage in the possibilities that were arising. Their design work was mostly focused on mainstream commercial product design and branding. Around this time, however, and along with designer Alejandro Sarmiento, they turned their attentions to more activist interventions. Specifically, they developed a cutting tool that could be used to slice up discarded drink bottles to create plastic 'threads' of varying gauges. They then established training workshops so that *cartoneros* and others could learn how to use the resultant material to design and make products they could then sell for themselves.

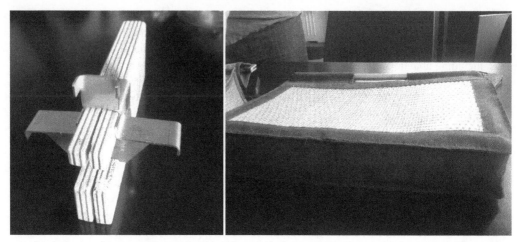

7.4   Friedenbach and Leavy cutting tool and handbag made from reclaimed plastic bottle material (Photos: Guy Julier)

These workshops looked to facilitate processes to help fellow citizens thrive better in the alternative economies that were coalescing at the time (Friedenbach 2013).

It would be an exaggeration to claim such design activities as being 'politically pure' in the sense that they subscribed wholeheartedly to the principles of *horizontalidad* and self-management. Rather, they can be best described as taking part in a general affective atmosphere (Anderson 2009; Stewart 2011) that prevailed at the time and had very much sat in the background of daily life in Argentina until then. Their work may also be viewed as an emotional or, even, aesthetic response to a situation that is collectively experienced. This has otherwise been termed as *politica afectiva* (affective politics). This involves putting emotional, human connections before the 'rationality' of a sense of external, moral obligation. In this, what is wrong in society is taken to be something that is felt before it is known (Dinerstein 2014: 137–9).

Activist design may be taken to be a general disposition to promote societal considerations ahead of commercial ones and yet its distinctions from mainstream practices may quickly become blurred. For example, it wasn't long before Friedenbach and Leavey's project formed the foundation of 'ScrapLab', which was sponsored by Coca-Cola. This programme was dedicated to developing high-quality products made from scrap that could be artisanally produced in homes and that could subsequently hatch micro-enterprises (Friedenbach 2013). Aside from the sponsorship of a global corporation, these good attentions may be read as playing into an ideal of 'the dignified worker and self-sufficient citizen, who responds to the neoliberal principles of self-responsibility and self-industriousness' (Sternberg 2013: 192).

The slippage from activist to mainstream practices may go further in these circumstances. Following the economic depression, the Buenos Aires municipality instigated a programme of regularising the *cartoneros*. This involved their registration, the design and provision of uniforms and tying them into official recycling centres. Again, this arose in part from civic concerns over the health and safety of *cartoneros*, but has equally been interpreted as a disciplining of labour – without relieving the sheer volume of work involved – into conceptions of the organised, neoliberal city (Whitson 2011; Sternberg 2013).

The failure of neoliberal systems can open up opportunities for alternative forms of design practice. These exploit the spaces that are left behind by economic crisis, both literally and symbolically.

Through Argentina's economic depression, as factories were closed by their owners, so some were occupied and re-opened by their workers and put back into production. These were run as cooperatives according to various, localised interpretations of *horizontalidad*. Two well-known examples, that also included the participation of designers, were the ceramics factory Zanon and the textile producer Brukman (Ledesma 2015). Among the first examples of these *empresas recuperadas* (recuperated businesses) was Industrias Metalúrgicas y Plásticas Argentina (IMPA) in Buenos Aires. This traditionally had manufactured a range of aluminium products, from paint tubes to light aircraft. Following its worker occupation in 1998, it was unable to run to its original, full production, but its vast building undertook other functions. Hence, in order to survive, it gradually included a cultural centre, educational, performance and rehearsal spaces. In a corner of this recuperated factory, the studio of Cooperativa de Diseño was established.

Cooperativa de Diseño is a multidisciplinary design studio, covering product and graphic design as well audio-visual production. Founded in 2011 as a cooperative by seven women, they work from a principle of *horizontalidad* and self-organisation. Their ethos is that of 'constructing design from and for people'. This is an awkward translation from the Spanish, but it expresses both the idea that this kind of design is undetermined and in constant development as a process and in ongoing dialogue with its publics. In terms of 'clients', Cooperativa de Diseño undertakes such projects as product development with cooperatives from other recuperated factories, or videos for womens' campaign groups (Cooperativa de Diseño 2013).

A particularly interesting facet of Cooperativa de Diseño, in terms of their economic processes, is in their internal costings and workflow procedures. Classically, in mainstream designing, a client brief is costed and then jobs are apportioned to studio members according to the 'envelope' of that commission. At Cooperativa de Diseño the polarities are reversed. The basic financial needs of each member of the cooperative are defined (according to such things as dependents, standing charges for services and each member's housing costs). This produces a guaranteed base (or 'floor') salary for each that is covered out of the cooperative's overall income. Outside work they may do, such as teaching, is calculated as part of this. The second income category is 'life', which includes daily living expenses such as food and clothing. The aim is that each member ends up with the same income above the 'floor' or base amount, making salaries non-hierarchical.

7.5   Cooperativa de Diseño, Buenos Aires: members, organisational spreadsheet and products (Photos: Guy Julier and Cooperativa de Diseño)

Necessary hours, divided between different kinds of tasks (whether directly income generating or not) are then divided equally among them as well, using Excel and iCalc digital tools.

In this way, Cooperativa de Diseño adjusts the processes and tools of mainstream, commercial work to a collective way of working that is consonant with their political outlooks. This shows that taking a measured approach to how they might survive and thrive, both individually and as a collective, is still necessary while adhering to activist aims.

CREATIVE TIMEBANKING

The example of Cooperativa de Diseño demonstrates how design practice may operate in different constellations from the traditional model of the designer who operates in a defer- ent, service mode to their client. While power relations may not be entirely absent from the frame, the studio seeks out a particular kind of dialogue and relationship. Internally, they have structured a way of costing for their worktime that ensures equality among its members. This example shows how alternative economies, while involving exchange, may produce their own norms and motivations that, in turn, open up spaces for alternative ways of practising design. In this section, we review an initiative that attempts to produce a parallel creative economy and politics in itself.

Timebanking is an economic system where the unit of exchange is time. This unit is usu- ally taken as an hour and is traded through a central bank of time by members who sign up to one. It is a service-based system in that it involves the exchange of members' time that is dedicated to a task rather than being tradeable for goods. The key principle within it is that everyone's time is valued equally, no matter what the different value that that time might have in the mainstream economy. The idea was first conceptualised by Josiah Warren in 1827, who thought of in terms of 'labor notes'. However, the term 'timebanking' was introduced in 1986 in the USA by Edgar Cahn, who went on to establish a network of timebanks there in 1995. By 2015 there were 288 timebanks in the UK (Timebanking UK 2015) and more than 120 timebanks in the USA (Shih et al. 2015: 1075).

With its 'hour for an hour' ethos, timebanking therefore produces a flat, egalitarian economy. It also gives value to skills such as care for older people or children that may not always be highly valued in the mainstream economy and, nonetheless, are abundant. In most cases, however, these non-market activities underpin the market economy. By way of illustration, the futurist Alvin Toffler was prone to asking company CEOs what effect on productivity there would be if their employees were not toilet trained (Ryan-Collins et al. 2008: 9).

Given that it is a service-based system involving close peer-to-peer exchanges, timebanking is invariably highly local in its operations. It can help build social relationships, creating support networks within a community. As such it is also viewed as important in its potential to address welfare and health challenges (Seyfang 2002; Glynos and Speed 2012).

In 2010, a group of artists and designers in the city of Leeds, UK, developed a timebanking system for creative professionals. Called the Leeds Creative Timebank (LCT), this was founded as both a practical and political response to the deepening challenges being felt as the result of the 2008 economic crisis. It was becoming abundantly clear that financial support from state sources for visual artists, performers, filmmakers and other creative professionals was rapidly disappearing. For designers, client work looked to be drying up as well. The Leeds Creative Timebank was thus conceived as a way by which these could continue to work together while removing the need for cash generation to pay each other. Therefore, a clear difference from other timebanks was that it was intended in the first place as a way of supporting a distinct professional sector rather than a wider community. The aim was therefore to increase the resilience of the creative sector in Leeds by maintaining the opportunities for collaboration within it while developing a mutually supportive, rather than competitive, alternative economy in parallel to mainstream modes.

By 2016, the Leeds Creative Timebank included 147 members, of which 136 had actively used it. It is supported by an external database, Timebanking UK, that they sign into to offer or search for collaboration with other LCT members. Design, in the more traditional conception of graphic, interior, product and so on, perhaps takes up a minority in the range of professional skills it embraces; choreography, circus skills, copywriting, stage management, storytelling and video-editing also figure on its list, for example. That said, practically all the 46 professional skills offered may at some time be of interest and usable by a designer (Ball 2016). Furthermore, another category of 'mentoring or training' provides just that to designers who want to broaden their own skills-base by learning from other members.

With its non-cash ethos, the Leeds Creative Timebank involves distinct value generation, producing what one participant has called 'non-risky risk'. Money is not lost if a collaboration doesn't work, just a few hours. This makes members more open to experimenting in open-ended ways with other disciplines, prototyping new ways of working or in novel media combinations. In turn, this may produce an experimental economy that is internal to the timebank. At the same time, the core skills of members – the activities that they normally get paid to do – do not always fully come into play within the timebank. They might if there isn't other work around but they are more likely to engage skills that are more peripheral to them within the LCT (Briggs et al. 2016).

In light of the above observations, it is important to recognise the specific qualities that a creative timebank produces. First, it engages a solidarity between its participants as they adhere to an ethos of sharing skills and expertise. Second, this also produces a space for creative practice that is more experimental and whose outcomes may then lie outside the commoditisation that the mainstream economy may insist on. Third, however, purely as an alternative economy, it is not separate from the main, cash economy; rather, complex knots between the two may result (Day et al. 2014).

CONCLUSION

Reviewing the four case studies presented in this chapter, it seems that design occupies a varied position in relation to informal and alternative economies.

In the case of *shanzhai*, we have seen that design begins in copying but that this copying is undertaken in knowing and even ironic ways. From this it is then deeply imbedded into systems of product development, production, distribution and repair to the point that it is difficult to define it separately. The borders between copying, innovation and design are fluid. The boundaries of intellectual property are also loose where *shanzhai* rests on open innovation. Thus, creativity takes on a distinct quality here: it is founded more on tinkering and sharing than according to Western notions of originality and individual authorship. Further, we may take *shanzhai*, and the role of design therein, to carry deep cultural connotations that may be taken to be at odds with economic development. As economic policy in China attempts to align itself with global, neo-liberal orthodoxies in intellectual property and the role of the creative industries, so these issues become increasingly problematic. Design, whether in tacit or explicit senses, appears to sit at the meeting points of informal and formal economies here.

In the case of *jugaad*, design also occupies a problematic position. It appears to figure in a move in India from grassroots adaptations and tinkering to its upscaling into consumer items. As such, it is taken to enact frugal innovation. This then becomes a symbolic metaphor for how entire economies may flourish. An abundance of ingenuity and risk-taking in the informal economy that is born out of material scarcity, is seen more generally to provide a route that the formal economy may follow. The idea of 'quick-fix' problem solving in *jugaad* may be an over-simplification of how design plays out in reality, however.

In the case of *horizontalidad*, the economic and political crises in Argentina has led to activism in egalitarian, community-based market and industrial systems. Although limited in size in relation to the ongoing neoliberalisation of the country's economic processes, it nonetheless provides an interesting space where alternative economies are experimented with. Importantly, this space is characterised by and articulated through a language of emotional appeal. Its key feature could be said to be its affective politics rather than any programmatic course of action. Activist design emerges as an act of generosity rather than for commercial gain here. One way this is done is in designing tools and systems that help others to survive in scarcity. Another is in rethinking the ways by which design work may be valorised and accounted for.

Finally, the example of the creative timebank in the UK is shown to produce a parallel economy that exists both independently of and in association with the mainstream economy. Conceived as a way of protecting the livelihoods of creative practitioners in a context of economic crisis and public funding cuts, work undertaken within the timebank is, however, seen to function differently and have different purposes than in the normal, commercial context. It results in greater risk-taking within collaborations between timebank members.

These examples have wide variations, both in their geographical locations and economic and political contexts. At the same time, it is clear that in all four cases, design takes on distinct functions and forms of practice as compared with mainstream economies. To push further, design in the informal and alternative economies both reconfigures what design work is and produces distinct aesthetic sensibilities against which it may be judged. This may be the result of the specific cultural contexts in which it operates. But it also suggests a conscious alterity in what is considered to be of value.

8

PUBLIC SECTOR
INNOVATION

In many countries, following the 2008 economic crisis, funding cuts to the public sector have stirred up interest in the use of design to reconfigure their services. Through this, new ways of designing that foreground the user experience have developed. To what extent do these developments reproduce commercial orthodoxies? Or does this allow for new thinking about civic participation in public life? Chapter 8 investigates changing approaches to governance and the different roles that design practice has there.

So far, this book has concentrated almost exclusively on commercial contexts of design. But several reasons compel us to discuss the ways by which design operates in the public sector and how this has changed according to developing economic and governance processes.

The first is, quite frankly, a matter of size. The public sector represents a significant, and often overlooked, element of design. In OECD countries, public sector employment of total employment was 21.3 per cent in 2013, with it touching 35 per cent in Denmark and Norway (OECD 2015: 84). In the same year, with 1.7 million employees, the UK National Health Service was the fifth largest employer in the world, the US Department of Defense being the biggest with 3.2 million (McCarthy 2015). The public sector represents massive but diverse fields of work, management and expenditure. For OECD countries in 2013, the production costs of goods and services in the public sector represented on average 21.3 per cent of GDP (OECD 2015: 80). The public sector is a major user and stimulant of design activities.

Second, the public sector is by no means independent of the private, commercial sector or other external bodies. Much of this connection is made by the outsourcing of government functions to private sector providers as well as external voluntary, charitable and/or not-for-profit organisations. In 2013, government outsourcing of OECD countries represented, on average, 8.9 per cent of GDP. Among these, Belgium, Japan, Germany and the Netherlands dedicated over 60 per cent of expenditure to the outsourcing of services to third-party provision (OECD 2015: 80). This stimulates competition among providers, in turn creating design opportunities.

Third, many public sector functions, such as education, health and defence, provide the basis for research, innovation and development that subsequently feeds into commercial applications. The Federal government of the USA was responsible for 26 per cent of research and development funding in 2008. The technologies that have brought us the Apple iPod, iPhone and iPad came about thanks to a mixture of US state investment support, prior research carried out in military initiatives, government procurement and academic scientific research (Mazzucato 2013: 60 and 93–5).

Fourth, and where much of this chapter focuses, developments in the ways by which governments manage the public sector, how policy is formulated, how services are delivered and the relationships they have with citizens have given way to an increased centrality of design. At the heart of this has been the rise of design thinking and many associated design approaches. This has been driven, as we shall see, by fiscal constraint on public budgets (otherwise known as austerity) but also by rising demand on public services. Design and, in particular, its person-centred methods have been drawn into public sector innovation and policymaking. We must therefore look into developments in design practice that meet changes in governance and what it means to be a citizen. In this, the relationship of public and private sectors becomes progressively more complex, as do the design frameworks and methods that are employed.

The following section plunges straight into the important changes that have taken place in design in relation to the public sector since around 2008. It reveals a development in the representation and expectations of design practices here. Having established the contemporary scene, the following sections then hop back to review changes that have taken place in the ways by which the public sector is formulated since the 1980s. They show that the public sector has progressively been subject to thinking derived from the private sector and the subsequent significance of this for design and design methods. The latter part of this chapter discusses different conceptions of citizenship as produced, in part, through design. In this, it moves beyond neoliberal conceptions of the citizen as a 'consumer' of public services to more complex arrangements of belonging and identity.

NEW OBJECTS OF DESIGN FOR PUBLIC SECTOR INNOVATION

We have become used to a rarefied language of design representation through the pages of popular design magazines and websites: singularised products floating in space; chairs accompanied by nothing but their own shadows; brand logos, posters or packaging without context; ready-to-use interiors, evacuated of the mess of people and clutter. These objects appear to come from nowhere, magicked into existence with no regard to their legions of creative workers, entrepreneurs, factory workers, dockers and truck drivers, retailers and, of course, design journalists.

But in the mid-2000s, another visual language began to circulate through blogs, tweets and PDF-ed institutional reports. These are populated with photographs of design in action: walls of Post-it notes map customer journeys; matchboxes, Play-Doh and string, annotated with marker-pens, model neighbourhoods; sketchnotes on A1 sheets expose the networks of 'issues'; breakout groups of concerned citizens discussing their concerns while a rapporteur busily takes notes; role plays with civil servants and service users.

Welcome to the new world of service design jams, policy prototyping days and design sprints. The old world of reified design objects has not gone away. But since about 2000, a whole new idiom for design has gained prominence. Here, transparency and inclusivity in processes dominate – hence the pictures of the studio or lab in action. These images also suggest a shift from design as a noun (an output of process) to design as a verbal noun (the process itself). They indicate a continual state of transformation, whose material culture is filled out with pointers and exploratory devices – prototypes that carry futurity as 'things-that-are-not-quite-objects-yet' (Corsin Jiménez 2013: 383).

Understanding the tools that are at play in this recent account of design practice in the public sector is fundamental to understanding the positioning of design here. Often their simulations of design in use point in two directions. One is in modelling current practices in, experiences of or perspectives onto products or services. Using ethnographic research, user-observation, focus groups or other modes of enquiry, these provide representations to help understand the networks of people and things at work. The other is where abduction comes into play. Plausible but provisional insights and possibilities are created (Reichertz 2010; Kimbell 2014, 2015). It thus looks beyond the singularised object of design to map the user journey through a service that is made up of a series of encounters. This is where this new material culture of a design process – the Post-its and Play-Doh – that maps this at work. This mapping may therefore be employed to understand how a service currently exists or for prototyping future possibilities. In either case, it pays attention to the human, material, spatial and temporal relationships of a system or service. In other words, it is concerned, at least in theory, with working with the *situated* realities of everyday life whether these actually exist or are speculations.

8.1   UK government Cabinet Office civil servants prototyping patient experience of GP surgeries (Photos: Lucy Kimbell)

Conceptually, there is a shift in the location of value here. Traditional and, if you like, twentieth-century conceptions of design regard it as putting added value *into* the object (by making it more attractive, more utilitarian or both). Instead, here, an evidence-base is used to understand 'value-in-use' (Kimbell 2014: 154). These mapping devices act as prototypes of services, things and people, and their relations, in an effort to understand how these are constituted, or could be constituted in future situations. Services engage many different types of actor and multitudes of environments and objects.

This shift in understanding value has a rich theoretical background. In particular, Shove et al. (2005) draw on the actor-network theory work of Latour (2005) and the practice theory of Schatzki (1996) and Reckwitz (2002) to posit that value is not inscribed in the objects themselves; rather it is mobile and contextual. It is contingent on assemblages of related material artefacts for it to have any value in use or exchange (Molotch 2003). It comes into being as the outcome of social processes such as its imbrication into everyday routines. Value cannot sit dormant; rather, it surfaces through its enacting in ways that are also configured by design itself. This observation promotes the contextual contingency of value in relation to the designed object in spatial and temporal terms. Value comes into being in the right place and at the right time.

In short, this design approach is typified by making its processes public, a shift towards thinking more rigorously in terms of the social practices of use and, following from this, the use of prototyping future possibilities as a way of producing an evidence-base.

CONSULTANT- AND GOVERNMENT-DRIVEN PUBLIC SECTOR INNOVATION

In their widest context, these (not-quite) objects belong to the field of 'design thinking', but also service design processes, co-creation, participatory design, design for community, design activism, design for social innovation and design for policy. Rather than pick apart the different usages and nuances of these methods according to distinct design headings – probably an impossible task given their interconnectivity – it is more useful to observe their overall, emergent power and think about the precise conditions that have given rise to them. They take place in both commercial and non-commercial settings and, as we shall see later in this chapter, their development in these two is not unrelated.

By 2015, several small-scale design consultancies had emerged to specialise in public sector innovation. Consultancies such as the Innovation Unit, FutureGov, Design Affects, Snook and Uscreates in the UK, STBY in the Netherlands, Nahman and Yellow Window in Belgium or the Greater Good Studio in the USA, were developing new forms of service delivery for the public sector. These came mostly from a background in service design mixed with experience in local government. At the other end of the scale, the large design company IDEO moved increasingly into public sector innovation for global clients in the 2000s.

Upstream, government-funded units such as MindLab in Denmark, TACSI in Australia, the PolicyLab in the UK, the Public Policy Lab in New York City or La 27e Región in France employed design methods in policymaking. There were around one hundred such innovation labs operating around the world in 2015. There is some diversity among these: some are focused on future scenario buildings, others have a stronger, core design focus while a third grouping foreground data, technology or behavioural economics more (Nesta 2015a).

Of these, MindLab has been particularly note-worthy as an influential pioneer. Understanding its development helps in appreciating the different levels at which a design-led approach in government can function. MindLab was established within the Danish government's (then) Ministry of Business Affairs in 2002 as an initiative that brought policy, qualitative research and innovation through design methods together. It subsequently took on a more cross-government role in stimulating policymaking that focused on its multiple implementers, users and stakeholders that could be, at the same time, disruptive of traditional public sector bureaucracies.

8.2 Uscreates working with healthcare professionals exploring challenges and change (Photo: Uscreates)

MindLab has moved through three cumulative phases in its development. The first was MindLab as a facilitation unit or otherwise a 'creative platform'. It provided, for example, graphic tools and representations for Ministry meetings to allow them to see the networks of actors engaged around policy. In the second phase, from 2006, MindLab became more clearly an innovation unit that integrated user-research into the processes of government policy development. In 2011, MindLab entered a third phase that began to put more emphasis on organisational change within Ministries to foster a culture that embraced and supported co-creative approaches. From around 2012, another major activity of MindLab was in training and development of similar labs in other countries (Carstensen and Bason 2012). Thus it developed increasingly sophisticated and complex roles and approaches with the Danish government.

Around both the consultant design studios and the government financed labs we also find a number of thinktanks and innovation groups that are often funded through endowments or sponsorships. These would include Nesta and the Young Foundation in the UK, GovLab in New York and MaRS in Toronto. In addition, quasi-government or independent design promotion organisations, such as the UK's Design Council or the European Union's SEE Platform, have been active in developing and supporting the idea of using design in public sector innovation.

There has therefore been a rapid rise of the specialist commercial consultancies, the government innovation labs and other organisations funded by diverse means since the early 2000s. Taken together these have produced a global ecosystem supported by conferences, meet-ups and online publication as well as live web events such as service or social design jams. In addition, movement, in terms of personnel and projects, is often fluid between these consultancies and labs; one becomes a training ground for the other and vice versa.

However, despite this rapidity, they have emerged in response to a number of developments in public sector practices in the neoliberal age. The next section rewinds to the beginning of public sector reform to set the scene for subsequent discussions of design in the context of changes in patterns of governance.

NEW PUBLIC MANAGEMENT

Since the 1980s, the organisation of the public sector has moved from a 'public administration' approach to the so-called New Public Management (NPM) (McLaughlin et al. 2002). The 'public administration' model is best described within notions of the welfare state that existed from around 1945. Here, citizen needs in terms of things like care for the elderly or the maintenance of public spaces are met almost entirely by the state. However, in the neoliberal era the reform of public services, be it health, education, the civil service, the police force or social services, has become increasingly based upon the application of market principles in most capitalist countries, in particular across Europe and Australasia. Indeed, this has become a coordinated programme that comes as a necessary condition of membership of cross-national arrangements such as the European Union (Metcalfe 1994; Blum and Manning 2009).

Within NPM there has been the requirement to achieve 'best value' in order to ensure that contributions made through taxation are spent prudently. This means the pursuit of continuous improvement in the way public sector functions are exercised (Martin 2000). Thus, performance measurement and ratings, responsiveness to public demand and contracting out to competitive tendering gradually become features that bring the culture of public services closer to the private sector (Whitfield 2006).

One public sector tactic to provide infrastructure at lower immediate cost, which was rolled out in particular in the UK, Spain, Australia and New Zealand, is the use of public–private partnerships (PPPs). This relates to public sector projects or services being undertaken in collaboration with commercial corporations. Building projects may be funded through private finance called private finance initiatives (PFIs). Typically, such projects have included schools, hospitals or transport infrastructure and involve a contract wherein government bodies usually enter into 25–30 year arrangements to either buy or lease back the development. Property developers will organise funding, often from institutional investors in similar ways as discussed in Chapter 6. In other cases, local governments have actually sold their buildings to property companies to lease them back. The UK government built up a commitment of £35.5bn to 563 PFI deals by 2004, while in Australia some A\$20bn was tied up in PFI around the same time (Hodge and Greve 2007: 546). While PFIs relate mostly to the built environment rather than design *per se*, they often have an indirect effect on design by locking buildings into specific patterns and hierarchies of use for the duration of a PFI contract. Conflicts between private contractors and public sector providers may emerge that contest what is considered the most efficient use of space and how a service should be designed (Gesler et al. 2004).

More directly to design, NPM provides opportunities for design consultancies to create money-saving systems. An example of this is the UK graphics company Corporate Document Services that provides print management services that helps local authorities reduce their costs and the efficiency of their publication processes (CDS 2008). If new roles for design have emerged here, then this hasn't necessarily been the result of any dramatic reorientation of its professional body towards public service; it is more the result of the public sector bringing itself closer to the commercially oriented practices and norms of design.

PUBLIC SECTOR MARKETISATION AND CONSUMPTION

The marketisation of public services also creates a denser landscape of management and, indeed, design opportunities. Delivery of services may be developed and managed through the alliance of local authority social services, semi-public agencies and the voluntary sector. This forms part of what Whitfield (2001, 2006) calls 'agentification'. For example, Whitfield (2006) shows how, prior to agentification, the management of a school involved simply inter-acting with a local authority. It previously provided all ancillary services by subcontracting to a plethora of agencies including privatised school meal providers, buildings and facilities maintenance companies, after-school care voluntary groups, outsourced school transport, ICT, special educational needs resources and teacher supply agencies. In the NPM model, as shown in Figure 8.1, the school and the local authority are effectively working as agents to external suppliers, configuring and contracting their services to run things.

This marketisation of services calls for a much greater number of relationships with external bodies as well as more frequent decision making on the part of school managers. It also creates ever more numbers of subcontractee organisations that might represent themselves within this system: more logos, more corporate documents, more public sector oriented products, more relations. It is small wonder, therefore, that the public sector was of increasing significance to designers in this period. By 2006–07 in the UK, the public sector and non-government organisations (NGOs) provided work for around half of design agencies, making it the fourth or fifth most important client to them (British Design Innovation (BDI) 2006, 2007).

The shift from a welfare state model that predominated from 1945 to NPM from the 1980s does not only mean more job opportunities for designers, it fundamentally changes the relationship of citizens to state services. Apart from the greater emphasis on managerialist practices and terms in the public sector, NPM also involves the promotion of the notion of 'choice' in the provision of services. In this account of public services, there is an increased emphasis laid on focusing on the service 'user' and their needs. Marketisation sees to the creation of a competitive field at the supply end as providers vie with one another for contractors. At the user end, citizens are remade as consumers of those services (Clarke 2007; Clarke and Newman 2007; Moor 2009).

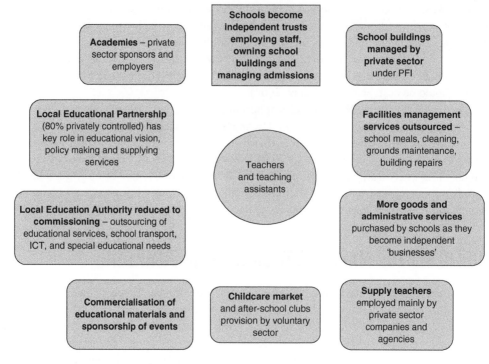

Figure 8.1 The marketisation of school education (Whitfield 2006)

This turn towards the consumption of public services – as opposed to their mere use – also involves the *making* of their consumers. Going to the doctor, getting the streets cleaned or putting children through schooling may involve making choices (which clinic? which school?) or, at least, the monitoring of service quality (how clean are the streets?). Here, there is an idea of exchange, in that taxes are paid and a level of service is expected. But this also involves a disciplining of citizens into taking responsibility for the choices they make (Malpass et al. 2007). They are active in shaping their everyday lives through the choices they make, and this includes welfare services, education or their local environments. Along with this, therefore, getting the right information and knowing what the choices are become part of this undertaking of citizen responsibility.

Public sector innovation is not only focused on the redesign of its services but also on the reconstitution of publics. It has involved the fashioning of varying forms of relationships between provider and user. The latter has been recast as 'consumer', 'partner' and active citizen through successive attempts to redesign the processes and functions of the public sector.

RESPONSES TO NEW PUBLIC MANAGEMENT

Criticisms of NPM are not difficult to raise. For example, NPM may be read as the needless application of private, commercial processes and interests to what is essentially a public asset. In this view, all the goodwill and sense of service that is seen as a necessary but unmeasurable aspect of the public sector is relegated. At the same time, therefore, the propensity towards the outsourcing of state functions gives its responsibilities over to companies whose first accountabilities are to their investors, not the public. Within state functions, managers expend more energy on sourcing and coordinating services than they could on ensuring the quality of outcomes. NPM also rests on the assumption that the outsourcing of services results in their being of better value, better quality and more innovative – an assumption that is partly drawn from a stereotype of state functionaries being the opposite.

In terms of design, there are three specific drawbacks of NPM. First, as we have seen, NPM recasts public sector service users as consumers with the attendant notions of choice and responsibility for making choices. This may result in different registers of presentation of services as they are rendered 'attractive' through various means either to citizens or commissioners. At the same time, one has to ask whether or not service users actually *want* to be treated as 'consumers'. Would they rather that design and other inputs be entirely focused on optimising the core of the service (Clarke and Newman 2007; Moor 2009)?

A second criticism of NPM in terms of design is that it may have the effect of making managers focus more on delivery improvement at the expense of thinking about the quality of the service itself at the point-of-use (Christensen 2013). Focusing on procurement, logistics or getting best value from suppliers is all very well, but this may detract from ensuring that the service being delivered is itself not poorly conceived and designed. This emphasis may not be particularly human-centred in that it is mostly concerned with the management of systems that are already configured rather than on what best functions *in use* and working back from there.

Third, the heavy requirement for demonstrating value creates a regime of constant measurement and audit of processes and outcomes. This results in a performative fix, whereby services are arranged in such a way to satisfy measurement criteria rather than thinking about their design as best serving citizens. A contradiction is constantly at play where public servants are pressured to be creative, innovative and agile while performing to centrally driven targets and being fully accountable (Gallop 2007; Parker and Bartlett 2008; Hill and Julier 2009). Risk-taking, trying out new ideas or prototyping new possibilities – core to design – do not find easy homes in this NPM environment.

In respect of these issues, from around 2010, some government organisational discourses have moved to thinking about public service delivery being reconfigured around outcome-based budgeting (OBB) or outcome based commissioning (OBC) (KPMG 2011; Law 2013). This takes the pragmatic ordering of services beyond NPM. Here, instead of thinking organisationally and financially in terms of the operations of a system of delivery, OBB looks to what one wants to achieve at the user end. As such, it is very user-centred in its emphasis on the desired results of services (healthier citizens, cared-for elderly, literate children, for instance) and 'reverse engineering' from there in thinking about how best to achieve these in terms of what combination of organisations, departments and institutions can best (and often, most cheaply) provide that solution. OBB may be read as being designerly in its approach through its end-on, problem-solving ethos.

This thinking recalls Manzini and Jégou's (2005) notion of 'results'-driven design wherein responses to problems are not predetermined in terms of their kind of design outcome; rather, the most effective and appropriate (particularly in environmental and social terms) response is sought. It calls for a radical reconceptualisation of design's aims, processes and outcomes. By prioritising results over means to achieve these, design is immediately taken outside its sub-disciplinary structures of 'graphics', 'interior', 'product' and so on. It becomes media agnostic where the 'best tool for the job' prevails over predetermined, specialist approaches.

Likewise, OBB may be disruptive of traditional public sector bureaucracies and processes: a parks and leisure department may become part of health and wellbeing aims or entirely new forms of administration may need to be created. Either way, it may push public administration into more innovative and flexible modes. Further, its highly pragmatic, results-driven approach has developed in the context of pressure on public budgets. This confluence of austerity and public sector innovation is developed in the next section.

AUSTERITY

The 2007–08 financial crisis had severe effects on global trade and investment. Naturally this resulted in a reduction of income to the state sector: tax receipts diminished as unemployment rose and business turnover dropped. Many governments, particularly across Europe, instigated austerity programmes in response to this, but also to clear the national debt that had risen, particularly through the years running up to the crisis. An alternative view to this 'official' line is that the crisis was used as an excuse to carry out further scaling down of the state in order to continue the ratcheting up of marketisation and the privileging of private business over state functions (Whitfield 2012; Fraser et al. 2013). It should be added here that the austerity of the post-crisis era may also be seen as a mere extension of an ongoing squeeze on public budgets felt since the 1980s (Peters 2012).

Whichever account of austerity is most accurate, it soon became clear that the ensuing public spending cuts across Europe would result in job losses, pay freezes and the reduction or disappearance of some services. In terms of personnel, for instance, a first wave of planned downsizing of the number of public sector employees would involve reductions of 12 per cent in Ireland, 15 per cent in the Netherlands, 20 per cent in Greece and 23 per cent (in terms of central government civil service) in the UK (Lodge and Hood 2012: 80). Between 2010 and 2014, public expenditure was to be cut by 40 per cent of GDP in Ireland, 20 per cent in the Baltic countries, 15 per cent in Hungary, 12 per cent in Spain and 11.5 per cent in the UK (Leschke and Jepsen 2012). How can frontline welfare services be continued against these challenges?

Budget cuts have taken many public sector interests to the point where service delivery requires wholesale redesign in order to survive at all. A range of policy-oriented thinktanks, foundations and institutions make the same claims that undertaking a more research-led, user-focused approach to the design of services results in efficiency gains and greater effectivity in their many reports (e.g. Lehki 2007; Design Commission 2012; Bason 2013; Design Council 2013; SEE Platform 2013). In 2008, the magazine of the UK Design Council ran a discussion entitled 'Can we deliver better public services for less money?' (Bichard 2008). In the context of post-credit crunch rising national debt and foreseeing the squeezing of public sector spending, this debate was apposite. Tellingly, Ben Reason, director of service design outfit Live|Work, remarked that 'we need to change our relationship with public services, from one where we just expect things to be there for us, to one where we're more engaged in ensuring we don't need them, or managing our way through them' (Reason, quoted in Bichard 2008). Avoiding 'unnecessary' use of services and making judicious choices within them is therefore also a way of saving public money.

Many consultant design outfits who specialise in this sector have promoted themselves on their effectiveness in making financial savings for them. For example, the Innovation Unit – a London-based consultancy specialising in public sector innovation that was spun out from the government's Department for Education – offers 'radical efficiency' and 'more for less' (Innovation Unit 2015). Their aim is in developing service delivery through focusing on service users, developing new insights and seeing how resources both within and without public sector organisations can be reconfigured and re-used. At the same time they are also interested in influencing the core processes of public sector institutions. An approach is promised in which long-term research relationships are established to generate 'an innovation culture' that enhances their internal efficacy. They are thus involved both outwardly in finding cheaper, effective forms of services and inwardly in capacity building among their public sector clients.

A tactic that is at play here, and which overlaps with social innovation, is in seeing how underused assets may be set to work in delivering such things as community cohesion, street security or neighbourly care. Examples of these include Participle's 'Circle' system to promote peer-to-peer support among the elderly (Cottam and Dillon 2014) or FutureGov's 'Casserole Club' network to provide home-cooked food by and for neighbours (Nesta 2015b). In both these, the quest is to find creative ways of making use of citizens' free time and skills to produce social benefits. In both these, the consultancies have designed digital and analogue networking and systems to facilitate peer-to-peer support.

Whether or not such developments actually result in budget savings for the public sector has been hotly debated. Participle's 'Circle' system was first rolled out in the London borough of Southwark in 2009, with six further 'Circles' being established in both urban and rural locations. The Circle developed social networks among the over-50s, with learning activities, a helpline for resources and low-level practical support from volunteer Circle helpers. These were initially supported by local council grants: £1m in the case of Southwark Circle, £680,000 for the Suffolk Circle (Brindle 2014). While Circle involved a membership fee of £20 or £30 per year, by 2014, both of these had closed as core support funding was terminated. Meanwhile, impact evaluation of the scheme argued that it generated 85,000 new social connections, 70 per cent of members reporting increased participation in social activities, 15 per cent feeling less unwell and 13 per cent visiting their doctor less (Cottam and Dillon 2014).

The Circle system did not directly provide medical support, therefore, but it did effect savings to health costs. Likewise, its peer-to-peer help for practical issues like household maintenance would mean a reduction on care support costs for local councils. In these circumstances, making the financial case for such innovations is complex and challenging. It calls into question the rigidities of traditional accounting systems that focus more on quantitative inputs and outputs. Nonetheless, the kinds of public sector innovations that have arisen through austerity contexts have a deep background in the rethinking of citizenship and governance.

TOWARDS NETWORKED GOVERNANCE

There is a demand for change by which the public sector formulates its relationship to citizens, regardless of the financial pressures of austerity economics. Indeed, some of the theory of what could come after NPM predates austerity, and even just as NPM was getting underway. A seminal text by Bryson and Crosby (1992) identified the need for collaborative working between state and citizens. They wrote:

> We live in a world where no one is 'in charge'. No one organisation or institution has the legitimacy, power, authority, or intelligence to act alone on important public issues and still make substantial headway against the problems that threaten us all … we live in a 'shared power' world, a world in which organisations and institutions must share objectives, activities, resources, power or authority in order to achieve collective gains or minimise losses. (Bryson and Crosby 1992, cited in Quirk 2007: 48)

In this quote we see a relinquishment of the notion that the state, or, indeed, any other organisation, can claim dominion. Following on, models of collaboration, co-production or, otherwise, co-creation are the only viable route to addressing complex, contemporary problems.

This turn towards 'co-creation' in relation to the public sector exists within a longer trajectory of thinking with respect to the state, its public and the contexts of post-industrial, neoliberal economies. In his analysis of the relationship of economic change and political reform, Claus Offe (1985) concludes his book *Disorganized Capitalism* with a discussion of the relationship of politics to administrative action. First, he identifies the incongruity of administrations that require norms of action within fluctuating systems of demand. Administrations have to correspond to their socio-economic environments and vice versa, he argues, in order to be fully functional. Rigid state bureaucracies only make sense if they serve an equally rigid economy and society, for example.

On the other hand, in the case of liberal democracy within disorganised capitalism, certain norms are still necessary, but administrative action is nonetheless much more 'goal oriented'. Fluctuations in demand, employment, exchange and so on make specific and irregular demands on administration. As a result, government is centred on the successful management of systems rather than on the strident enforcement of ideological priorities. Here, the relationship between politics and administration partially reverses as governments are made increasingly reactive to the latter's demands where bargaining and cooperation are necessary. In this respect, Offe further argues that in the course of the production of state-organised services, the distinction between 'consumption' and 'production' is blurred (Offe 1985: 311). Users enter into partnerships with agents in 'productive interactions'.

From around 2000, this thinking about 'productive interactions' was picked up by a range of academics, practitioners and organisations and developed further. Of particular influence on UK government policy was Charles Leadbeater, who was also a co-founder of Participle, the public service innovation agency (Leadbeater 2008). It figures under various other headings such as 'co-production' (Brandsen and Pestoff 2006), 'digital-era governance' (Dunleavy et al. 2005), 'the collaborative state' (Parker and Gallagher 2007) and the 'relational state' (Cooke and Muir 2012). As an umbrella term, we may think of these as sitting under the heading of 'networked governance' or, alternatively, new public governance (NPG). Conceptually, networked governance rests on, as the words suggest, the idea that all actors in society (citizens, public servants, organisations etc.) rely on mutually sustained systems. Governing structures (i.e. national, regional or local governments) are engaged in the management of networks in such a way as to include the interdependencies of actors, directed towards shared goals. Thus, partnerships, cooperation and collaboration become ways to create, produce and maintain public service systems (Christensen 2013).

While there may be subtle differences in their backgrounds and aspirations, all these terms may suffer the accusation that they don't amount to much more than 'policy cheerleading' (Hodge and Greve 2007; Christensen 2013). It is all very well to envision more democratic, open forms of governance where citizens and public servants collaborate in the fashioning of policies and services and where 'citizen engagement' goes beyond the voting turns, but in the sometimes necessarily grinding world of public administration and accountability the actual carrying out of these may be over-ambitious. Further, it may be that this public administration and academic jargon is really just a set of policy 'language games', created to obfuscate something else (Teisman and Klijn 2002) – that is, the relinquishment of responsibility by the state for welfare and other public services.

In terms of citizen representation, and the claim to open out and democratise governance, there are other quandaries. How are we sure whose particular interests are being represented among those 'representing' or represented citizens (Swyngedouw 2005)? How do the results include and exclude individuals and groups in their membership of society? How is design sometimes used to iron out difference or dissent in what it means to be a citizen (Fortier 2010)? Governmental interests may privilege certain networks over others. While it may appear to build decision making and designing outside its own bureaucracies, one has to consider which groups it is choosing to foreground over others. What groups that were previously represented through other systems are now excluded in networked governance?

DESIGN IN NETWORKED GOVERNANCE

The sticky questions that revolve around networked governance that arise here may be regarded as challenges that can never go away. They are things that we should be constantly vigilant to and that constantly reconstitute themselves as problems as we address them. They emerge, it could be argued, through the ongoing consideration of high-level challenges that governments, policymakers and their designers confront. In the meantime, multiple, complex problems have to be addressed.

While earlier in this chapter I have stressed the austerity driver of public sector innovation and a move towards networked governance, the pressure on public sector budgets is also met by an intensification of demand on governments due to a series of challenges being felt across the developed world. Aside from climate change (something affecting the entire world), health and care are among the most significant. While the predominant concern for mid-twentieth century health was acute illness, today it is for chronic illness and 'lifestyle diseases'. In the UK, for example, diabetes accounts for 9 per cent of the National Health Service's budget and was projected to increase to 25 per cent by 2020 (Parker 2007: 178). In terms of care, the ageing population combined with a pensions crisis and growth in the number of women and men working full-time creates impossible demand on the formal care sector. The ageing timebomb is not just confined to the West. In 2009, China had 167 million over-60s – around one-tenth of the population; by 2050 this is expected to reach 480 million – about one-third of inhabitants (Branigan 2012; Sun 2014).

In broad terms, the potential for networked governance to address such issues had already been recognised in theory but without practical application and testing. For instance, the UK Government's White Paper 'Innovation Nation' (Department for Innovation, Universities and Skills 2008) listed climate change, the ageing population, globalisation and higher expectations of public sector users as drivers of the need for innovatory approaches to service delivery. It represented a concern to optimise service delivery at local levels by instilling a sense of innovation and autonomy on the part of the public sector workers who configure and provide it as well as in including end-users in their co-creation and operationalisation. However, it would not be until 2014 that the UK Cabinet Office would establish its PolicyLab, which was set to experiment with ways of working through design approaches to policy (Kimbell 2015).

Design has therefore moved to the centre of grey literature reports and other publications produced by organisations concerned with social innovation and change in the public sector. These include the Institute of Public Policy Research (e.g. Rogers and Houston 2004), Demos (e.g. Parker and Gallagher 2007) and Nesta (e.g. Murray et al. 2010). However, again this move may be seen as part of a longer design history. In the UK, the recession of the early 1990s led to a radical overhaul of the Design Council. John Sorrell, who was chair of the branding company Newell and Sorrell, produced a review and policy document for it (Sorrell 1994) that ushered in a leaner version, scaling down from 200 employees nationally to just 40 located in a new London office. The Design Centre, which exhibited examples of 'good design', was closed. Instead, the Design Council was to act more as a thinktank for the dissemination of new knowledge in design. It was also to carry a greater emphasis on its role in the public sector.

In its role as a thinktank on new knowledge, it cultivated a particular approach to the processes and uses of design that keyed in with changes in public sector discourse. Between 2004 and 2006, the Design Council housed RED, a unit was set up to tackle social and economic issues through design-led innovation. Spearheaded by its director, Hilary Cottam (who was later to become the head of the aforementioned Participle), RED developed co-creation approaches to the design of public services such as health, schools and prisons. Such projects foregrounded the intermediary role that design may play between citizens and the state. This way of thinking was set out in RED's document *Touching the State* (2004). It argued that

> [d]esign, after all, is not just about producing effective and attractive objects. Designers ... are trained to analyse and improve processes, exchanges and encounters – between customer and products, clients and services or, potentially, between citizens and States. They are, or should be, rehearsed at looking at the larger picture, and identifying where an object, or process, fits in the user's life ... government institutions don't for the most part look at civic encounters in this way. No one seems to be thinking about the citizen's journey through even a single encounter – from, say, the arrival of the first summons letter from the jury service, to the final goodbye – let alone through the course of a life.

This statement reflects the growing importance of service design as a specialism. Indeed, arch proponents of service design such as the agencies Engine Service Design and Live|Work had close relationships to many Design Council projects from 2000 onwards.

Why else should a particularly designerly approach to the problem solving of such policy challenges emerge in any case? Why should such a plethora of design-oriented innovation labs become an almost standardised response here? Christian Bason lists three possible reasons. First, design research allows the 'architecture of problems' – how different components that constitute challenges fit together – to be revealed. The designer's tools of ethnographic, qualitative, user-centred research, experimentation and probing through prototyping solutions and data visualisation help this understanding. Second, design, he claims, stimulates group creativity. Through their tools, designers are able to provide usable meeting points between policymakers, interest and lobby groups as well as citizens and business representatives. Third, designers can articulate policy so that its user experience can be understood and engaged with (Bason 2014: 4–5). As such, it allows for new hybrid spaces between government and its partners in policymaking (Bailey et al. 2016; Kimbell 2016).

It is also where all that service-user journey mapping and all that Play-Doh and Post-its, as described at the beginning of this chapter, comes into play.

Design may be seen to provide a cheap and quick fix for structural problems that are produced through the shrinkage of the state sector within neoliberal governance. However, some design interventions produce substantive changes and re-imaginings of what the state, publics and their relationships might be.

VIRTUALISM

Two related difficulties remain to be discussed in this narrative of design in networked governance. The first is that it can lead to a perception that design-led public sector innovation suffers a surfeit of workshops and Post-its whose results rarely find their way through to implementation. Put otherwise, its emphasis on process and collaboration, its customer experience mapping or its frequent use of workshops, hackathons and jams makes it appear to contribute to a kind of virtualism where things are made real but not actual (Miller and Carrier 1998). In this, abstracted accounts of social and economic activity then become the accepted model of how things should be, regardless of how they would play out in the messy friction of actuality. Negotiating a project through public sector bureaucracies and power systems or, even, the legacies of NPM and its audit culture, certainly present challenges that, as we have already seen in terms of 'Circle', the designer has to understand and surmount.

A second difficulty, not unrelated to this notion of virtualism, is in the institutional infrastructures that give voice to design-led public sector innovation. We have noted the number of organisations, either supported as foundations, through endowments or directly by governments, who are engaged in developing and promoting this specialism. There is the danger here that orthodoxies flow like memes through and between these, without focusing on what is possible or, even, politically desirable. One of the founders of the Social Innovation Lab for Kent (SILK), Sophia Parker, has noted with regard to both these difficulties that

it can feel a bit like the same group of people talking to each other about the same ideas, with a bit too much affection for Post-it notes and bunting and with not enough focus on impact.... the real challenge to anyone working in this space is to ensure that at the beginning of a project, you aren't just creating a great piece of work, you're also anticipating how the change is actually going to happen. Who do you need to line up? How does spending need to be redirected, and who will decide on that? Unless we focus on impact and what that looks like, there's a danger that Lab work just ends up as some really nice Post-it notes on a wall somewhere. (Parker 2015)

Notwithstanding these internal challenges within design-led public sector innovation, the context of networked governance orients a particular relationship to value and futurity. In a sense, it creates design economies wherin value is co-produced with citizens and other stakeholders (Sangiorgi 2015). In short, this may be read as involving the tapping into under-used resources that exist among citizens –sometimes colloquially referred to as 'sweat assets'. As shown in the earlier example of 'Circle' and 'Casserole Club', designers and public servants are looking to leverage social arrangements and practices – to nudge or re-scale them for social benefit by developing communications and working infrastructures. In this, the general approach as well as its tools exhibit something of that sense of futurity. They look to things as they could be. The prototyped service models the value of things in use.

In the final sections of this chapter, we analyse how design has actually been mobilised and implemented in two contrasting contexts. One is destined to impact on very personal, behavioural practices. The other takes a place-based approach that invokes a kind of 'design citizenship'.

BEHAVIOUR CHANGE

Behaviour change appears as a frequent, if not core trope in the offer of many public sector oriented design consultancies. For example, the Chicago-based Greater Good Studio announced on its website that 'We believe that research changes design, design changes behavior, and behavior changes the world' (Greater Good Studio 2015). Notwithstanding this rather ambitious view with regard to 'changing the world', the message is clear that their work is directed towards influencing the ways by which individuals undertake their lives. As a consultancy that is focused on social impact, they are taking the concept of behaviour change that actually derives from the study of economics and importing it into the non-commercial world of everyday practices.

Behaviour change has its origins in mid-twentieth century thinking, particularly in the USA, around the limits of the 'utility-maximisation' (Sent 2004). This latter model makes the assumption that citizens are going to be entirely rational in the way they spend their money to get the most out of this expenditure for their daily lives. The departure from this assumption began to look at deviations – how seemingly irrational behaviours lead to consumer practices that appeared to defy utility-maximisation. Out of this the specialism of behavioural economics grew that focused on the actual, empirical description of personal conduct. In terms of commercial advertising and design, tapping into this apparent 'irrationality' has been an important aspect of their practices and specialisms. Indeed, it could be said to sit at the heart of concepts such as styling and high design that try to capture the subjective, even whimsical desires of consumers (Haug 1986; Julier 2014: chs 5 and 6). A hugely influential text that extended from this conception was *Nudge: Improving Decisions about Health, Wealth and Happiness* by Thaler and Sunstein (2008). Here, as the title suggests and using 'nudge' as another term for behaviour change, the aims of behavioural economics were extended into how individuals could improve their wellbeing, conduct with regard to environmental responsibility and other behaviours that coincide with public policy concerns.

Within Thaler and Sunstein's 'nudge' thinking, the idea is that people make repeated mistakes in their decision making, often being poorly informed and impulsive. Out of this they built the idea of providing 'choice architecture' – a structured series of possible options through which citizens may navigate their actions. In effect, this is not far from commercial operations to be found in the presentation of products on supermarket shelves or through shopping websites (Leggett 2014). In this, people are supposedly empowered by allowing choices, but which lead to overall improvements. Thaler and Sunstein thus claim that 'nudge' offers a third way that is neither domineeringly statist nor subject to the openness of the marketplace. They call this third way 'libertarian paternalism' (Thaler and Sunstein 2008: 14).

The concept of behaviour change had been under discussion within the UK government since 2004 (Halpern et al. 2004). 'Nudge theory' was put into practice at the heart of government with the foundation of the Behavioural Insights Team in 2010 (Dolan et al. 2010). It was also established in Australia within the New South Wales government.

In terms of design, many projects whose aim is towards behaviour change have taken place within health, with the aim of prevention rather than cure. One example of this is a project developed by Uscreates in 2009 to increase awareness and rates of chlamydia testing among 15 to 24 year olds in the city of Birmingham (rates of chlamydia in this age group were 10 per cent at the time). It included an advertising and social media campaign ahead of thousands of self-testing kits that were sent out. From this, the agency reflected that campaigns are more effective where communications are linked to well run and usable services that support the message (Cook 2011).

The use of design for behaviour change may be read as a straightforward transfer of mainstream market mechanisms of behavioural economics to the policy and social sphere, working with a normative concept of the individual as consumer. It could be that governments, in deploying behaviour change approaches, are using techniques that stem from the market sphere to interfere in micro-level decision making of people. At the same time, it may lack an adequate understanding of the social background of the individuals it addresses. It appears, perhaps, to avoid considerations such as shared socio-cultural practices, as in specific neighourhoods, family or religion. Further, Leggett (2014) argues that behaviours are themselves the result of the historical formation of an environment and its ideas and practices. They also create an environment. Decoupling behaviour and environment may be easier said than done.

A further issue may lie in 'nudge' becoming an end in itself. Design for behaviour change may lead to improved engagement with state priorities such as filling out tax forms correctly, paying fines on time, using health services wisely. But once this is achieved and becomes normalised, who is to say that this 'new normal' doesn't become the new base to be improved on? Dunleavy (2016) argues that there is the danger then that past innovations 'wear off' and 'become overfamiliar'. This means that government then has to continuously market itself to harness citizen awareness. In this way, design for behaviour change could, again, play into private sector notions of the attention economy in which marketing and communications dominate rather than consolidating and deepening its own processes and understandings.

These challenges suggest that design for behaviour change should necessarily be slow-moving, involving deep understanding and analysis of the contexts in which it is to be enacted. Indeed, the same could be said for any form of public sector innovation that engages the co-production processes of networked governance. Since so many of these projects address very specific problems in the public sphere, it is difficult to see how they might add up to a wider social or political programme, if at all. The next section considers an example where a programmatic approach is taken to this issue in the expectation of engaging what I call 'design citizenship'.

DESIGN CITIZENSHIP

Design citizenship does not exist as an 'official' term. It does not appear as a 'core aim' in 'city visions'; nor is it taught in schools or universities. It might be taken as a way by which the material and immaterial features of everyday life, and the processes that produce these, make and unmake citizens (Weber 2010: 11). By contrast with the more top-down processes of spatial planning that consider the arrangement of built form and functions in towns and cities, design citizenship begins at the experiential frontline of everyday practices. Design citizenship is about being and acting in various modes where the artefactual field (both material and immaterial) is understood to be active and acted on. If, then, these are followed up on, its actors can work backwards to understand or even change the bigger systems, bureaucracies or regulations that frame these. In other words, design citizenship may also invoke the participatory, co-creative process of networked governance.

A little-known, but programmatic example where there has been an attempt to revive a city through design policies has been in Kolding, a small city of some 57,600 inhabitants located on the southeast coast of the Danish peninsula of Jutland. While Kolding includes one of Denmark's two dedicated design schools, a university campus focused primarily on design-related studies and an international business academy, few of the city's 4,500 students settle in Kolding while their lecturers mostly commute from Copenhagen, Aarhus or Odense. It has had an ageing population as skilled younger citizens have largely deserted the city. With an extensive seaport and with good motorway links to northern Germany, the city was an important logistics hub. However, the global economic crisis from 2008 impacted negatively on this sector. Further, the building of a 62,000 sq m shopping centre on the city's outskirts in the early 1990s, with 120 shops, contributed to the hollowing out of its centre. Shops with 'to let' signs flanked many of its streets while its night-time economy is markedly quiet. A survey of the city's population revealed that 20 per cent of the respondents would not recommend others to live or work there (Jungersen and Hansen 2014). Something had to be done.

The outcome of deliberations in view of this crisis may prove to be an object lesson in design-led urban regeneration. In 2012, the Kolding Municipal Council unanimously adopted a new vision for the city and municipality: 'Together, we design a better life through entrepreneurship, social innovation and education.' In a subsequent, shorter version, this became 'Kolding – We design for life'. Design was to be at the centre of all city development activities within a 10-year programme.

This new vision came through a distillation process that resulted in a clear direction for future policy and strategy development. A private consultancy, Copenhagen-based Stagis, was

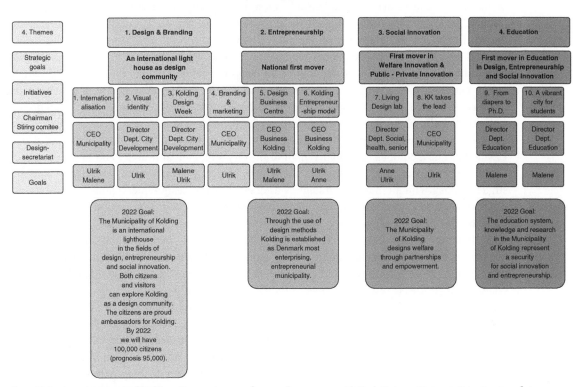

Kolding - We Design for Life
*Together we design options for a good life through entrepreneurship,
social innovation and education*

	1. Design & Branding				2. Entrepreneurship		3. Social innovation		4. Education	
4. Themes										
Strategic goals	An international light house as design community				National first mover		First mover in Welfare Innovation & Public - Private Innovation		First mover in Education in Design, Entrepreneurship and Social Innovation	
Initiatives	1. Internationalisation	2. Visual identity	3. Kolding Design Week	4. Branding & marketing	5. Design Business Centre	6. Kolding Entrepreneur-ship model	7. Living Design lab	8. KK takes the lead	9. From diapers to Ph.D.	10. A vibrant city for students
Chairman Stiring comitee	CEO Municipality	Director Dept. City Development	Director Dept. City Development	CEO Municipality	CEO Business Kolding	CEO Business Kolding	Director Dept. Social, health, senior	CEO Municipality	Director Dept. Education	Director Dept. Education
Design-secretariat										
Goals	Ulrik Malene	Ulrik	Malene Ulrik	Ulrik	Ulrik Malene	Ulrik Anne	Anne Ulrik	Ulrik	Malene	Malene

2022 Goal:
The Municipality of Kolding is an international lighthouse in the fields of design, entrepreneurship and social innovation. Both citizens and visitors can explore Kolding as a design community. The citizens are proud ambassadors for Kolding. By 2022 we will have 100,000 citizens (prognosis 95,000).

2022 Goal:
Through the use of design methods Kolding is established as Denmark most enterprising, entrepreneurial municipality.

2022 Goal:
The Municipality of Kolding designs welfare through partnerships and empowerment.

2022 Goal:
The education system, knowledge and research in the Municipality of Kolding represent a security for social innovation and entrepreneurship.

8.3 Main shopping street of Kolding, Denmark; one of many shop spaces with 'to let' sign; citizen participation in refining a new vision for Kolding; strategy diagram for 'Kolding: We Design For Life' (Photos: Guy Julier; Stagis; Kolding Municipality)

hired to guide the process of creating the new vision. This in itself was conceived as a design process and included an anthropological mapping, creative workshops with local politicians, with local representatives from business, education, public institutions and culture and leisure associations and, finally, two huge community meetings for all citizens of the municipality that engaged some 900 people. Stagis's methodology is based on the principle that in order to create a strong vision, a vision that would distinguish Kolding from other cities and munici-palities, it is necessary to look inwards to identify particular geographical, historical, cultural, social or economical characteristics – in Stagis's terminology, these characteristics describe authentic strengths, which make up the local identity (Stagis 2012).

The detailing of the vision led to the creation of a series of specific strategies that was to develop the three themes of entrepreneurship, social innovation and education, with design thinking at the centre of each of these. A fourth, of design and branding, was directed more internally in terms of raising local awareness of the programme. Part of this was operational-ised through appointing 50 civic actors from local business, education, culture and community associations who were enrolled in the Design Network Kolding (Julier and Leerberg 2014). They would be ambassadors for the vision and network by contributing citing to the development and implementation of its initiatives. Thus a strategy of developing design thinking and awareness beyond design specialists was adopted. In addition, 25 municipality employees were enrolled on an innovation course that included visualisation, prototyping and user research (Jungersen and Hansen 2014). By 2015, the Kolding Municipality claimed that the strategy was already saving the city €6.6m per year (Kolding Municipality 2015).

What is particularly notable about the strategy is that it is conceived to last over a 10-year period, initially stretching over two municipal election cycles. The relatively slow and partici-patory nature of its development ensures, to some degree, wider and deeper commitment from citizens, politicians and other stakeholders to it. In turn, this produces a measure of background stability that allows for longer-term initiatives. On the output side of this process, for example, an innovation centre linking the university, the design school and local SMEs was established. Design became a compulsory subject in all of the city's municipal primary and lower secondary schools, and an international design summer camp for young people was established. A 'city life strategy' along with an 'outdoor strategy' was created, using design interventions to link its cul-tural infrastructure, physical activities, the urban realm and wellbeing (Højdam 2015).

In this Kolding example, there is a turn away from a conception of design as manifested exclusively through objects. In other words, design is seen, in part, as a skill, attitude or even disposition that may be embedded into the organisation (Michlewski 2008). The relationship of these notions to innovativeness and organisational performance has been examined in terms of commercial entities (Press and Cooper 2003; Boland and Collopy 2004). In the public domain, this has been pushed through more general appeals to creativity and innovation as part of city boosterism (Stevenson 2004; Evans 2009; UNESCO 2015). However, the Kolding example demonstrates a more focused attempt to garner a sense of purpose and identity through design as a skill and outlook, through both private and public channels among its citizens and stakehold-ers. These begin with the deployment of design skills and understanding within the municipal authority, but also with the ambition that these are carried through multiple channels in the civic life of the city. Thus, they are intended to course through business activities, various forms of welfare provision and also act as a focus for all levels of education and training. They are expected to be engaged among multi-agency, multi-actor and multilayered interests that go beyond the single organisation.

Contrasting the behaviour change approach discussed in the previous section with this notion of design citizenship, we can see how the former attempts to move away from public sector innovations that have their longer historical roots in the private sector and that treats citizens as largely non-social beings. Constrastingly, this approach to design citizenship draws out some of the background social networks, outlooks and practices that constitute a place while taking into account institutional and business linkages. Nonetheless, it has the potential for a radical redirection of citizenry away from any pure dominance of commercial interests to collective, societal concerns that are also entangled with localised design economies and vice versa.

CONCLUSION

Design sits at the interface between government and citizens. It provides the conduit through which governments reach people and the material culture within which people understand themselves and act as citizens. One may go so far as to say that design configures publics, producing different contexts and scales within which people find themselves socially connected. Design is entangled with varying administrative approaches to the public sector, which in turn reflect different orthodoxies of political economy.

In contemporary capitalism, the public sector has largely been dominated by modalities of the so-called NPM. In this, it has been compelled to adopt many of norms of the private sector, attempting to fulfil efficiency targets, engaging in widespread outsourcing of provision to private or voluntary organisations and being bound by systems of audit and measurement. Within this paradigm, the citizen may be reframed as a consumer of public services. This has also resulted in a stimulation to consultant design while, at the same time, contributed to the fragmentation of state functions while, arguably, limiting opportunities for innovations in how services are conceived and configured.

Such criticisms, combined with budget pressures created through austerity, have led to attempts to shift away from NPM towards co-producing public sector services. In this, designers, particularly extending service design processes, have been increasingly active in working closely with citizens, public servants and stakeholder organisations to re-think services and, consequently, the relationship between government and people. This puts the ambitions of 'networked governance' into practice. The scale and volume of this kind of design work is relatively small compared to standard NPM. Cutting across many of the traditional bureaucratic divisions of the public sector makes the impact of this kind of design work difficult to demonstrate. However, it does strike out into new sets of economic arrangements between the state and citizens. At the same time, it should be recognised that this approach is also driven by thinktanks and foundations and that the amount of promotion it receives outweighs much of its actual implementation.

Finally, this chapter has pushed a concept of 'design citizenship' as a possible outcome of these kinds of challenges. Here, an understanding of design is extended beyond the domain of specialised professionals to figure in the toolbox of municipal functionaries, to become embedded in the dispositions and everyday lives of citizens and to be supported through key cultural, educational and entrepreneurial supports. It also emerges out of deep, considered research and analysis of a location's pre-existing assets. It is a heady ambition, not without its own difficulties. However, it may suggest a turn towards bringing citizen life back into control.

STUDYING ECONOMIES
OF DESIGN

How can a meaningful and useful approach to the study of economies of design be built upon? How might we link the small-scale case study of a design project to wider understandings of economic processes? What disciplinary tools are to hand to help us with these challenges? First, this chapter discusses the limitations that design management studies place on understanding the varied contexts in which design operates. It then makes a case for thinking in terms of design cultures and economic sociology rather than design management in order to get closer to these. The chapter ends by reviewing some core questions that have sat in the background of this book. These include how design operates in economies in both utilitarian and symbolic ways, how it produces certain economic behaviours and how it materialises finance.

Neoliberalism unfolds in multiple forms. It involves constant processes of change in which new technologies, publics, resources and relations are reformatted. Meanwhile, design is a key agent in the differentiation of the goods and services that are active in the economy (Doyle and Broadbridge 1999; Grinyer 2001). It does the work of filling niche markets, slicing up consumer groups across national boundaries, and producing distinctive business models or novel places to invest in. Design also plays a semiotic role in communicating that change is happening. It shapes the stuff but also tells us about it.

Much of this book has paid attention to the specific ways by which design functions through different economic scales, locations and relationalities. A danger, though, is that its analysis then gets reduced to endless sets of case studies. While pursuing 'the dignity of the particular' (Stark 1998) may be a noble and important cause, it is also productive to build some overarching under-standings, not least in order to have a broader framework through which we understand those case studies.

Here lies a crucial challenge for studying economies of design. On the one hand, we must comprehend the macro-economic processes that come to bear on the everyday world and its design. These might include the influence of interest rate fluctuations, commodity prices, the impacts of national and international legal frameworks regarding intellectual property and transnational trade agreements. On the other, there are the micro-economic practices that take place, and within which designers, producers and consumers act. These may encompass how entrepreneurialism is conceived and played out, the ways that resources are combined in specific places or the implementation of government policies at local levels. As we drill down to the particular, the roles of design become ever more apparent. Looping these observations to the bigger picture is necessary. Without this process, the account becomes fragmentary and incomplete.

This chapter is given over to reflecting on how we might best work with these two levels that define economies of design. This is initially done through a critique of some orthodoxies that are at play in the academic field of design management. While this specialism is mostly concerned with the analysis of current practices in order to provide guidance for future action in design, its expressed concern for the economic roles of design should, in theory, provide routes into a sophisticated understanding of their connections. However, the connec-tions that are made between case study analysis and generalisations appear to be problematic here. We thus turn to the emergent disciplinary field of 'design culture' that provides a way of unpicking the economic interactions between design, production and consump-tion. Stemming from this, its potential connections to economic sociology, particularly in exploring the relationships between the macro- and the micro-economic contexts of design, are discussed.

The final three sections are dedicated to exploring three fundamental questions that sit behind many of the earlier chapters. The first is, quite simply, why are design and neoliberal-ism so 'good' together? The second focuses on how we might talk about economics in terms of the qualitative functions of design. The third concerns how finance is materialised through design. In responding to these, I recapitulate on some of the key examples that are given in different chapters. In so doing, I hope to draw them together while providing some thoughts for further study.

BEYOND DESIGN MANAGEMENT

The discipline of design management is redolent with initiatives and publications that champion the use of design in the strategic direction of firms, design and the commercial frameworks within which it operates are taken as givens. In other words, design management largely presents a conventional view of what both design and management are there for. However, it is rare in design management studies for the definition of 'business success' to be opened up for inspection.

For example, the USA-based Design Management Institute (DMI), a membership association that brings together researchers, designers and businesspeople in its field, defines design management by the way it 'seeks to link design, innovation, technology, management and customers to provide competitive advantage across the triple bottom line: economic, social/cultural, and environmental factors' (DMI 2015). However, the vast majority of articles published in its journal, the *Journal of Design Management*, are directed at the first of these: that is, economic factors. Perhaps the key words in its definition to focus on are 'to provide competitive advantage'. It is difficult, here, to appreciate this 'competitive advantage' in the spheres of the social/cultural and the environmental without these in turn being connected to their roles in achieving business success. Thus the way that design management is imprinted into particular economic and ideological frameworks of understanding goes unquestioned.

Judged by the university courses in design management that are imparted and its academic conference and publishing content, its chief motivational focus is in building techniques for design success. Three recurring formats for presenting research appear there. One is through undertaking a close survey of business practices in relation to design or of business practitioners' views on design and, from these, creating a taxonomy of collective features which often then turned into a summarising diagram (e.g. Stoll 1991; Bohemia and Harman 2008). This is intended in some way to provide a framework for future action for other design managers. Another is through developing particularised conceptual terms, often turned into an acronym, such as PDL (personal design leadership) (Bianchini and Maffei 2012) or the DDA (design-driven approach) (Lee and Evans 2012). These are meant to guide the design manager to prioritising their way of approaching enterprise over others, such as from marketing. In the third, the effectiveness of particular formal aspects of design are surveyed. Hence, for example, analysing the use of symmetry in brand marks and their commercial effectiveness (Orth and Malkewitz 2008; Marsden and Thomas 2013). In these approaches, the researchers are seeking to synthesise studied, real-life situations into ideal models. In so doing, they are invariably emptied out of the friction that is part of the behavioural, affective and thing-based subjectivities that take place in organisations, institutions and public life.

Put otherwise, it is important to consider that design practice is *situated* (Deserti and Rizzo 2014) – as is design production and design consumption. It is the product of specific conjunctions of many features including material constraints and opportunities both in terms of where and how design is done, available technologies and knowledge, discursive and attitudinal markers among the design team, interactions with external actors such as clients, financial backers, supporting design practices and other specialists. It is also subjected to varying frameworks such as differing legal parameters set by intellectual property law in different countries, environmental, health and safety standards or logistical questions.

One may well look to economic motivations as constant drivers in delivering differentiation between brands, products, services and, indeed, design studios; however, at the same time, the very situatedness of design practice gives rise to endless variations in its processes and, thus, outcomes. Contrastingly, many design management studies appear to be often more engaged in the pursuit of normative understandings around design. These may be successful in filling out lectures in business schools, but their abstraction ignores the messy contingencies that exist in business.

The analysis of design within design management studies may be useful in providing structures against which everyday action might be compared. It might be helpful in knowing the various start and end points of undertaking product or service development. It might be handy in providing a baseline for then looking out for the subtleties and differences within organisational, institutional and everyday cultures and how these are expressed in designerly ways. But in order to move beyond its abstractions, we might turn to design culture studies.

Economies of design rest on many variables that are observable but often elusive – too elusive to sit comfortably in abstracted certainties of 'best practice' models and diagrams.

DESIGN CULTURE STUDIES

Design culture describes an object, an academic discipline and a practice (Julier 2014: ch. 1). As an object, we might view it as an ecology that features the interaction of the economic work of designers, design production (including its mediation and circulation) and design consumption in which design artefacts are active within and between them. As a discipline we might take it to engage a range of related scholarly fields of the social sciences and humanities in researching and understanding such ecologies. As a practice, we might take it as a way of intervening in the world that is self-knowing of its position in and effect on the ecologies in which this action takes place. Studying economies of design within a design culture framework puts emphasis on particular actors within this.

Figure 9.1 presents some of the entry points for studying economies of design through a design culture lens. In reality, the practices of each node – designer, production, consumption – are more complex than is presented here. After all, designers are also consumers, as are people who work in production. Intellectual property is something that impacts also on designers and consumers, not just among production. The node of 'consumption' is problematic as it implies that citizenry is reduced to transactions in the marketplace rather than a wider set of activities that are both individual and collective, that involve public processes of participation in civil society as well as the everyday, routine practices of acting and being. So it is important to be flexible in the interpretation and use of this construction.

All of these are affected by and form part of macro-economic and micro-economic landscapes. Inflation, taxation levels, unemployment, interest rates, rates of exchange, the stock markets, growth: these are some of the big features that go together to be studied within macro-economics. These features influence the supply and availability of money, the affordability of things, how much can be borrowed and many other aspects of our daily lives. Changes in the macro-economic context mean changes in what we can buy, where we spend our leisure time or how we perform

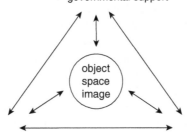

DESIGNER
- education/training
- ambitions/outlooks
- capitalisation
- professional networks/representation
- client relationships
- innovation cycles
- governmental support

object
space
image

PRODUCTION
- Intellectual Property Rights
- capitalisation and investment
- business networks
- business cycles
- education/training/know-how
- legal constraints and affordances
- governmental support

CONSUMPTION
- demographic factors (age, family, cultural etc.)
- habits/routines
- expendable income
- investment
- political outlooks

Figure 9.1 Domains of design culture and economies of design factors

in our working lives. The design of products, of bars and restaurants, video games or company brochures is therefore closely tied into this.

The study of the small-scale of economic practices is called, rather obviously, micro-economics. This is where individual consumer decisions, the management of households, the activities of firms or, for example, the processes of localised markets come into view. In this, the emphasis often shifts from talking about statistical data in macro-economics towards behaviours in micro-economics. In macro-economics there are buttons to press that change the processes of the economy as a whole. Interest rates are cut by central banks. Taxation is raised by governments. Stocks are bought and sold according to agreed prices. It's all about graphs, indices and percentages that are often viewed historically in terms of their change over time. In part, micro-economics studies the effects of these changes in the real, everyday worlds of people. Design is active in helping to shape them.

In this, we might, to start with, think of macro-economics as studying the influences that the big picture of national and global processes of policy and finance have *on* design while viewing design itself mostly to be more influential *within* the smaller scales found in the study of micro-economics. But there are also individual and social behaviours and everyday practices *in* those worlds that may even appear to exist independently of the bigger economic frameworks or might deliberately attempt to create their own ones (we saw this with the Transition Towns and the Slow City movements in Chapter 4). This is where an understanding of the aims of economic sociology provides a useful underpinning to exploring economies of design.

ECONOMIC SOCIOLOGY

Since the mid-1980s there has been a revival of academic interest in exploring the social processes that are embedded within economic activities. The foundations of this lie in the work of Durkheim (1933 [1893]), Weber (2002 [1905]) and Simmel (2004 [1900]) that appeared around the turn of the twentieth century. However, through much of that century, work in this field concentrated mostly on industrial sociology, labour relations and the effects of capitalist economies on social life (Dobbin 2004). By the mid-twentieth century, the dominant emphasis of such research was mainly on questions of large-scale manufacture and bureaucracies, management systems and class. The revival of economic sociology in the 1980s saw a reorientation of it towards subjects that were more varied, however. This took in, for example, gender relations (e.g. England and Folbre 2005), small- and medium-scale business relationships (e.g. Piore and Sabel 1986) or entrepreneurship (e.g. Burt 1992). The earlier twentieth-century approach is sometimes called 'old economic sociology' while its revival is referred to as 'new economic sociology' (Granovetter 1990).

The new economic sociology took its cue from the work of Karl Polanyi (1957 [1944]), who coined the term 'embeddedness'. Disembeddedness assumes that markets are free of any 'backgrounds' and have their own logic – that they override or, even, undermine social processes and structures. Polanyi didn't actually use the term 'embeddedness' a lot, but it came to be reinterpreted and re-used, in particular by Granovetter (1985). In economic terms, it refers to the social constraints and affordances of institutions. These may, for instance, be religious, kinship or informal social structures that play parts in organising economic activities. To this, one should note that the relationship of the economic and the social is a two-way street – markets produce social relationships as well (Beckert and Streeck 2008). Further, socialities may be consciously facilitated in order to benefit economic interests.

The revival of economic sociology in the 1980s is partially explained by a number of profound changes in the organisation of economic and social life in capitalist contexts. It also coincided with changes in the culture of design in general and designing in particular, as we have seen in Chapter 2. To briefly summarise here, however, in neoliberal economic practices these contexts included increased privatisation of state resources, institutions and assets, deregulation of legal constraints on financial and industrial processes and the promotion of competitivity. These macro-economic changes provide some of the frameworks for micro-economic practices that emerged from the 1980s, particularly with respect to the creative industries and design. It is where a particular culture of design emerges that engages closer and tighter relationships and 'fit' between its own professional world and its publics.

Connectedly, this was also the moment that 'endogenous growth theory' was promoted by Paul Romer (1986) and Robert Lucas (1988). Here, broad technological explanations of economic developments (in other words, exogenous growth) are relegated to focusing on human capital – what skills, knowledge, motivations and social relations that engender these are available in any one context. This leads to a greater emphasis on considering policy areas such as education, research and subsidies to economic sectors within notions of the knowledge economy. In both these cases, this does not mean to say that technological issues are unimportant. Rather, attempts are made to show their complex entanglement with other factors.

An economic sociology of design culture thus provides a useful line of enquiry for several reasons. First, it reminds us to look beyond the market itself and the profit-motive in explaining how the economic work of design and designers is carried out. There are other, social forces at play as well. Second, it challenges us to explore the role of design in creating socialities and the relationship of these to economic activities. Third, it encourages us to undertake research at a number of scales that may work across design, production and/or everyday life. Fourth, it is suited to the breadth and flexibility of economic practices within which design operates.

How is design active in forming socially shared adherences to certain ways of working and thinking in the economic world?

With regard to the last point, one might even go beyond accounts of mainstream economic practices to look at other economic frames in which designers sometimes operate. These might include circular, green, social or feminist economies and many other formations and organisations of economics that prioritise concerns that exist instead of, beyond or in addition to commercial gain. New economic sociology prompts us to dispense with the abstractions of classical approaches to economics, where input/output or investment/profit conceptions dominate, in order to consider the multifarious motivations and forms of economic activity where social, environmental and cultural questions must also be brought into view.

It is late in this book to raise the subject of further, heterodox economies of design such as circular, green, social or feminist economies. Heterodox economics studies of non-mainstream activities has its own methodologies and applications (Lee and Cronin 2016). The discussion of *horizontalidad* and timebanking in Chapter 7 began to push in this direction. Further research in uncovering the role of design in similar situations would be productive in uncovering the multiple ways by which it shapes heterodox economic practices. In the meantime, let us turn, for the remainder of this chapter, to those three background questions of design and neoliberalism, the qualitative elements of economics and the materialisation of finance by way of reaffirmation some of the core issues in economies of design. This takes us away from the above questions of method and discipline to a set of speculations and suggestions that are synthesised from earlier chapters.

DESIGN AND NEOLIBERALISM

Why are design and neoliberalism so 'good' together? In Chapters 1 and 2, I established a connection between the rise of design since the 1980s and the economic turn to neoliberalism. This was divided into four organising elements: deregulation, New Economy, financialisation and austerity. They all relate closely to one another but, to briefly review them individually, they go as follows.

Deregulation ushers in increased competitivity. As state enterprises get privatised and marketised, so competition between the providers of similar goods and services (e.g. domestic energy) means that design comes into play in order to differentiate their offers. As rules that govern the activities of corporations are relaxed, so they are increasingly required to make their case themselves, leading to an increased emphasis on product and service differentiation and branding, for instance. In turn, as explained in Chapter 3, the design profession itself steps up several gears to compete in the marketplace. This is in terms of its speed in processing projects, its ability to manage complex briefs and in delivering and showing its value to clients.

New Economy involves greater flexibility and speed in the relationships between production and consumption. In particular, it gives rise to higher degrees of subcontracting, partly facilitated by information technologies, but also global transport systems becoming more wide-reaching and efficient. Faster iterations between design, production and consumption result, as argued in Chapter 4. Therefore more designing gets done.

Financialisation involves the search for and investment in sources of future value. Corporate and 'lay' investors look for places for their capital to render profit. Design both adds value to those locations (be they buildings, technologies, primary resources and so on) by, for instance, making them more attractive, novel, useable or cheaper to produce. But it also functions in a symbolic way by signalling that changes are happening. We saw in Chapter 5 how homes and shopping centres are designed in such a way to attract buyers or inward investment, thus pushing up their overall value. Finance can often be seen hanging around in other design intensities such as airports, research and development facilities and modern tourist resorts. In Chapter 6, we saw how the participation of design in investments in and developments of intellectual property produces future value, shoring up sector monopolies. Intellectual property becomes another kind of asset.

Austerity is where the state gets rolled back even further. This is, in part, by way of response to economic crises where government spending is reduced. In extreme cases and as recounted in Chapter 7, alternative economies may fill the void left behind by the retreat of the state. Design may be active in a reconfiguration of labour relations here or, more simply, be an instrument for shoring up everyday lives. Chapter 8 showed how design becomes a quick, cost-saving fix for spending cuts in the public sector. But austerity may also be seen to loop back to deregulation in that it is a dimension of increasing the presence of the private sector in the delivery of public services. Whichever way, design business comes out as a winner.

ECONOMIES OF QUALITIES

Copious reports are in evidence that address the contribution of design to GDP (e.g. Europe Economics 2015), its influence on shareholder value (e.g. Design Council 2007) or its role in public sector innovation (e.g. Thomas 2008). We have the numbers and the stories. However, in recalling the influence of the new economic sociology discussed earlier, Callon et al. (2002) argue that economists are not the only ones who are invited to undertake the analysis of economic practices. They state that economists, these days, find themselves alongside anthropologists, sociologists, political scientists and others in the investigation. Further, their work is mixed with 'lay' expertise of marketing specialists, designers, businesspeople and others who are involved in the making of those economies. In short, attention is paid to their qualitative features and processes. So how do we talk about economics in terms of the qualitative functions of design?

Callon et al.'s essay, entitled 'The economy of qualities', goes on to talk about this in terms of singularisation and attachment. First, goods do not exist on their own in the marketplace.

Drawing on Chamberlin (1946), they state that goods are part of a continuum that includes 'brands, packaging or special recipients, particular sales conditions such as location, seller's reputation or personal relations between the salesperson and customers' (Callon et al. 2002: 200). Thus it is the constellation of these – and many other factors – that define, differentiate and therefore singularise (or otherwise define their uniqueness) the good, not the object merely on its own. Second, the attachment of consumers comes about as the result of these collective features, but also the influence of their own social practices and their processes of judgement.

While their argument is somewhat convoluted, it nonetheless brings us to the complex, subtle and contingent features that make up economies of qualities. Beyond merely concluding that 'no object is an island' and that, instead, they function as part of assemblages of a range of phenomena, we can get a sense of the 'push and pull' that constitutes the finely-tuned relationships of producer and consumer practices here, with design often working at the interface between the two.

There are several other ways we could be talking about the qualitative functions of economics through design. While drawing from the transfer of goods as the starting point for their argument, the propositions of Callon and colleagues are generalisable to other economic relations. It is as well to remember that, for instance, design may be employed to serve several 'social worlds' or, otherwise, publics. In the case of shopping centres in Chapter 5, we saw how their design and its mediation is formulated to appeal to shoppers, but also to investors in the scheme as well as civic interests and pressure groups. In this, economic relations are multidirectional just as the clients of the design are multiply accountable.

Much of the literature on creative and cultural industries builds an accounts of the role of professionals in these sectors as economic agents (e.g. Caves 2000; Scase and Davis 2000; Hartley 2005). This may involve consideration of how cultural activities lead to economic ones or may focus on specific, strategic moves to leverage creative capital for economic benefits. Callon et al. (2002) are not necessarily talking about these kinds of causality, however; their focus is on the cultural activities that go on *within* economic processes. By 'culture' they are not just talking about its professional exponents (designers, artists, craftspeople etc.) but the cultural processes that exist in the everyday social practices of consumers and, indeed, the cultural meeting point between production and consumption. Thus their interests are in the nexus between the culturally-informed knowledge and thinking of professionals in marketing, design and so on and the 'lay', quotidian cultural world of people.

We might take this notion of the workings of cultural processes *within* economics further, beyond the production and consumption of goods. One way that this book has considered this has been in the cultural construction of a general disposition towards neoliberal living, and the roles of design therein. This may be found, for example, in the disciplining of homeowners to regimes of capital accumulation. This is done in part through media events such as home improvement TV programmes and their background networks of objects such as DIY knowledge and stores. There are 'experts' here (e.g. TV presenters, writers of home makeover books, shopfloor workers in DIY stores). Expertise is also deployed through the cultural and social practices of householders engaged in home improvements. Design is where this gets materialised while, at the same time, the materialising that goes on (painting walls, choosing furniture, installing lighting etc.) is also the *doing of neoliberalism.*

Alternatively, we might think outwards in terms of the cultural roles that design plays in shaping certain attitudes to economic life. City branding schemes, urban regeneration, the championing of creativity and creative quarters all take part in signalling trajectories of innovation and growth for localities (Julier 2005). They are part of what in Chapter 1 was identified as 'cultural political economy' (Best and Paterson 2010; Sum and Jessop 2013). This semiotic role of design in neoliberal processes of transformation may be explained via Jessop's notion of 'economic imaginaries' – practices and even objects that stand in for wider practices of economic change, particularly when that change is complex and unstructured, as, indeed, contemporary capitalism often is (Jessop 2004).

Design shapes products, environments or images. It also makes 'economic imaginaries'.

These are just a few of the many ways by which we might approach the role of design in the qualitative dimension of economics. The key issue here is to foreground that none of these processes – or other ones – is frictionless, effortless or consistent. The design object provides a moment of resistance in the meeting of economies and people. It has to be worked at or with. It will perform differently according to the where, when and how. Thus it is more useful to talk of economies of qualities rather than *the* economy of qualities.

MATERIALISATION AND FINANCE

To repeat a witty observation: design is a laxative – it helps move things through the system quicker (Reavley 1998). For example, we saw in Chapter 6 how Amazon's '1-click' interface design speeds up the online purchasing process. But it isn't always about speed. Some retail spaces may be configured to slow people down, to get them to browse and maybe make unplanned purchases. Here, by contrast to the '1-click' example, a certain friction is deliberately introduced. In either case, designers attend to the micro-practices of consumers, producing habits that result in the movement of finance.

At a few points in this book, I have drawn attention to the global flows of finance within contemporary capitalism. We have touched on the rise in the amount that has moved across national borders, the policy and legal adjustments that have allowed the movement of goods and finance and the technologies, such as containers or fibre-optic cabling, that have encouraged this. Beyond these devices, though, how and in what other ways is finance materialised through design?

In consideration of this question, it is useful to take an expanded view onto what production includes. Classically we might think of factories or workshops here. However, we may also expand to all those agents who operate in the broader shaping of design artefacts: this would include those involved in the production of meanings through mediation such as advertising, packaging or design journalism. Or we might consider the networks of distribution that move objects or symbols from one place to another as part of production. Everything that comes after the design work and before reception by people comes within the domain of production.

Within thinking about economies of design, we can push further to consider the financial interests and processes that are at work as part of this production domain, though. Here, it is not merely a case of the basic fact that money provides investment for commerce or the public sector to do things. It is the very structures and expectations of investing that can have roles in shaping artefacts. This became most evident in Chapter 5 where we looked at how home improvement and the design of shopping centres was handled to align with particular concerns for return on investment. More broadly, these come within Harvey's (1989b, 2001) notion of the spatial fix. They provide investment nodes for surplus capital. Design is a cash converter.

Finance is materialised through design in other ways. While the improved home or the new shopping centre may be conceived as rent or equity-bearing assets, so can intellectual property in the form of patents, design registrations or trademarks, as we saw in Chapter 6. These are what have been termed 'intensities' that lead to 'extensities'. In other words, intensive design input is made so that artefacts may render future value through their licensing, serial reproduction or franchising.

It isn't just a one-way street, though. Design also functions in environments of disinvestment and austerity. One example here is in the phenomenon of shrinking cities. Neoliberal orthodoxies often employ regeneration programmes to urban centres to attract inward investment. This might include urban design programmes such as new street lighting and paving to revive flagging town centres and encourage new businesses to locate there. Alternatively, places may be subject to evolutionary decline within which new design functions are established, often due to a mix of communitarian activism and local government planning (Giorda 2012; Walker 2015). For example, Detroit has become well known for the development of urban agriculture, reassigning spaces left by depopulation and industrial decay. Alternatively, cultural interventions and economic and spatial planning may be employed in order to manage decline, as has been the case across 19 cities of Saxony-Anhalt in eastern Germany (Altrock and Huning 2014). In more localised ways, social innovation strategies may be adopted that 'plug the leaks' of finance from neighbourhoods to create more resilient and self-supporting places to live (New Economics Foundation 2008; Unsworth et al. 2011).

Design or design-like activities often fill out the voids left by disinvestment, austerity or decline. They can work in the fissures that neoliberal macro-economic processes cause. These may involve activist attempts to formulate alternative economic spaces and practices. Contrastingly, design may be mobilised as a quick fix to regenerate places or problem solve the societal challenges that recession or austerity make. Design also *makes* new spaces for financial in-flow. This may be in the urbanisation process through its role in shaping spaces of investment. It may be through its role in particular creative intensities where, for example, design and production become co-located or, otherwise, re-localised. This has emerged in the new global landscape of fast fashion, as we saw in Chapter 4, for example.

In either case of the loose gaps or the concentrated nodes of neoliberalism, materialisations take place to fill them out. This 'filling out' also involves frictions and resistances that create further financial heat as the many cogs of production turn. To put it perhaps less poetically, design work is involved in ongoing, unfinished transformations whether, for example, we are talking about products that are subject to continuous upgrading or localities that compete in the global marketplace for a share of tourism, shopping or inward business investment.

CONCLUDING REMARKS

In design, as in economics, there is an inevitable component of change at work. Other facets of life, such as social or religious practices, may remain largely the same. But design and economics involve people in the deliberate making of change. There is an intentional 'before' and 'after'. It follows, therefore, that while this book has attempted mostly to focus on contemporary manifestations of economies of design, an historical angle has been unavoidable.

Neoliberalisation has been under way in its mature sense since the 1980s. However, since the 2008 global economic crisis, there has sometimes been talk of our entering a new period of post-neoliberalism. Parallels were drawn between the rupture of the fall of Berlin Wall in 1989 with the collapse of major financial institutions and processes of 2008 (Peck et al. 2009). Soon after, it was suggested that the major world economic powers had entered into a period of 'zombie capitalism' in which neoliberalism was essentially dead but was continuing to twitch and stagger onwards (Harman 2010). Yet, all indications suggest that its chief proponents, leaders and institutions endure as does the design that results.

A key difference between the events of 1989 and 2008 is that the fall of the Berlin Wall and the collapse of communism in Europe was largely unforeseen by those on the outside. Meanwhile, a crisis of what became neoliberalism, by contrast, was calculated and foreseen even at its birth and again shortly before the financial crisis of 2008 (e.g. Meadows et al. 1972, 2004). Just as neoliberalism engages continuous calculation of its quantitative and qualitative mechanisms and assets, so calculation and analysis can reveal its limits, greed, untruths and violence (e.g. Dorling et al. 2008).

Design practice may shape products, lifestyles and relationships that sit outside or, at least, parasitically live off, the mainstream of contemporary capitalism. Plenty of examples of these exist, some of which have been featured in this book. However, it is stunning to consider that the roots of many of these alternative practices emerged just as the orthodoxies of neoliberalism were being shaped in the 1970s. In 1971, Victor Papanek's *Design for the Real World* first appeared in English calling for design that responded to real need rather than produced desire. In 1973, Schumacher's *Small is Beautiful* first appeared, calling for the creation of localised, resilient human and material ecologies. Mollison and Holmgren's book *Permaculture One* followed in 1978, with its instruction on creating sustainable food and living systems. One might also cite the rise of community architecture and planning and appropriate technology movements of this period. These all shared activist concerns for engaging the dignity and needs of ordinary people in design.

Neoliberal orthodoxies and these alternative pathways emerged at the same time as responses to widescale economic crises of the early 1970s. At that time, crises of capitalism or, more prosaically, economic recession appeared to spur on new, politicised directions in design. They also provoked a rebooting of capitalism itself. Thirty years later, as the world of financialist capitalism appeared to falter, so a new impetus to activist design also emerged (Fuad-Luke 2009; Thorpe 2012; Julier 2013). Overall, whether in the 1970s or the 2000s, these approaches might be taken as attempts to stabilise everyday life, to provide for continuity and locality against the turbulence and globalising processes of capitalism.

The re-emergence of activist thinking in design may lead to new arrangements for daily life that either maintain their independence or may be altered and gradually subsumed into the mainstream processes of capitalism. However, there is another role for design practice and discourse that does not necessarily enter directly into the construction of everyday life. This could be in showing what is there, in articulating the systems that are at work in economies.

Concealment and obfuscation often run through the tactics of capitalism in general and financialisation specifically. They account for the shady subterfuges of tax havens (Urry 2014). They supply the sometimes impermeable language of global banking (Lanchester 2015). Design is at work here too. Finance may flow in ways that are sometimes difficult to decipher, but it has to flow to somewhere or something. These places and things are shaped for this flow. They are not merely vessels to be filled, however. They are the transmutation of that flow, turning that finance into other calculable forms of value.

Economies of design are never static. They are in constant flux. This doesn't mean to say that they are autonomous. They are the result of explicit and tacit agreements and action that make them go on changing and developing. Nor are economies of design homogenous. Showing their variance is a theme that has coursed through this book. Exposing what is behind this variance and what drives it has also been a key task. This process of revealing can take place through texts such as this one. Making the material and informational infrastructures, the systems of power or the financial logics of economies of design visible and knowable might also be one of the tasks of design practice itself.

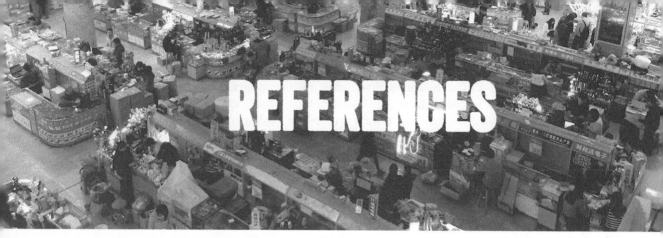

REFERENCES

Abrams, Fran and Astill, James (2001) 'Story of the Blues', *Guardian*, 29 May (www.theguardian.com/g2/story/0,,497788,00.html, accessed 26/10/15).

AHRC Newton Fund (2016) 'China's Creative Communities: making value and the value(s) of making' (https://chinascreativecommunities.wordpress.com/2016/04/18/about-the-project/, accessed 04/08/16).

Akrich, Madeleine (1995) 'The de-scription of technological objects', in W.E. Bijker and J. Law (eds), *Shaping Technology/Building Society – Studies in Sociotechnical Change*. Cambridge, MA: MIT Press. pp. 205–24.

Allegro, Sander and de Graaf, Rob (2008) 'Innovation and strategy implementation: the key challenge in today's competitive atmosphere', in M. Olsen and J. Zhao (eds), *Handbook of Hospitality Strategic Management*. Oxford: Elsevier. pp. 407–24.

Allon, Fiona (2010) 'Speculating on everyday life: the cultural economy of the quotidian', *Journal of Communication Inquiry*, 34(4): 366–81.

Altrock, Uwe and Huning, Sandra (2014) 'Cultural interventions in urban public spaces and performative planning: insights from shrinking cities in Eastern Germany', in C. Tornaghi and S. Knierbein (eds), *Public Space and Relational Perspectives: New Challenges for Architecture and Planning*. London: Routledge. pp. 148–66.

Anders, George (2013) 'Amazon's 1,263 patents reveal retailing's high-tech future' (www.forbes.com/sites/georgeanders/2013/11/14/amazons-1263-patents-reveal-retailings-high-tech-future, accessed 22/05/15).

Anderson, Ben (2009) 'Affective atmospheres', *Emotion, Space and Society*, 2(2): 77–81.

Anderson, Chris (2006) *The Long Tail: How Endless Choice is Creating Unlimited Demand*. London: Random House Business Books.

Andonov, A., Kok, N. and Eichholtz, P. (2013) 'A global perspective on pension fund investments in real estate', *Journal of Portfolio Management*, 39(5): 32.

Antia, K.D., Zheng, X. and Frazier, G.L. (2013) 'Conflict management and outcomes in franchise relationships: the role of regulation', *Journal of Marketing Research*, 50(5): 577–89.

Appadurai, Arjun (1990) 'Disjuncture and difference in the global cultural economy', *Theory, Culture and Society*, 7: 295–310.

Armstrong, Leah (2015) 'Steering a course between professionalism and commercialism: the Society of Industrial Artists and the Code of Conduct for the Professional Designer 1945–1975', *Journal of Design History*, epv038.

Arrighi, Giovanni (2006) 'Spatial and other "fixes" of historical capitalism', *Journal of World-Systems Research*, 10(2): 527–39.

Arsenault, Mike (2012) 'How valuable is Amazon's 1-click patent? It's worth billions' (http://blog.rejoiner.com/2012/07/amazon-1clickpatent, accessed 19/05/15).

Ash, James (2010) 'Architectures of affect: anticipating and manipulating the event in processes of videogame design and testing', *Environment and Planning D: Society and Space*, 28(4): 653–71.

Ash, James (2012) 'Attention, videogames and the retentional economies of affective amplification', *Theory, Culture and Society*, 29(6): 3–26.

Aspara, Jaakko (2010) 'How do institutional actors in the financial market assess companies product design? The quasi-rational evaluative schemes', *Knowledge, Technology and Policy*, 224: 241–58.

Aspara, Jaakko (2012) 'The influence of product design evaluations on investors' willingness to invest', *Design Management Journal*, 6(1): 79–93.

Augé, Marc (1995) *Non-places: An Introduction to an Anthropology of Supermodernity* (trans. J. Howe). New York: Verso.

Autor, David H. and Dorn, David (2013) 'The growth of low-skill service jobs and the polarization of the US labor market', *American Economic Review*, 103(5): 1553–97.

Bagwell, Susan (2008) 'Creative clusters and city growth', *Creative Industries Journal*, 1(1): 31–46.

Bailey, J., Lloyd, P. and Julier, G. (2016) 'The introduction of design to policymaking: Policy Lab and the UK government', paper presented at the Design Research Society Conference, University of Brighton.

Bakshi, H., Freeman, A. and Higgs, P. (2013) 'A dynamic mapping of the UK's creative industries' (report). London: NESTA.

Baldwin, Richard (2011a) '21st century regionalism: filling the gap between 21st century trade and 20th century trade rules', *CEPR Policy Insight*, No. 56.

Baldwin, Richard (2011b) 'Trade and industrialisation after globalisation's 2nd unbundling: how building and joining a supply chain are different and why it matters', National Bureau of Economic Research, Working Paper 17716 (www.nber.org/papers/w17716, accessed 31/03/16).

Ball, Sue (2016) Founder of Leeds Creative Timebank; communication with the author, 12 February.

Barberis, Peter and May, Timothy (1993) *Government, Industry and Political Economy*. Buckingham: Open University Press.

Bardi, Ugo (2009) 'Peak oil: the four stages of a new idea', *Energy*, 34(3): 323–6.

Bason, Christian (2013) *Powering European Public Sector Innovation: Towards a New Architecture Report of the Expert Group on Public Sector Innovation*. Luxembourg: Publications Office of the European Union.

Bason, Christian (2014) 'Introduction: the design for policy nexus', in C. Bason (ed.), *Design for Policy*. Farnham: Gower. pp. 1–7.

Batchelor, Ray (1994) *Henry Ford, Mass Production, Modernism, and Design*. Manchester: Manchester University Press.

Bathelt, Hareld and Schuldt, Nina (2010) 'International trade fairs and global buzz. Part I: Ecology of global buzz', *European Planning Studies*, 18(12): 1957–74.

Bathelt, Hareld and Schuldt, Nina (2011) 'International trade fairs and global buzz. Part II: Practices of global buzz', *European Planning Studies*, 19(1): 1–22.

Baudrillard, Jean (1995 [1968]) *The System of Objects*. London: Verso.

Baum, Tom (2007) 'Human resources in tourism: still waiting for change', *Tourism Management*, 28(6): 1383–99.

Bauman, Zygmunt (2000) *Liquid Modernity*. Cambridge: Polity Press.

Beckert, Jens and Streeck, Wolfgang (2008) 'Economic sociology and political economy: a programmatic perspective', MPIfG Working Paper 08/4. Cologne: Max Planck Institute for the Study of Societies.

BEDA (Bureau of European Design Associations) (2014) 'Positioning paper BEDA: Supporting innovation and opportunity in EU design IPR'. Brussels: BEDA. (www.beda.org/resources/position-papers/supporting-innovation-and-opportunity-in-eu-design-ipr.html, accessed 11/02/15).

Beebe, Barton (2014) 'Shanzhai, sumptuary law, and intellectual property law in contemporary China', *University of California Davis Law Review*, 47: 849–74.

Bell, David and Hollows, Joanne (2005) 'Making sense of ordinary lifestyles', in D. Bell and J. Hollows (eds), *Ordinary Lifestyles: Popular Media, Consumption and Taste*. Maidenhead: Open University Press. pp. 1–18.

Bellamy, Robert and Walker, James (1996) *Television and the Remote Control: Grazing on a Vast Wasteland*. New York: Guilford Press.

Berman, Bruce (ed.) (2006) *Making Innovation Pay: People who Turn IP into Shareholder Value*. Hoboken, NJ: Wiley.

Best, Jacqueline and Paterson, Matthew (eds) (2010) *Cultural Political Economy*. London: Routledge.

Bhabha, Homi (1984) 'Of mimicry and man: the ambivalence of colonial discourse', *Discipleship: A Special Issue on Psychoanalysis*, 28: 125–33.

Bianchini, Massimo and Maffei, Stefano (2012) 'Could design leadership be personal? Forecasting new forms of "Indie Capitalism"', *Design Management Journal*, 7(1): 6–17.

Bichard, Martin (2008) 'Can we deliver better public services for less money?', *Design Council Magazine*, 4: 16–21.

Birtchnell, Thomas (2011) '*Jugaad* as systemic risk and disruptive innovation in India', *Contemporary South Asia*, 19(4): 357–72.

Birtchnell, Thomas and Urry, John (2012) '3D, SF and the future', *Futures*, 50(June): 25–34.

Birtchnell, Thomas and Urry, John (2013) 'Fabricating futures and the movement of objects', *Mobilities*, 8(3): 388–405.

Birtchnell, T., Urry, J., Cook, C. and Curry, A. (2013) 'Freight miles: the impact of 3D printing on transport and society' (report), University of Lancaster (http://eprints.lancs.ac.uk/66198/1/Freight_Miles_Report.pdf, accessed 01/11/15).

Blackwell, Lewis (1986) 'Question marks over AGGI Hall', *Design Week*, 3 October, p. 8.

Blessi, G.T., Grossi, E., Sacco, P.L., Pieretti, G. and Ferilli, G. (2016) 'The contribution of cultural participation to urban well-being: a comparative study in Bolzano/Bozen and Siracusa, Italy', *Cities*, 50: 216–26.

Blum, Jürgen and Manning, Nick (2009) 'Public management reforms across OECD countries', in T. Bovaird and E. Loffler (eds), *Public Management and Governance*, 2nd edn. London: Routledge. pp. 41–58.

Boards of Appeal of the European Patent Office (2011) 'Datasheet for the decision of 27 January 2011' (www.epo.org/law-practice/case-law-appeals/recent/t071244eu1.html, accessed 19/05/15).

Bobel, Ingo (2012) 'Jugaad: a new innovation mindset', *Journal of Business and Financial Affairs*, 1(3): 4.

Bochner, Arthur and Bochner, Rose (2007) *The Totally Awesome Money Book for Kids*. New York: Newmarket Press.

Bohemia, Erik and Harman, Kerry (2008) 'Globalization and product design education: the global studio', *Design Management Journal*, 3(2): 53–68.

Boland, Richard and Collopy, Fred (eds) (2004) *Managing as Designing*. Stanford, CA: Stanford University Press.

Boulard, Denis (2013) 'Domino's Pizza en guerre avec ses franchisés', *L'Obs*, 2 January (http://tempsreel.nouvelobs.com/societe/20130102.OBS4158/domino-s-pizza-en-guerre-avec-ses-franchises.html, accessed 02/06/15).

Bound, Kirsten and Thornton, Ian (2012) *Our Frugal Future: Lessons from India's Innovation System*. London: Nesta.

Bourdieu, Pierre (1984a) *Distinction: A Social Critique of the Judgement of Taste* (trans. Richard Nice). Cambridge, MA: Harvard University Press.

Bourdieu, Pierre (1984b) *The Field of Cultural Production: Essays on Art and Literature*. New York: Columbia University Press.

Bowman, Paul (2007) *Post-Marxism versus Cultural Studies: Theory, Politics and Intervention*. Edinburgh: Edinburgh University Press.

Brands, Raina (2014) 'Why women are fighting an uphill battle on military language', *Guardian*, 24 March (www.theguardian.com/women-in-leadership/2014/mar/24/why-women-are-fighting-an-uphill-battle-on-military-language, accessed 27/05/15).

Brandsen, Taco and Pestoff, Victor (2006) 'Co-production, the third sector and the delivery of public services: an introduction', *Public Management Review*, 8(4): 493–501.

Branigan, Tania (2012) 'China faces "timebomb" of ageing population', *Guardian* (www.theguardian.com/world/2012/mar/20/china-next-generation-ageing-population, accessed 23/12/15).

Briggs, J., Lury, C. and Teasley, S. (2016) 'Creative temporal costings: a collaborative study of Leeds Creative Timebank' (https://protopublics.files.wordpress.com/2015/05/creative-temporal-costings-academic-report.pdf, accessed 01/01/16).

Brindle, David (2014) 'London elderly scheme's closure fuels row over care-gap crisis', *Guardian* (www.theguardian.com/society/2014/apr/24/london-elderly-scheme-closure-care-gap-crisis, accessed 23/12/15).

British Design Innovation (BDI) (2004) 'The British Design Industry valuation survey – 2003 to 2004' (report). Brighton: BDI.

British Design Innovation (BDI) (2005) 'The British Design Industry valuation survey – 2004 to 2005' (report). Brighton: BDI.

British Design Innovation (BDI) (2006) 'The British Design Industry valuation survey – 2005 to 2006' (report). Brighton: BDI.

British Design Innovation (BDI) (2007) 'The British Design Industry valuation survey – 2006 to 2007' (report). Brighton: BDI.

Bryson, John (1997) 'Obsolescence and the process of creative reconstruction', *Urban Studies*, 34(9): 1439–1458.

Bryson, John and Crosby, Barbara (1992) *Leadership for the Common Good: Tackling Problems in a Shared-power World*. San Francisco, CA: Jossey-Bass.

Bryson, John and Rusten, Grete (2010) *Design Economies and the Changing World Economy: Innovation, Production and Competitiveness*. Abingdon: Routledge.

Bryson, John R., Daniels, Peter W. and Warf, Barney (2004) *Service Worlds: People, Organisations and Technologies*. London: Routledge.

Buchanan, Richard (1992) 'Wicked problems in design thinking', *Design Issues*, 8(2): 5–21.

Buderi, Charles (1986) 'Conflict and compromise: the Shipping Act of 1984', *International Taxation and Business Law*, 3(2): 311–44.

Burnard, Pamela and White, Julie (2008) 'Creativity and performativity: counterpoints in British and Australian education', *British Educational Research Journal*, 34(5): 667–82.

Burt, R.S. (1992) *Structural Holes: The Social Structure of Competition*. Cambridge, MA: Harvard University Press.

Business Ratio Plus (1998) *Design Consultancies*. London: ICC Business Publications.

Butler, Judith (1997) *Excitable Speech: A Politics of the Performative*. London: Routledge.

Cachon, Gérard and Swinney, Robert (2011) 'The value of fast fashion: quick response, enhanced design, and strategic consumer behavior', *Management Science*, 57(4): 778–95.

CADA Design (2013) 'Our work/Domino's pizza' (www.cada.co.uk/dominos-pizza, accessed 01/06/15).

Cairncross, Frances (2001) *The Death of Distance: How the Communications Revolution is Changing Our Lives*. Boston, MA: Harvard Business Press.

Callon, Michel and Law, John (2005) 'On qualculation, agency and otherness', *Environment and Planning D: Society and Space*, 23(5): 717–33.

Callon, M., Méadel, C. and Rabeharisoa, V. (2002) 'The economy of qualities', *Economy and Society*, 31(2): 194–217.

Campbell, Beatrix and Wheeler, Wendy (1988) 'Filofaxions', *Marxism Today*, 32(12): 32–3.

Campbell, Colin (1987) *The Romantic Ethic and the Spirit of Modern Consumerism*. Oxford: Basil Blackwell.

Carstensen, Helle Vibeke and Bason, Christian (2012) 'Powering collaborative policy innovation: can innovation labs help?', *The Innovation Journal: The Public Sector Innovation Journal*, 17(1): 1–26.

Caves, Richard E. (2000) *Creative Industries: Contracts between Art and Commerce*. Cambridge, MA: Harvard University Press.

CDS (2008) 'CDS wins Essex local authorities print framework contract' (www.cds.co.uk/news.asp#essex, accessed 22/12/10).

Chamberlin, E.H. (1946) *The Theory of Monopolistic Competition: A Reorientation of the Theory of Value*, 5th edn. Cambridge, MA: Harvard University Press.

Chambers, M., Garriga, C. and Schlagenhauf, D. (2009) 'Accounting for changes in the home ownership rate', *International Economic Review*, 50(3): 677–726.

Chaney, David (1996) *Lifestyles*. London: Routledge.

Chang, Shaun (2009) 'Great expectations: China's cultural industry and case study of a government-sponsored creative cluster', *Creative Industries Journal*, 1(3): 263–73.

Chatterton, Paul (2014) *Low Impact Living: A Field Guide to Ecological, Affordable Community Building*. London: Earthscan.

Chatzky, Jean (2010) *Not Your Parents' Money Book: Making, Saving, and Spending Your Own Money*. New York: Simon and Schuster.

Chesbrough, Henry William (2003) *Open Innovation: The New Imperative for Creating and Profiting from Technology*. Boston, MA: Harvard Business Press.

Christensen, Jesper (2013) 'The irrealities of public innovation: exploring the political epistemology of state interventions and the creative dimensions of bureaucratic aesthetics in the search for new public futures', PhD dissertation, University of Aarhus.

Chronopoulos, Themis (2006) 'The cartoneros of Buenos Aires, 2001–2005', *City*, 10(2): 167–82.

Chubb, Andrew (2015) 'China's Shanzhai culture: "grabism" and the politics of hybridity', *Journal of Contemporary China*, 24(92): 260–79.

Cidell, Julie (2012) 'Flows and pauses in the urban logistics landscape: the municipal regulation of shipping container mobilities', *Mobilities*, 7(2): 233–45.

Cietta, Enrico (2008) *La Rivoluzione del Fast Fashion: Strategie e modelli organizzativi per competere nell industrie ibride*. Milan: FrancoAngeli.

Cittaslow (2015) 'Cittaslow International Network: 201 Città presenti in 30 Paesi nel Mondo' (www.cittaslow.org/download/DocumentiUfficiali/CITTASLOW_LIST_october_2015.pdf, accessed 20/10/15).

City of London Corporation (2011) 'Insurance companies and pension funds as institutional investors: global investment patterns' (www.cityoflondon.gov.uk/business/support-promotion-and-advice/promoting-the-city, accessed 18/11/15).

Clarke, John (2007) 'Unsettled connections: citizens, consumers and the reform of public services', *Journal of Consumer Culture*, 7(2): 159–78.

Clarke, John and Newman, Janet (2007) 'What's in a name? New Labour's citizen-consumers and the remaking of public services', *Cultural Studies*, 21(4–5): 738–57.

Clemons, Eric and Weber, Bruce (1990) 'London's big bang: a case study of information technology, competitive impact, and organizational change', *Journal of Management Information Systems*, 6(4): 41–60.

Coates, Nigel (1988) 'Street signs', in J. Thackara (ed.), *Design after Modernism: Beyond the Object*. London: Thames and Hudson. pp. 95–114.

Coates, Nigel (2012) *Narrative Architecture*. Chichester: Wiley.

Cochoy, Franck (2008) 'Calculation, qualculation, calqulation: shopping cart arithmetic, equipped cognition and the clustered consumer', *Marketing Theory*, 8(1): 15–44.

Cochrane, Ian (2010) Managing Director, Fitch 1979–1990, interview with the author, 29 October.

Colliers International (2014) 'A rising tide stirs cautiously optimistic markets' (www.colliers.com/-/media/files/global/pdf/global-retail-highlights-2014.pdf?campaign=Global-Retail-Report-2014-PDF, accessed 18/11/15).

Communities and Local Government (2009) 'Housing statistics live table 801: tenure trend' (www.communities.gov.uk/documents/housing/xls/141491.xls, accessed 21/06/12).

Concilio, Grazia and Rizzo, Francesca (eds) (2016) *Human Smart Cities: Rethinking the Interplay between Design and Planning*. Basel: Springer.

Constant, Amelie (2014) 'Do migrants take the jobs of native workers?', *IZA World of Labor* (http://wol.iza.org/articles/do-migrants-take-the-jobs-of-native-workers/long, accessed 27/10/15).

Cook, Mary Rose (2011) 'Opportunities to design "sustainable communities": an investigation into an emerging design market, shaped by the UK Government's "Sustainable Communities" Agenda', *Design Principles and Practices: An International Journal*, 4(6): 209–19.

Cooke, Graeme and Muir, Rick (eds) (2012) *The Relational State: How Recognising the Importance of Human Relationships Could Revolutionise the Role of the State*. London: IPPR.

Cooke, Philip and Lazzeretti, Luciana (eds) (2008) *Creative Cities, Cultural Clusters and Local Economic Development*. Aldershot: Edward Elgar.

Cooperativa de Diseño (2013) Interview with the author, 22 October.

Corsin Jiménez, Alberto (2013) 'Introduction: the prototype, more than many and less than one', *Journal of Cultural Economy*, 7(4): 381–98.

Cottam, Hilary and Dillon, Cath (2014) 'Learning from London Circle' (www.participle.net, accessed 18/12/15).

Court of Justice of the European Union (2014). 'Press Release No. 98/14: The representation of the layout of a retail store, such as an "Apple" flagship store, may, subject to certain conditions, be registered as a trade mark' (http://curia.europa.eu/jcms/upload/docs/application/pdf/2014-07/cp140098en.pdf, accessed 27/05/15).

Coyle, Diane (1999) *The Weightless World: Strategies for Managing the Digital Economy*. Cambridge, MA: MIT Press.

Creative Industries Task Force (CITF) (2001) *Creative Industries Mapping Document*. London: Department of Culture, Media and Sport.

Cresswell, Tim (2010) 'Mobilities I: catching up', *Progress in Human Geography*, 35(4): 550–58.

Cross, Nigel (2001) 'Designerly ways of knowing: design discipline versus design knowledge', *Design Issues*, 17(17): 49–55.

Cross, Nigel (2006) *Designerly Ways of Knowing*. London: Springer.

Crowley, David (1992) *Design and Culture in Poland and Hungary, 1890–1990*. Brighton: University of Brighton.

Currah, Andrew (2003) 'Digital effects in the spatial economy of film: towards a research agenda', *Area*, 35(1): 64–73.

Currah, Andrew (2007) 'Hollywood, the internet and the world: a geography of disruptive innovation', *Industry and Innovation*, 14(4): 359–84.

Dalton, M.M. (2004) *The Hollywood Curriculum: Teachers in the Movies*. New York: Peter Lang.

Darby, Michael and Karni, Edi (1973) 'Free competition and the optimal amount of fraud', *Journal of Law and Economics*, 16(1): 67–88.

Day, S., Lury, C. and Wakeford, N. (2014) 'Number ecologies: numbers and numbering practices', *Distinktion: Scandinavian Journal of Social Theory*, 15(2): 123–54.

Department for Culture, Media and Sport (DCMS) (2014) 'Creative industries economic estimates, January 2014, statistical release' (report). London: DCMS.

Department for Innovation, Universities and Skills (2008) *Innovation Nation*. London: HMSO.

Deserti, Alessandro and Rizzo, Francesca (2014) 'Design and the cultures of enterprises', *Design Issues*, 30(1): 36–56.

Design Commission (2012) *Restarting Britain 2: Design and Public Services*. London: Policy Connect.

Design Council (1998) *Design in Britain 1998–9: Facts, Figures and Quotable Quotes*. London: Design Council.

Design Council (2003) *Design in Britain 2003–2004*. London: Design Council.

Design Council (2007) *The Value of Design Factfinder Report*. London: Design Council.

Design Council (2010a) *Design Industry Research 2010*. London: Design Council.

Design Council (2010b) *International Design Research*. London: Design Council.

Design Council (2013) *Design for Public Good*. London: Design Council.

Design Council (2015) *The Design Economy 2015: The Value of Design to the UK*. London: Design Council.

Design Industry Voices (2013) 'Design Industry Voices 2013: how it feels to work in British digital and design agencies right now' (www.designindustryvoices.com, accessed 29/01/15).

Design Management Institute (2015) 'What is design management?' (www.dmi.org/?What_is_Design_Manag, accessed 18/08/16).

Design Skills Advisory Panel (2007) 'High level skills for higher value' (report). London: Design Council and Creative and Cultural Skills.

Design Week (2002) 'Attack is the only form of defence' (www.designweek.co.uk/news/attack-is-the-only-form-of-defence/1103750.article, accessed 07/02/15).

Dezeen (2013) 'Milan is a breeding ground for people who copy our products' (www.dezeen.com/2013/04/22/milan-is-a-breeding-ground-for-people-who-copy-our-products, accessed 02/06/15).

Dinerstein, Ana Cecilia (2014) *The Politics of Autonomy in Latin America: The Art of Organising Hope*. London: Palgrave Macmillan.

Dobbin, Frank (2004) 'The sociological view of the economy', in F. Dobbin (ed.), *The New Economic Sociology: A Reader*. Oxford: Princeton University Press. pp. 1–45.

Docquier, F., Lowell, B.L. and Marfouk, A. (2009) 'A gendered assessment of highly skilled emigration', *Population and Development Review*, 35(2): 297–321.

Doctorow, Cory (2009) *Makers*. London: HarperCollins.

Dolan, P., Hallsworth, M., Halpern, D., King, D. and Vlaev, I. (2010) *MINDSPACE: Influencing Behaviour through Public Policy*. London: Cabinet Office and Institute for Government.

Dorland, AnneMarie (2009) 'Routinized labour in the graphic design studio', in G. Julier and L. Moor (eds), *Design and Creativity: Policy, Management and Practice*. Oxford: Berg. pp. 105–21.

Dorling, D., Newman, M. and Barford. A. (2008) *The Atlas of the Real World: Mapping the Way We Live*. London: Thames and Hudson.

Doyle, Stephen and Broadbridge, Adelina (1999) 'Differentiation by design: the importance of design in retailer repositioning and differentiation', *International Journal of Retail and Distribution Management*, 27(2): 72–83.

Drake, Graham (2003) '"This place gives me space": place and creativity in the creative industries', *Geoforum*, 34(4): 511–24.

Drèze, Jacques and Sen, Amyrata (2013) *An Uncertain Glory: India and Its Contradictions*. Princeton, NJ: Princeton University Press.

Du Gay, Paul (1996) *Consumption and Identity at Work*. London: Sage.

Du Gay, Paul and Pryke, Martin (eds) (2002) *Cultural Economy: Cultural Analysis and Commercial Life*. London: Sage.

Dubois, G., Peeters, P., Ceron, J. P. and Gössling, S. (2011) 'The future tourism mobility of the world population: emission growth versus climate policy', *Transportation Research, Part A: Policy and Practice*, 45(10): 1031–42.

Dunleavy, Patrick (2016) '"Big data" and policy learning', in G. Stoker and M. Evans (eds), *Methods that Matter: Social Science and Evidence-Based Policymaking*. Bristol: Policy Press. ch. 8.

Dunleavy, P., Margetts, H., Bastow, S. and Tinkler, J. (2005) 'New public management is dead – long live digital-era governance', *Journal of Public Administration Research and Theory*, 16(3): 467–94.

Durkheim, Émile (1933 [1893]) *The Division of Labor in Society*. New York: Macmillan.

Dzidowski, Adam (2014) 'The map and the territory: sensemaking and sensebreaking through the organisational architecture', *Problemy Zarzadzania*, 12(4): 29–44.

easyHotel (2014) 'Franchising – how does it work?' (www.easyhotel.com/franchising/how_does_it_work.html, accessed 16/05/14).

Ehrman, John (2006) *The Eighties: America in the Age of Reagan*. New Haven, CT: Yale University Press.

Elzenbaumer, Bianca (2013) 'Designing economic cultures: cultivating socially and politically engaged design practices against procedures of precarisation', PhD dissertation, Goldsmiths College, University of London.

England, Paula and Nancy Folbre (2005) 'Gender and economy in economic sociology', in N.J. Smelser and R. Swedberg (eds), *The Handbook of Economic Sociology*, 2nd edn. Princeton, NJ: Princeton University Press. pp. 627–49.

Europe Economics (2015) *The Economic Review of Industrial Design in Europe — Final Report.* London: Europe Economics.

European Commission (2010) 'Green Paper: Unlocking the potential of cultural and creative industries' (report). Brussels: COM.

Evans, Graham (2009) 'Creative cities, creative spaces and urban policy', *Urban Studies*, 46(5–6): 1003–40.

Exeter City Council (2008) 'A summary of the redevelopment in Exeter's city centre' (report). Exeter: Exeter City Council.

Express and Echo (2012) 'Princesshay tracks shoppers via mobile phones' (www.exeterexpressand-echo.co.uk/Princesshay-tracks-shoppers-mobile-phones/story-14334332-detail/story.html, accessed 31/03/16).

Fairs, Marcus (2005) 'Dead end at the Design Museum', *Evening Standard* (www.standard.co.uk/home/dead-end-at-the-design-museum-7439381.html, accessed 11/11/15).

Fallan, Kjetil (2008) 'De-scribing design: appropriating script analysis to design history', *Design Issues*, 24(4): 61–75.

Featherstone, Mike (1991) *Consumer Culture and Postmodernism.* London: Sage.

Fejos, Zoltan (2000) 'Coca-Cola and the Chain Bridge of Budapest: a multi-ethnographic experiment', *Ethnologia Europaea*, 30(1): 15–30.

Ferdows, K., Lewis, M.A. and Machuca, J.A. (2005) 'Zara's secret for fast fashion', *Harvard Business Review*, 82(11): 98–111.

Findeli, Alain (2001) 'Rethinking design education for the 21st century: theoretical, methodological, and ethical discussion', *Design Issues*, 17(1): 5–17.

FindLaw (2008) 'One-click or two? The war over business method patents' (http://corporate.findlaw.com/intellectual-property/one-click-or-two-the-war-over-business-method-patents.html, accessed 22/05/15).

FIRJAN (2014) 'Mapeamento Da Indústria Criativa No Brasil' (report). Rio de Janeiro: Sistema FIRJAN.

Fitch, Rodney and Knobel, Lance (1990) *Fitch on Retail Design.* London: Phaidon.

Fladmoe-Lindquist, Karin and Jacque, Laurent (1995) 'Control modes in international service operations: the propensity to franchise', *Management Science*, 41(7): 1238–49.

Fletcher, Kate, Grose, Lynda and Hawken, Paul (2012) *Fashion and Sustainability: Design for Change.* London: Laurence King.

Flew, Terry (2011) *The Creative Industries: Culture and Policy.* London: Sage.

Flood, Chris (2013) 'Pension funds drawn to property', *Financial Times*, 13 January.

Folkmann, Mads Nygaard (2013) *The Aesthetics of Imagination in Design.* Cambridge, MA: MIT Press.

Foord, Jo (2009) 'Strategies for creative industries: an international review', *Creative Industries Journal*, 1(2): 91–113.

Fortier, Anne-Marie (2010) 'Proximity by design? Affective citizenship and the management of unease', *Citizenship Studies*, 14(1): 17–30.

Foster, Hal (ed.) (1985) *Postmodern Culture.* London: Pluto.

Foster, John and McChesney, Robert (2012) *The Endless Crisis: How Monopoly-finance Capital Produces Stagnation and Upheaval from the USA to China.* New York: NYU Press.

Foster, John and Szlajfer, Henryk (eds) (1984) *The Faltering Economy: The Problem of Accumulation under Monopoly Capitalism.* New York: Monthly Review Press.

Foucault, Michel (1988) 'Technologies of the self', in L.H. Martin, H. Gutman and P.H. Hutton (eds), *Technologies of the Self: A Seminar with Michel Foucault.* Amherst, MA: University of Massachusetts Press. pp. 17–49.

Foucault, Michel (1998 [1976]) *The History of Sexuality, Vol. 1: The Will to Knowledge.* London: Penguin.

Foucault, Michel (2008) *The Birth of Biopolitics: Lectures at the Collège de France 1978–1979* (ed. M. Sennelart, trans. G. Burchell). Basingstoke: Palgrave.

Fraser, A., Murphy, E. and Kelly, S. (2013) 'Deepening neoliberalism via austerity and "reform": the case of Ireland', *Human Geography*, 6(2): 38–53.

Freeman, Alan (2011) 'Current Issues Note 33: London's creative industries 2011 update' (report). London: GLA Economics.

Friedenbach, Miki (2013) Interview with the author, 21 October.

Friedman, Ken (2003) 'Theory construction in design research: criteria, approaches and methods', *Design Studies*, 24(6): 507–22.

Friedman, Thomas (2006) *The World is Flat: The Globalized World in the Twenty-first Century*. London: Penguin.

Frith, Simon and Horne, Howard (1987) *Art into Pop*. London: Routledge.

Froud, J., Haslam, C., Johal, S. and Williams, K. (2000) 'Shareholder value and financialization: consultancy promises, management moves', *Economy and Society*, 29(1): 80–110.

Froud, J., Johal, S., Leaver, A. and Williams, K. (2006) *Financialization and Strategy: Narrative and Numbers*. London: Routledge.

Fuad-Luke, Alastair (2009) *Design Activism: Beautiful Strangeness for a Sustainable World*. London: Earthscan.

Gabriel, Yiannis (2003) 'Glass palaces and glass cages: organizations in times of flexible work, fragmented consumption and fragile selves', *Ephemera*, 3(3): 166–84.

Gallop, Geoff (2007) 'Strategic planning: is it the new model?', *Public Administration Today*, 10: 28–33.

Galloway, Susan and Dunlop, Steward (2007) 'A critique of definitions of the cultural and creative industries in public policy', *International Journal of Cultural Policy*, 13(1): 17–31.

Gardner, Gareth (2007) 'The Princess and the maze', *BD Magazine*, Issue 6.

Garnham, Nick (1990) *Capitalism and Communication – Global Culture and the Economics of Information*. London: Sage.

Garriga, C., Gavin, W. and Schlagenhauf, D. (2006) 'Recent trends in homeownership', *Federal Reserve Bank of St. Louis Review*, 88(5): 397–412.

Gemser, Gerda and Wijnberg, Nachoem (2001) 'Effects of reputational sanctions on the competitive imitation of design innovations', *Organization Studies*, 22(4): 563–91.

Gerth, Karl (2010) *As China Goes, So Goes the World: How Chinese Consumers are Transforming Everything*. New York: Hill and Wang.

Gesler, W., Bell, M., Curtis, S., Hubbard, P. and Francis, S. (2004) 'Therapy by design: evaluating the UK hospital building program', *Health and Place*, 10(2): 117–28.

Gibson, Lisanne and Stevenson, Deborah (2004) 'Urban space and the uses of culture', *International Journal of Cultural Policy*, 10(1): 1–4.

Gilbert, David (2013) 'A New World Order? Fashion and its capitals in the twenty-first century', in S. Bruzzi and P. Church Gibson (eds), *Fashion Cultures Revisited: Theories, Explorations and Analysis*. Abingdon: Routledge. pp. 11–30.

Giorda, Erica (2012) 'Farming in Motown: competing narratives for urban development and urban agriculture in Detroit', in A. Viljoen and J. Wiskerke (eds), *Sustainable Food Planning: Evolving Theory and Practice*. Wageningen: Wageningen Academic Publishers. pp. 271–81.

Glasmeier, A., Thompson, J. and Kays, A. (1993) 'The geography of trade policy: trade regimes and location decisions in the textile and apparel complex', *Transactions of the Institute of British Geographers*, 18: 19–35.

Global Language Monitor (2015) 'Paris towers over world of fashion as top global fashion capital for 2015' (www.languagemonitor.com/category/fashion/fashion-capitals, accessed 02/11/15).

Glynos, Jason and Speed, Ewen (2012) 'Varieties of co-production in public services: time banks in a UK health policy context', *Critical Policy Studies*, 6(4): 402–33.

Goffman, Erving (1959) *The Presentation of Self in Everyday Life*. New York: Double Day Anchor.

Gordon, I., Travers, T. and Whitehead, C.M. (2007) *The Impact of Recent Immigration on the London Economy*. London: London School of Economics.

Granovetter, Mark (1985) 'Economic action and social structure: the problem of embeddedness', *American Journal of Sociology*, 91(3): 481–510.

Granovetter, Mark (1990) 'The old and the new economic sociology: a history and an agenda', in R. Friedland and A.F. Robertson (eds), *Beyond the Market Place: Rethinking Economy and Society*. New York: Aldine de Gruyter. pp. 89–112.

Grattan, Robert (2002) *The Strategy Process: A Military–Business Comparison*. London: Palgrave Macmillan.

Greater Good Studio (2015) 'Theory of change' (www.greatergoodstudio.com/theoryofchange, accessed 08/12/15).

Grimshaw, Mike (2004) '"Soft modernism": the world of the post-theoretical designer' (www.ctheory.net/articles. aspx?id=418, accessed 21/06/12).

Grinyer, Clive (2001) 'Design differentiation for global companies: value exporters and value collectors', *Design Management Journal (Former Series)*, 12(4): 10–14.

Grodach, Carl and Seman, Michael (2013) 'The cultural economy in recession: examining the US experience', *Cities*, 33: 15–28.

Grubbauer, Monika (2014) 'Architecture, economic imaginaries and urban politics: the office tower as socially classifying device', *International Journal of Urban and Regional Research*, 38(1): 336–59.

Hadjimichalis, Costis (2006) 'The end of the third Italy as we knew it', *Antipode*, 38: 82–106.

Hall, Kevin (2010) 'A chronology of the Filofax' (www.philofaxy.com/files/filofax-chronology.pdf, accessed 17/09/15).

Hall, Stuart (1988) 'Brave new world', *Marxism Today*, 32(12): 24–30.

Halpern, D., Bates, C., Mulgan, G. and Aldridge, S. with Beales, G. and Heathfield, A. (2004) *Personal Responsibility and Changing Behaviour: The State of Knowledge and its Implications for Public Policy*. London: Prime Minister's Strategy Unit.

Hannam, K., Sheller, M. and Urry, J. (2006) 'Editorial: Mobilities, immobilities and moorings', *Mobilities*, 1(1): 1–22.

Hanson, Gordon and Slaughter, Mathew (2002) 'Labor-market adjustment in open economies: evidence from US states', *Journal of International Economics*, 57(1): 3–29.

Haraway, Donna (2006 [1985]) 'A cyborg manifesto: science, technology, and socialist-feminism in the late 20th century', in J. Weiss, J. Nolan, J. Hunsinger and P. Trifonas (eds), *The International Handbook of Virtual Learning Environments*. Dordrecht: Springer. pp. 117–58.

Hardie, Michael and Perry, Frederick (2013) 'Economic review, May 2013' (report). London: Office for National Statistics.

Harman, Chris (2010) *Zombie Capitalism: Global Crisis and the Relevance of Marx*. Chicago, IL: Haymarket.

Harper, Krista (1999) 'Citizens or consumers? Environmentalism and the public sphere in postsocialist Hungary', *Radical History Review*, 74: 96–111.

Harrison, Bennett (1994) *Lean and Mean: The Changing Landscape of Corporate Power in the Age of Flexibility*. New York: Basic Books.

Hartley, John (ed.) (2005) *Creative Industries*. Oxford: Blackwell.

Hartley, John, Wen, Wen and Li, Henry Siling (2015) *Creative Economy and Culture: Challenges, Changes and Futures for the Creative Industries*. London: Sage.

Hartwich, Oliver Marc and Razeen, Sally (2009) 'Neoliberalism: the genesis of a political swearword', Occasional Paper 114. Sydey: Centre for Independent Studies.

Harvey, David (1989a) *The Condition of Postmodernity: An Enquiry into the Origins of Cultural Change*. Oxford: Basil Blackwell.

Harvey, David (1989b) *The Urban Experience*. Oxford: Basil Blackwell.

Harvey, David (2001) 'Globalization and the "spatial fix"', *Geographische Revue*, 2(3): 23–30.

Harvey, David (2003) *The New Imperialism*. Oxford: Oxford University Press.

Harvey, David (2005) *A Brief History of Neoliberalism*. Oxford: Oxford University Press.

Harvey, David (2010) *The Enigma of Capital and the Crisis of Capitalism*. London: Profile.

Haug, W.F. (1986) *Critique of Commodity Aesthetics: Appearance, Sexuality and Advertising in Capitalist Society*. London: Polity Press.

Haughton, G., Deas, I. and Hincks, S. (2014) 'Making an impact: when agglomeration boosterism meets antiplanning rhetoric', *Environment and Planning A*, 45(2): 265–70.

Healy, Stephen (2009) 'Alternative economies', in N. Thrift and R. Kitchin (eds), *The International Encyclopedia of Human Geography*. Oxford: Elsevier. pp. 338–44.

Hebdige, Dick (1985) 'The impossible object: toward a cartography of taste', *Block*, 12: 13–14.

Hebdige, Dick (1988) *Hiding in the Light: On Images and Things*. London: Comedia.

Hennessey, William (2012) 'Deconstructing *Shanzhai*-China's copycat counterculture: catch me if you can', *Campbell Law Review*, 34(3): 609–60.

Herod, Andrew (1997) 'From a geography of labor to a labor geography: labor's spatial fix and the geography of capitalism', *Antipode*, 29(1): 1–31.

Heskett, John (2008) 'Creating economic value by design', *International Journal of Design*, 3(1): 71–84.

Hesmondhalgh, David (2007) *The Cultural Industries*, 2nd edn. London: Sage.

Hilbert, Martin and López, Priscila (2011) 'The world's technological capacity to store, communicate, and compute information', *Science*, 332(60): 60–65.

Hill, Katie and Julier, Guy (2009) 'Design, innovation and policy at local level', in G. Julier and L. Moor (eds), *Design and Creativity: Policy, Management and Practice*. Oxford: Berg. pp. 57–73.

Hirsch, R.L., Bezdek, R. and Wendling, R. (2005) 'Peaking of world oil production', in ASPO, *Proceedings of the IV International Workshop on Oil and Gas Depletion*. Evora: Centro de Geofísica de Évora. pp. 19–20.

Hochschild, Arlie Russell (2003 [1983]) *The Managed Heart: Commercialization of Human Feeling*. Berkeley, CA: University of California Press.

Hodge, Graeme A. and Greve, Carsten (2007) 'Public–private partnerships: an international performance review', *Public Administration Review*, 67(3): 545–58.

Højdam, Jonny (2015) 'Design Community Kolding' (https://prezi.com/rlgfcwfzgpqg/design-community-kolding-en-final, accessed 23/12/15).

Hopkins, Rob (2008) *The Transition Handbook: From Oil Dependency to Local Resilience*. Totnes: Green Books.

Horolets, Anna (2015) 'Finding one's way: recreational mobility of post-2004 Polish migrants in West Midlands, UK', *Leisure Studies*, 34(1): 5–18.

Howkins, John (2001) *The Creative Economy: How People Make Money from Ideas*. London: Penguin.

Hozic, Aida (1999) 'Uncle Sam goes to Siliwood: of landscapes, Spielberg and hegemony', *Review of International Political Economy*, 6(3): 289–312.

Hsu, Tiffany (2013) 'See's, Topshop, Topman opening at the Grove in February', *LA Times*, 5 February (www.latimes.com/business/la-fi-mo-sees-topshop-grove-20130204-story.html, accessed 31/03/16).

Hurdley, Rachel (2006) 'Dismantling mantelpieces: narrating identities and materializing culture in the home', *Sociology*, 40(4): 717–33.

Huyssen, Andreas (1986) *After the Great Divide: Modernism, Mass Culture, Postmodernism*. Chicago, IL: Indiana University Press.

IFIClaims® (2015) 'IFI CLAIMS® 2014 Top 50 US patent assignees' (www.ificlaims.com/index.php?page=misc_top_50_2014, accessed 27/05/15).

Innovation Unit (2015) 'Different, better, lower cost: innovation support for public services' (www.innovationunit.org, accessed 01/04/15).

Insurance Europe and Oliver Wyman (2013) 'Funding the future: insurers' role as institutional investors' (www.insuranceeurope.eu/sites/default/files/attachments/Funding%20the%20future.pdf, accessed 31/03/16).

Intellectual Property Office (2012) 'Copyright protection for designs: final impact assessment' (www.gov.uk/government/uploads/system/uploads/attachment_data/file/31970/12-866-copyright-protection-designs-impact-assessment.pdf, accessed 21/04/16).

Intellectual Property Office (2015) *Registered Designs Act 1949*. Newport: IPO (https://www.gov.uk/government/uploads/system/uploads/attachment_data/file/498821/Registered_Designs_Act_1949.pdf, accessed 11/08/16).

IP Australia (2008) *Protect Your Creative: A Guide to Intellectual Property for Australia's Graphic Designers*. Victoria: IP Australia.

Jansson, Johan and Power, Dominic (2010) 'Fashioning a global city: global city brand channels in the fashion and design industries', *Regional Studies*, 44(7): 889–904.

Jeffcutt, Paul and Pratt, Alex (2002) 'Managing creativity in the cultural industries', *Creativity and Innovation Management*, 11(4): 225–33.

Jessop, Bob (2004) 'Critical semiotic analysis and cultural political economy', *Critical Discourse Studies*, 1(2): 159–74.

Jessop, Bob (2006) 'Spatial fixes, temporal fixes, and spatio-temporal fixes', in N. Castree and D. Gregory (eds), *David Harvey: A Critical Reader*. Oxford: Blackwell. pp. 142–66.

Johnson, Stephen (2015) *Guide to Intellectual Property: What it is, How to Protect it, How to Exploit it*. London: The Economist.

Julier, Guy (1991) *New Spanish Design*. London: Thames and Hudson.

Julier, Guy (2005) 'Urban designscapes and the production of aesthetic consent', *Urban Studies*, 42(5–6): 869–88.

Julier, Guy (2010) 'Playing the system: design consultancies, professionalisation and value', in B. Townley and N. Beech (eds), *Managing Creativity: Exploring the Paradox*. Cambridge: Cambridge University Press. pp. 237–59.

Julier, Guy (2013) 'From design culture to design activism', *Design and Culture*, 5(2): 215–36.

Julier, Guy (2014) *The Culture of Design*, 3rd edn. London: Sage.

Julier, Guy and Leerberg, Malene (2014) 'Kolding – we design for life: embedding a new design culture into urban regeneration', *The Finnish Journal of Urban Studies*, 52(2): 29–56.

Jungersen, Ulrik and Hansen, Poul (2014) 'Designing a municipality', in M. Laakso and K. Ekman (eds), *Proceedings of Norddesign 2014 Conference*. Aalto: Aalto University. pp. 610–19.

Kar, Dev and Spanjers, Joseph (2014) *Illicit Financial Flows from Developing Countries: 2003–2012*. Washington, DC: Global Financial Integrity.

Kasarda, John and Lindsay, Greg (2011) *Aerotropolis: The Way We'll Live Next*. London: Macmillan.

Kasperkevic, Jana (2015) 'McDonald's franchise owners: what they really think about the fight for $15', *Guardian*, 14 April (www.theguardian.com/business/2015/apr/14/mcdonalds-franchise-owners-minimum-wage-restaurants, accessed 02/02/15).

Katatomic (2015) 'SUBWAY® The largest sandwich franchise in the world' (www.katatomic.co.uk/our-work/subway, accessed 02/06/15).

Kaygan, Harun (2016) Ankara-based design historian; communication with the author, 10 April.

KEA European Affairs (2006) 'The economy of culture in Europe' (report) (http://ec.europa.eu/culture/library, accessed 13/01/15).

Keane, Michael (2007) *Created in China: The Great New Leap Forward*. London: Routledge.

Keane, Michael (2009) 'Creative industries in China: four perspectives on social transformation', *International Journal of Cultural Policy*, 15(4): 431–43.

Keane, Michael (2013) *Creative Industries in China: Art, Design and Media*. Cambridge: Polity Press.

Keith, M., Lash, S., Arnoldi, J. and Rooker, T. (2014) *China Constructing Capitalism: Economic Life and Urban Change*. London: Routledge.

Kelly, Kevin (1999) *New Rules for the New Economy*. London: Penguin.

Kent, Anthony and Stone, Dominic (2006) 'Retail design management: the creation of brand value', in *Proceedings of D2B: The 1st International Design Management Symposium*, March 2006, Jiao Tong University, Shanghai, China.

Kerr, Hui-Ying (2016) 'Envisioning the bubble: creating and consuming lifestyles through magazines in the Japanese bubble economy (1986–1991)', PhD dissertation, Royal College of Art.

Kim, Tae K. (2010) 'How Nintendo's NES console changed gaming' (www.pcworld.idg.com.au/article/367375, accessed 07/11/14).

Kimbell, Lucy (2014) *The Service Innovation Handbook: Action-oriented Creative Thinking Toolkit for Service Organisations*. Amsterdam: BIS.

Kimbell, Lucy (2015) *Applying Design Approaches to Policy Making: Discovering Policy Lab*. Brighton: University of Brighton.

Kimbell, Lucy (2016) 'Design in the time of policy problems', paper presented at the Design Research Society Conference, University of Brighton.

Knorr Cetina, Karin (1997) 'Sociality with objects: social relations in postsocial knowledge societies', *Theory, Culture and Society*, 14(4): 1–30.

Knorr Cetina, Karin (2001) 'Objectual practice', in T.R. Schatzki, K. Knorr Cetina and E. Von Savigny (eds), *The Practice Turn in Contemporary Theory*. London: Routledge. pp. 184–96.

Knorr Cetina, Karin (2003) 'From pipes to scopes: the flow architecture of financial markets', *Distinktion: Scandinavian Journal of Social Theory*, 4(2): 7–23.

Knorr Cetina, Karin and Bruegger, Urs (2000) 'The market as an object of attachment: exploring postsocial relations in financial markets', *Canadian Journal of Sociology/Cahiers canadiens de sociologie*, 25(2): 141–68.

Knorr Cetina, Karin and Preda, Alex (eds) (2004) *The Sociology of Financial Markets*. Oxford: Oxford University Press.

Knox, Paul and Mayer, Heike (2013) *Small Town Sustainability: Economic, Social, and Environmental Innovation*, 2nd edn. Basel: Birkhäuser.

Kolding Municipality (2015) 'EPSA Ansøgning' (internal document).

Koskinen, Ilpo (2005) 'Semiotic neighborhoods', *Design Issues*, 21(2): 13–27.

KPMG (2011) 'Making the transition: outcome-based budgeting: a six nation study' (www.kpmg-institutes.com/content/dam/kpmg/governmentinstitute, accessed 23/12/15).

Kuehn, Kathleen and Corrigan, Thomas (2013) 'Hope labor: the role of employment prospects in online social production', *Political Economy of Communication*, 1(1): 9–25.

Laclau, Ernesto and Mouffe, Chantal (1985) *Hegemony and Socialist Strategy: Towards a Radical Democratic Politics*. London: Verso.

Lanchester, John (2015) *How to Speak Money*. London: Faber and Faber.

Land Securities (2007) 'Princesshay launches in Exeter' (press release) (www.landsecurities.com/website files/Princesshay_launch_200907.pdf, accessed 18/11/15).

Land Securities (2013a) 'Investor tour of Trinity Leeds – presentation and QandA' (www.land securities.com/documentlibrary/Trinity_Leeds_tour_presentation_transcript_with_QA.pdf, accessed 18/08/15).

Land Securities (2013b) 'Tour of Trinity Leeds' (www.landsecurities.com/documentlibrary/Trinity_Leeds_investor_tour_-_WEBSITE_FINAL.PDF, accessed 18/08/15).

Land Securities (2014) 'Land Securities exits Princesshay, Exeter and takes full control of Buchanan Galleries, Glasgow' (press release) (http://landsecurities.com/media/press-releases?MediaID=1861, accessed 31/03/16).

Land Securities (2015) 'Annual Report 2015' (http://annualreport2015.landsecurities.com/pdf/Full_Report.pdf, accessed 18/08/15).

Lash, Scott (2002) *Critique of Information*. London: Sage.

Lash, Scott (2010) *Intensive Culture: Social Theory, Religion and Contemporary Capitalism*. London: Sage.

Lash, Scott and Urry, John (1987) *The End of Organized Capitalism*. London: Polity Press.

Latour, Bruno (2005) *Reassembling the Social: An Introduction to Actor-Network Theory*. Oxford: Oxford University Press.

Law, Jennifer (2013) 'Do outcomes based approaches to service delivery work? Local authority outcome agreements in Wales'. University of South Wales: Centre for Advanced Studies in Public Policy (http://

caspp.southwales.ac.uk/media/files/documents/2013-06-24/publication-local-authority-outcome.pdf, accessed 27/02/15).

Lawson, Julie and Milligan, Vivienne (2007) 'International trends in housing and policy responses', report for the Australian Housing and Urban Research Institute No. 110. Sydney: Sydney Research Centre.

Lazzarato, Maurizio (1996) 'Immaterial labour', in M. Hardt and P. Virno (eds), *Radical Thought in Italy: A Potential Politics*. Minneapolis, MN: University of Minnesota Press. pp. 133–47.

Leadbeater, Charles (2008) *We-think: The Power of Mass Creativity*. London: Profile.

Ledesma, María (2015) 'Empoderamiento y horizontalidad en nuevos emergentes en el diseño social', *Inventio*, 24(11): 41–7.

Lee, Frederic and Cronin, Bruce (eds) (2016) *Handbook of Research Methods and Applications in Heterodox Economics*. Cheltenham: Edward Elgar.

Lee, Younjoon and Evans, Martyn (2012) 'What drives organizations to employ design-driven approaches? A study of fast-moving consumer goods', *Design Management Journal*, 7(1): 74–88.

Lees, L., Slater, T. and Wyly, E. (2013) *Gentrification*. Abingdon: Routledge.

Leggett, Will (2014) 'The politics of behaviour change: nudge, neoliberalism and the state', *Policy and Politics*, 42(1): 3–19.

Lehki, Rohit (2007) *Public Service Innovation: A Research Report for The Work Foundation's Knowledge Economy Programme*. London: The Work Foundation.

Leonard, Andrew (2014) 'Amazon's ridiculous photography patent makes Mark Cuban happy', *Salon*, 9 May (www.salon.com/2014/05/09/amazons_ridiculous_photography_patent_makes_mark_cuban_happy, accessed 22/02/16).

Lerner, Fern (2005) 'Foundations for design education: continuing the Bauhaus Vorkurs vision', *Studies in Art Education*, 46(3): 211–26.

Leschke, Janine and Jepsen, Maria (2012) 'Introduction: crisis, policy responses and widening inequalities in the EU', *International Labour Review*, 151(4): 289–312.

Levitsky, Steven and Murillo, María Victoria (2003) 'Argentina weathers the storm', *Journal of Democracy*, 14(4): 152–66.

Lewis, Justin (1990) *Art, Culture and Enterprise: The Politics of Art and the Cultural Industries*. London: Routledge.

Li, David (2014) 'The new *Shanzhai*: democratizing innovation in China', *ParisTech Review* (www.paris techreview.com/2014/12/24/shanzhai-innovation-china, accessed 01/04/16).

Li, David (2016) CEO of Shenzhen Open Innovation Lab; conversation with the author, 14 March.

Liao, Lit and Li, David (2016) Founder of Litchee Lab, Shenzhen, and CEO of Shenzhen Open Innovation Lab. Interventions in MadLab, Manchester roundtable event, 20 April.

Lin, Yi-Chieh Jessica (2011) *Fake Stuff: China and the Rise of Counterfeit Goods*. London: Routledge.

Lindtner, Silvia (2014) 'Hackerspaces and the internet of things in China: how makers are reinventing industrial production, innovation, and the self', *China Information*, 28(2): 145–67.

Lindtner, Silvia and Greenspan, Anna (2014) '*Shanzhai*: China's collaborative electronics-design ecosystem', *The Atlantic* (www.theatlantic.com/technology/archive/2014/05/chinas-mass-production-system/370898/, accessed 20/04/16).

Lindtner, Silvia and Li, David (2012) 'Created in China: the makings of China's hackerspace community', *Interactions*, 19(6): 18–22.

Lipton, Jacqueline (2009) 'To © or not to ©? Copyright and innovation in the digital typeface industry', *University of California Davis Law Review*, 43: 143–82.

Lodge, Martin and Hood, Christopher (2012) 'Into an age of multiple austerities? Public management and public service bargains across OECD countries', *Governance*, 25(1): 79–101.

Lucas, Robert (1988) 'On the mechanics of economic development', *Journal of Monetary Economics*, 22(1): 3–42.

Lury, Celia (2004) *Brands: The Logos of the Global Economy*. Abingdon: Routledge.

Lyotard, Jean-François (1987) *The Postmodern Condition: A Report on Knowledge* (trans. G. Bennington and B. Massumi). Manchester: Manchester University Press.

MacKenzie, Donald (2008) *Material Markets: How Economic Agents are Constructed*. Oxford: Oxford University Press.

MacKenzie, Donald (2014) 'At Cermak', *London Review of Books*, 36(23): 25.

MacLaren, Andrew (ed.) (2014) *Making Space: Property Development and Urban Planning*. Abingdon: Routledge.

Maeckelbergh, Marianne (2013) 'What comes after democracy?,' *Open Citizenship*, 4(1): 74–9.

Mair, James (2015) Managing Director, Viaduct Furniture, London; correspondence with the author, 24 June.

Malpass, A., Barnett, C., Clarke, N. and Cloke, P. (2007) 'Problematizing choice: responsible consumers and sceptical citizens', in M. Bevir and F. Trentmann (eds), *Governance, Consumers and Citizens: Agency and Resistance in Contemporary Politics*. Basingstoke: Palgrave Macmillan. pp. 231–56.

Manyika, J., Bughin, J., Lund, S., Nottebohm, O., Poulter, D., Jauch, S. and Ramaswamy, S. (2014) 'Global flows in a digital age: how trade, finance, people, and data connect the world economy' (www.mckinsey.com/mgi, accessed 20/03/16).

Manzini, Ezio (2015) *Design, When Everybody Designs: An Introduction to Design for Social Innovation*. Cambridge, MA: MIT Press.

Manzini, Ezio and Jégou, François (2005) *Sustainable Everyday: Scenarios of Urban Life*. Milan: Edizione Ambiente.

Marsden, Jamie and Thomas, Briony (2013) 'Brand values: exploring the associations of symmetry within financial brand marks', *Design Management Journal*, 8(1): 62–71.

Marres, Noortje (2014) 'Introduction to "Inventing the Socials"', Inventing the Social Conference, Centre for the Study of Invention and Social Process, Goldsmiths College, University of London, 29–30 May.

Marsh, Peter (2012) *The New Industrial Revolution: Consumers, Globalization and the End of Mass Production*. New Haven, CT and London: Yale University Press.

Marshall, Ben (2011) 'Property shows: room for improvement?', *Guardian*, 10 August.

Martin, Craig (2013) 'Shipping container mobilities, seamless compatibility, and the global surface of logistical integration', *Environment and Planning A*, 45(5): 1021–36.

Martin, Randy (2002) *Financialization of Daily Life*. Philadelphia, PA: Temple University Press.

Martin, Steve (2000) 'Implementing "best value": local public services in transition', *Public Administration*, 78(1): 209–27.

Mau, Bruce (2004) *Massive Change: A Manifesto for the Future of Global Design Culture*. London: Phaidon.

Mayer, Heike and Knox, Paul (2006) 'Slow cities: sustainable places in a fast world', *Journal of Urban Affairs*, 28(4): 321–34.

Mazzucato, Mariana (2013) *The Entrepreneurial State: Debunking Public vs. Private Sector Myths*. London: Anthem Press.

McAlhone, Beryl (1987) 'British design consultancy' (report). London: Design Council.

McCarthy, Niall (2015) 'The world's biggest employers', *Forbes Business* (www.forbes.com/sites/niallmccarthy/2015/06/23/the-worlds-biggest-employers-infographic, accessed 09/12/15).

McCormack, Derek (2008) 'Engineering affective atmospheres on the moving geographies of the 1897 Andree Expedition', *Cultural Geographies*, 15(4): 413–30.

McCormack, Lee (2005) *Designers are Wankers*. London: About Face.

McCurdy, Howard E. (2001) *Faster, Better, Cheaper: Low Cost Innovation in the US Space Program*. Baltimore, MD: Johns Hopkins University Press.

McDowell, L., Batnitzky, A. and Dyer, S. (2007) 'Division, segmentation, and interpellation: the embodied labors of migrant workers in a greater London hotel', *Economic Geography*, 83(1): 1–25.

McLaughlin, Kate, Osborne, Stephen P. and Ferlie, Ewan (eds) (2002) *New Public Management: Current Trends and Future Prospects.* London: Routledge.

McLuhan, Marshall (1964) *Understanding Media: The Extensions of Man.* New York: McGraw-Hill.

McMurdo, George (1989) 'Filofax, personal organizers and information society', *Journal of Information Science*, 15(6): 361–4.

McRobbie, Angela (2002) 'Clubs to companies: notes on the decline of political culture in speeded up creative worlds', *Cultural Studies*, 16(4): 516–31.

McRobbie, Angela (2004) '"Everyone is creative": artists as pioneers of the new economy?', in T. Bennett and E. Silva (eds), *Contemporary Culture and Everyday Life.* London: Routledge. ch. 4.

Meadows, D.H., Meadows, D.L. and Randers, J. (2004) *Limits to Growth – the 30 Year Update.* London: Earthscan.

Meadows, D.H., Meadows, D.L., Randers, J. and Behrens, W.W. (1972) *The Limits to Growth: A Report for the Club of Rome's Project on the Predicament of Mankind.* New York: Universe Books.

Metcalfe, Les (1994) 'International policy co-ordination and public management reform', *International Review of Administrative Sciences*, 60(2): 271–90.

Michaëlis, Sabina (2013) Assistant Manager to Tom Ressau Design; personal interview 30 September in Kolding, Denmark.

Michaëlis, Sabina (2015) Correspondence with the author, 5 June.

Michlewski, Kamil (2008) 'Uncovering design attitude: inside the culture of designers', *Organization Studies*, 29(3): 373–92.

Miekle, Jeffrey (2005) *Design in the USA.* Oxford: Oxford University Press.

Migration Advisory Committee (2014) 'Migrants in low-skilled work: the growth of EU and non-EU labour in low-skilled jobs and its impact on the UK' (www.gov.uk/government/uploads/system/uploads/attachment_data/file/333083/MAC-Migrants_in_low-skilled_work__Full_report_2014.pdf, accessed 29/10/15).

Miller, Daniel (1987) *Material Culture and Mass Consumption.* Oxford: Blackwell.

Miller, Daniel and Carrier, James G. (eds) (1998) *Virtualism: A New Political Economy.* Oxford: Berg.

Ministry of Foreign Affairs of Denmark (2012) 'Design originals and intellectual property issues surrounding replica product from the UK' (unpublished report).

Minton, Anna (2012) *Ground Control: Fear and Happiness in the Twenty-first-century City.* London: Penguin.

Mollison, Bill and Holmgren, David (1978) *Permaculture One: A Perennial Agriculture for Human Settlements.* Perth: Corgi.

Molotch, Harvey (2003) *Where Stuff Comes From: How Toasters, Toilets, Cars, Computers and Many Other Things Come to Be as They are.* London: Routledge.

Mommaas, Hans (2004) 'Cultural clusters and the post-industrial city: towards the remapping of urban cultural policy', *Urban Studies*, 41(3): 507–32.

Money, Annemarie (2007) 'Material culture and the living room: the appropriation and use of goods in everyday life', *Journal of Consumer Culture*, 7(3): 355–77.

Montgomery, Angus (2015) 'Design's value to UK economy soars' (www.designweek.co.uk/news/designs-value-to-uk-economy-soars/3039636.article, accessed 13/01/15).

Montgomery, Lucy (2010) *China's Creative Industries: Copyright, Social Network Markets and the Business of Culture in a Digital Age.* Cheltenham: Edward Elgar.

Montgomery, Lucy and Fitzgerald, Brian (2006) 'Copyright and the creative industries in China', *International Journal of Cultural Studies*, 9(3): 407–18.

Moon, Christina (2014) 'The slow road to fast fashion', *Pacific Standard*, 17 March (www.psmag.com/business-economics/secret-world-slow-road-korea-los-angeles-behind-fast-fashion-73956, accessed 17/10/15).

Moor, Liz (2009) 'Designing the state', in G. Julier and L. Moor (eds), *Design and Creativity: Policy, Management and Practice.* Oxford: Berg. pp. 23–39.

Moor, Liz (2012) 'Beyond cultural intermediaries? A socio-technical perspective on the market for social interventions', *European Journal of Cultural Studies*, 15(5): 563–80.

Moreno, Louis (ed.) (2008) *The Architecture and Urban Culture of Financial Crisis*. London: Bartlett School of Architecture.

Morgan, Louise and Birtwistle, Grete (2009) 'An investigation of young fashion consumers' disposal habits', *International Journal of Consumer Studies*, 33(2): 190–98.

Moulaert, Frank and Swyngedouw, Erik (1989) 'Survey 15: a regulation approach to the geography of flexible production systems', *Environment and Planning D: Society and Space*, 7(3): 327–45.

Murphy, David and Hall, Charles (2011) 'Energy return on investment, peak oil, and the end of economic growth', *Annals of the New York Academy of Sciences*, 1219(1): 52–72.

Murray, Feargus (1987) 'Flexible specialization in the "Third Italy"', *Capital and Class*, 11(3): 84–95.

Murray, R., Caulier-Grice, J. and Mulgan, G. (2010) *The Open Book of Social Innovation*. London: Nesta.

Myerson, Jeremy (1986) 'In with the in crowd', *Design Week*, 26 September, pp. 20–21.

Myerson, Jeremy (2011) Founding Editor, *Design Week* 1986–1989; interview with the author, 19 January.

Nainan, Shihn (2010) *The Water Margin: The Outlaws of the Marsh* (trans. J.H. Jackson). North Clarendon, VT: Tuttle.

NDTV (2011) 'The "Mitticool" revolution: fridge for the poor' (www.ndtv.com/india-news/the-mitticool-revolution-fridge-for-the-poor-459588, accessed 10/01/16).

Nederveen Pieterse, Jan (1995) 'Globalization as hybridization', in M. Featherstone, Scott Lash and R. Robertson (eds), *Global Modernities*. London: Sage. pp. 45–68.

Neff, G., Wissinger, E. and Zukin, S. (2005) 'Entrepreneurial labor among cultural producers: cool jobs in hot industries', *Social Semiotics*, 15(3): 307–34.

Negus, Keith (2002) 'The work of cultural intermediaries and the enduring distinction between production and consumption', *Cultural Studies*, 16: 501–15.

Neidik, Binnur and Gereffi, Gary (2006) 'Explaining Turkey's emergence and sustained competitiveness as a full-package supplier of apparel', *Environment and Planning A*, 38(12): 2285–303.

Nelson, Harold and Stolterman, Erik (2003) *The Design Way: Intentional Change in an Unpredictable World: Foundations and Fundamentals of Design Competence*. Trenton, NJ: Educational Technology.

Nesta (2015a) 'World of labs' (www.nesta.org.uk/blog/world-labs, accessed 08/12/15).

Nesta (2015b) 'Casserole Club building networks and saving money through community meal-sharing' (www.nesta.org.uk/casserole-club, accessed 30/03/15).

Neuwirth, Robert (2011) *The Stealth of Nations: The Global Rise of the Informal Economy*. New York: Anchor.

New Economics Foundation (2005) *Clone Town Britain: The Survey Results on the Bland State of Britain*. London: NEF.

New Economics Foundation (2008) *Plugging the Leaks: Local Economic Development as if People Matter*. London: NEF.

Nixon, Sean (2003) *Advertising Cultures: Gender, Commerce, Creativity*. London: Sage.

Nonini, Donald (2008) 'Is China becoming neoliberal?', *Critique of Anthropology*, 28(2): 145–76.

Norman, Donald (2010) *Living with Complexity*. Cambridge, MA: MIT Press.

North, Peter (2005) 'Scaling alternative economic practices? Some lessons from alternative currencies', *Transactions of the Institute of British Geographers*, 30(2): 221–33.

North, Peter (2010) 'Eco-localisation as a progressive response to peak oil and climate change – a sympathetic critique', *Geoforum*, 41(4): 585–94.

O'Connor, Justin and Xin, Gu (2006) 'A new modernity? The arrival of "creative industries" in China', *International Journal of Cultural Studies*, 9(3): 271–83.

Oakley, Kate (2004) 'Not so cool Britannia: the role of the creative industries in economic development', *International Journal of Cultural Studies*, 7(1): 67–77.

OECD (2009) *Is Informal Normal? Towards More and Better Jobs*. Paris: OECD.

OECD (2015) *Government at a Glance 2015*. Paris: OECD (www.oecd-ilibrary.org/governance/government-at-a-glance-2015_gov_glance-2015-en, accessed 03/08/16).

Offe, Claus (1985) *Disorganized Capitalism*. Oxford: Polity Press.

Office for National Statistics (2010) *Social Trends 40*. Basingstoke: Palgrave Macmillan.

Oltermann, Philip and McClanahan, Paige (2014) 'Tata Nano safety under scrutiny after dire crash test results', *Guardian* (www.theguardian.com/global-development/2014/jan/31/tata-nano-safety-crash-test-results, accessed 10/01/16).

Ondaatje, Michael (2012 [1987]) *In the Skin of the Lion*. Toronto: Random House.

Ouellette, Laurie and Hay, James (2009) 'Makeover television, governmentality and the good citizen', in T. Lewis (ed.), *TV Transformations: Revealing the Makeover Show*. London: Routledge. pp. 31–44.

Orth, Ulrich and Malkewitz, Keven (2008) 'Holistic package design and consumer brand impressions', *Journal of Marketing*, 72(3): 64–81.

Pang, Laikwan (2012) *Creativity and its Discontents: China's Creative Industries and Intellectual Property Rights Offences*. Durham, NC and London: Duke University Press.

Papanek, Victor (1971) *Design for the Real World: Human Ecology and Social Change*. London: Thames and Hudson.

Papanek, Victor (1995) *The Green Imperative: Ecology and Ethics in Design and Architecture*. London: Thames and Hudson.

Parker, Simon and Bartlett, Jamie (2008) *Towards Agile Government*. London: Demos.

Parker, Simon and Gallagher, Naimh (2007) *The Collaborative State: How Working Together Can Transform Public Services*. London: Demos.

Parker, Sophia (2007) 'The co-production paradox', in S. Parker and N. Gallagher (eds), *The Collaborative State*. London: Demos. pp. 176–87.

Parker, Sophia (2015) 'Lab Notes interview with Sophia Parker, founder of Social Innovation Lab for Kent' (www.nesta.org.uk/blog/lab-notes-interview-sophia-parker-founder-social-innovation-lab-kent#sthash.7exkK6Hy.dpuf, accessed 22/12/15).

Parkins, Wendy and Craig, Geoffrey (2006) *Slow Living*. Oxford: Berg.

Pawley, Martin (1998) *Terminal Architecture*. London: Reaktion.

Peck, Jamie (2013) 'Explaining (with) neoliberalism', *Territory, Politics, Governance*, 1(2): 132–57.

Peck, Jamie and Tickell, Adam (2007) 'Conceptualizing neoliberalism, thinking Thatcherism', in H. Leitner, J. Peck and E. Sheppard (eds), *Contesting Neoliberalism: Urban Frontiers*. New York: Guilford Press. pp. 26–50.

Peck, J., Theodore, N. and Brenner, N. (2009) 'Postneoliberalism and its malcontents', *Antipode: A Radical Journal of Geography*, 41(6): 94–116.

Peri, Giovanni (2012) 'The effect of immigration on productivity: evidence from U.S. states', *Review of Economics and Statistics*, 94(1): 348–58.

Perry, Grayson (2014) *Playing to the Gallery: Helping Contemporary Art in its Struggle to be Understood*. London: Particular Books.

Peters, John (2012) 'Neoliberal convergence in North America and Western Europe: fiscal austerity, privatization, and public sector reform', *Review of International Political Economy*, 19(2): 208–35.

Pfiffner, Pamela (2002) *Inside the Publishing Revolution: The Adobe Story*. San Jose, CA: Adobe.

Picard, Kezia (2013) 'The uniqueness of late capitalism: biopower and biopolitics', in T. Dufresne and C. Sacchetti (eds), *The Economy as Cultural System: Theory, Capitalism, Crisis*. London: Bloomsbury. pp. 141–52.

Pickles, John and Smith, Adrian (2011) 'Delocalization and persistence in the European clothing industry: the reconfiguration of trade and production networks', *Regional Studies*, 45(2): 167–85.

Piketty, Thomas (2014) *Capital in the Twenty-first Century*. London: Belknap Press.

Pine, Joseph and Gilmore, James (1999) *The Experience Economy: Work is Theatre and Every Business a Stage*. Boston, MA: Harvard Business Press.

Piore, Michael J. and Sabel, Charles (1986) *The Second Industrial Divide: Possibilities for Prosperity*. New York: Basic Books.

Polanyi, Karl (1957 [1944]) *The Great Transformation*. Boston, MA: Beacon Press.

Pollert, Anna (1988) 'Dismantling flexibility', *Capital and Class*, 12(1): 42–75.

Portas, Mary (2011) *The Portas Review: An Independent Review into the Future of Our High Streets*. London: Department for Business, Innovation and Skills.

Power, Dominic and Jansson, Johan (2008) 'Cyclical clusters in global circuits: overlapping spaces in furniture trade fairs', *Economic Geography*, 84(4): 423–48.

Power, Dominic and Scott, Allen (2004) *Cultural Industries and the Production of Culture*. London: Routledge.

Prahalad, Coimbatore Krishnarao and Mashelkar, Raghunath Anant (2010) 'Innovation's holy grail', *Harvard Business Review*, 88(7–8): 132–41.

Press, Mike and Cooper, Rachel (2003) *The Design Experience: The Role of Design and Designers in the Twenty-first Century*. Aldershot: Ashgate.

PriceWaterhouseCoopers (2005) 'Lifestyle hotels survey' (report). London: PriceWaterhouseCoopers.

PriceWaterhouseCooper (2015) 'UK economic outlook' (www.pwc.co.uk/assets/pdf/ukeo-jul2015.pdf, accessed 05/11/15).

Quirk, Barry (2007) 'Roots of cooperation and routes to collaboration', in S. Parker and N. Gallagher (eds), *Our Collaborative Future: Working Together to Transform Public Services*. London: Demos. pp. 48–60.

Quito, Anne (2014) 'Casting Jessica Walsh', *Intern*, Summer Issue (2): 22–53.

Radjou, Navi, Prabhu, Jaideep and Ahuja, Simone (2012) *Jugaad Innovation: Think Frugal, Be Flexible, Generate Breakthrough Growth*. Chicago, IL: Wiley.

Rai, Amit (2015) 'The affect of *Jugaad*: frugal innovation and postcolonial practice in India's mobile phone ecology', *Environment and Planning D: Society and Space*, 33(6): 985–1002.

Rantisi, Norma (2004) 'The designer in the city and the city in the designer', in D. Power and A. Scott (eds), *Cultural Industries and the Production of Culture*. London: Routledge. pp. 91–109.

Raustiala, Kal and Sprigman, Christopher (2006) 'The piracy paradox: innovation and intellectual property in fashion design', *Virginia Law Review*, 92(8): 1687–777.

Reavley, Gordon (1998) 'Inconspicuous consumption', paper presented at *Design Innovation: Conception to Consumption*, 21st International Annual Conference of the Design History Society, University of Huddersfield.

Reckwitz, Andreas (2002) 'Toward a theory of social practices: a development in culturalist theorizing', *European Journal of Social Theory*, 5(2): 243–63.

RED (2004) *Touching the State*. London: Design Council.

Reich, Robert (2002) *The Future of Success: Working and Living in the New Economy*. London: Vintage.

Reichertz, Jo (2010) 'Abduction: the logic of discovery of grounded theory', in A. Bryant and K. Charmaz (eds), *The SAGE Handbook of Grounded Theory*. London: Sage. pp. 214–28.

Reimer, S., Pinch, S. and Sunley, P. (2008) 'Design spaces: agglomeration and creativity in British design agencies', *Geografiska Annaler: Series B, Human Geography*, 90(2): 151–72.

Reinach, Simona Segre (2005) 'China and Italy: fast fashion versus prêt-à-porter: towards a new culture of fashion', *Fashion Theory*, 9(1): 43–56.

Rinallo, D., Borghini, S. and Golfetto, F. (2010) 'Exploring visitor experiences at trade shows', *Journal of Business and Industrial Marketing*, 25(4): 249–58.

Ritzer, George (2000) *The McDonaldization of Society*. Thousand Oaks, CA: Pine Forge Press.

Rogers, Ben and Houston, Tom (2004) *Re-inventing the Police Station: Police–Public Relations, Reassurance and the Future of the Police Estate*. London: Institute of Public Policy Research.

Rolnik, Raquel (2013) 'Late neoliberalism: the financialization of homeownership and housing rights', *International Journal of Urban and Regional Research*, 37(3): 1058–66.

Romer, Paul (1986) 'Increasing returns and long-run growth', *Journal of Political Economy*, 94(5): 1002–37.

Rosenberg, Buck Clifford (2005) 'Scandinavian dreams: DIY, democratisation and IKEA', *Transformations*, 11 (www.transformationsjournal.org/issues/11/articles_02.shtml, accessed 01/12/16).

Rosenberg, Buck Clifford (2011) 'Home improvement: domestic taste, DIY, and the property market', *Home Cultures*, 8(1): 5–24.

Ross, Andrew (2009) *Nice Work If You Can Get It: Life and Labor in Precarious Times*. New York: New York University Press.

Rossi, Ugo (2013) 'On life as a fictitious commodity: cities and the biopolitics of late neoliberalism', *International Journal of Urban and Regional Research*, 37(3): 1067–74.

Rozentale, Ieva and Lavanga, Mariangela (2014) 'The "universal" characteristics of creative industries revisited: the case of Riga', *City, Culture and Society*, 5(2): 55–64.

Ruddick, Susan (2010) 'The politics of affect: Spinoza in the work of Negri and Deleuze', *Theory, Culture and Society*, 27(4): 21–45.

Ryan, John (2012) 'Design talk: Guy Smith, head of design, Arcadia' (www.retail-week.com/stores/design-talk-guy-smith-head-of-design-arcadia/5038247.article, accessed 31/03/16).

Ryan-Collins, J., Stephens, L. and Coote, A. (2008) *The New Wealth of Time: How Timebanking Helps People Build Better Public Services*. London: NEF.

Saad-Fiho, Alfredo and Johnston, Deborah (2005) 'Introduction', in A. Saah-Fiho and D. Johnston (eds), *Neoliberalism: A Critical Reader*. London: Pluto Press. pp.1–6.

Sabel, Charles (1982) *Work and Politics: The Division of Labor in Industry*. Cambridge: Cambridge University Press.

Salone del Mobile (2014) 'Exhibition factsheet' (http://salonemilano.it/en-us/VISITORS/Salone-Internazionale-del-Mobile/Exhibition-fact-sheet, accessed 04/06/16).

Sangiorgi, Daniela (2015) 'Designing for public sector innovation in the UK: design strategies for paradigm shifts', *Foresight*, 17(4): 332–48.

Sapsed, J., Camerani, R., Masucci, M., Petermann, M. and Rajguru, M. (2015) 'The BrightonFuse2: free-lancers in the creative digital IT economy' (www.brightonfuse.com/wp-content/uploads/2015/01/brighton_fuse2_online.pdf, accessed 17/11/15).

Sassen, Saskia (2003) 'Reading the city in a global digital age: between topographic representation and spatialized power', in L. Kraus and P. Petro (eds), *Global Cities: Cinema, Architecture and Urbanism in a Digital Age*. New Brunswick, NJ: Rutgers University Press. pp. 15–30.

Saunders, Joel (2016) 'Projects: EasyHotel' (http://joelsandersarchitect.com/project/easyhotel, accessed 25/02/16).

Saunders, Tom and Kingsley, Jeremy (2016) *Made in China: Makerspaces and the Search for Mass Innovation*. London: Nesta.

Scafidi, Susan (2006) 'Intellectual property and fashion design', in P.K. Yu (ed.), *Intellectual Property and Information Wealth: Issues and Practices in the Digital Age*. Westport, CT: Praeger. pp. 115–31.

Scase, Richard and Davis, Howard (2000) *Managing Creativity: The Dynamics of Work and Organization*. Milton Keynes: Open University Press.

Schatzki, Theodore (1996) *Social Practices: A Wittgensteinian Approach to Human Activity and the Social*. London: Routledge.

Scheltens, Harm (2015) Director of Pastoe 1981–2006; conversation with the author, 25 June.

Schiuma, Giovanni, (2012) 'Managing knowledge for business performance improvement', *Journal of Knowledge Management*, 16(4): 515–22.

Schlosser, Eric (2002) *Fast Food Nation*. London: Penguin.

Schmidt, Florian (2015) 'The design of creative crowdwork: from tools for empowerment to platform capitalism', PhD Dissertation, Royal College of Art, London.

Schneider, Friedrich (2014) 'In the shadow of the state – the informal economy and informal economy labor force', *DANUBE: Law and Economics Review*, 5(4): 227–48.

Schneider, Friedrich and Enste, Dominik (2013) *The Shadow Economy: An International Survey*. Cambridge: Cambridge University Press.

Schoenberger, Erica (2004) 'The spatial fix revisited', *Antipode*, 36(3): 427–33.

Scholz, Trebor (2012) *Digital Labor: The Internet as Playground and Factory.* New York: Routledge.

Schor, Juliet (2004) *Born to Buy: The Commercialized Child and the New Consumer Culture*. New York: Simon and Schuster.

Schumacher, E.F. (1993 [1973]) *Small is Beautiful: A Study of Economics as if People Mattered*. New York: Vintage.

Scott, Allen (2002) 'Competitive dynamics of Southern California's clothing industry: the widening global connection and its local ramifications', *Urban Studies*, 39(8): 1287–306.

Scott, Allen (2007) 'Capitalism and urbanization in a new key?: The cognitive-cultural dimension', *Social Forces*, 85(4): 1465–82.

SEE Platform (2013) 'An overview of service design for the private and public sectors' (www.seeplatform. eu/docs, accessed 01/04/15).

Sent, Esther-Mirjam (2004) 'Behavioral economics: how psychology made its (limited) way back into economics', *History of Political Economy*, 36(4): 735–60.

Seth, Sarang (2014) 'Indian psyche and *Jugaad*: the Gabbar and Mogambo to modern design in India' (https:// medium.com/@sarangsheth/indian-psyche-jugaad4b6dd1d1caf5#.3ig63h975, accessed 01/04/16).

Seyfang, Gill (2002) 'Tackling social exclusion with community currencies: learning from LETS to time banks', *International Journal of Community Currency Research*, 6(1): 1–11.

Shaughnessy, Adrian (2005) *How to be a Graphic Designer without Losing Your Soul*. London: Laurence King.

Sheller, Mimi and Urry, John (2006) 'The new mobilities paradigm,' *Environment and Planning A*, 38(2): 207–26.

Shelter (2013) 'Shelter reveals unaffordable housing costs' (http://england.shelter.org.uk/news/february_2013/ shelter_reveals_unaffordable_housing_costs, accessed 17/08/15).

Shepherd, Jessica (2010) 'China's top universities will rival Oxbridge, says Yale president', *Guardian* (www. theguardian.com/education/2010/feb/02/chinese-universities-will-rival-oxbridge, accessed 04/11/15).

Shepherd, William G. (1997) *The Economics of Industrial Organization*. Prospect Heights, IL: Waveland Press.

Shih, P.C., Bellotti, V., Han, K. and Carroll, J. (2015) 'Unequal time for unequal value: implications of differing motivations for participation in timebanking', *Proceedings of the 33rd Annual ACM Conference on Human Factors in Computing Systems*, 18–23 April, Seoul. pp. 1075–84.

Shove, E., Watson, M. and Ingram, J. (2005) 'The value of design and the design of value', *Joining Forces International Conference on Design Research, Helsinki* (www.lancaster.ac.uk/fass/projects/dnc/wkshp sjan06/papers/12-13th/shove.pdf, accessed 04/01/16).

Siegle, Lucy and Burke, Jason (2014) *We Are What We Wear: Unravelling Fast Fashion and the Collapse of Rana Plaza*. London: Guardian Shorts.

Silver, Jonathan Derek (2007) 'Hollywood's dominance of the movie industry: how did it arise and how has it been maintained?', PhD Dissertation, Queensland University of Technology.

Simmel, Georg (2004 [1900]) *The Philosophy of Money* (ed. David Frisby). London: Routledge.

Singh, Ramendroa, Gupta, Vaibhav and Mondal, Akash (2012) '*Jugaad* – from "making do" and "quick fix" to an innovative, sustainable and low-cost survival strategy at the bottom of the pyramid', *International Journal of Rural Management* 8(1–2): 87–105.

Sinha, Vivek (2014) 'Mitticool: son of the soil keeps things cool with his "desi gadget"' (www. hindustantimes.com/india/mitticool-son-of-the-soil-keeps-things-cool-with-his-desi-gadget/story-GQdAuKJNOOEoU7kfObZJoK.html, accessed 10/01/16).

Sitrin, Marina (ed.) (2006) *Horizontalism: Voices of Popular Power in Argentina*. Edinburgh: AK Press.

Skov, Lise (2006) 'The role of trade fairs in the global fashion business', *Current Sociology*, 54(5): 764–83.

Sleigh, A., Stewart, H. and Stokes, K. (2015) *Open Dataset of UK Makerspaces: A User's Guide*. London: Nesta (www.nesta.org.uk/publications/open- dataset-uk-makerspaces-users-guide, accessed 23/02/16).

Sorrell, John (1994) *The Future Design Council: A Blueprint for the Design Council's Future: Purpose, Objectives, Structure and Strategy*. London: Design Council.

Southerton, Dale (2003) '"Squeezing time": allocating practices, coordinating networks and scheduling society', *Time and Society*, 12(1): 5–25.

Southgate, Paul (1994) *Total Branding by Design: How to Make Your Brand's Packaging More Effective*. London: Kogan Page.

Space Caviar (ed.) (2014) *SQM: The Quantified Home*. Zurich: Lars Muller.

Sparviero, Sergio (2013) 'The business strategy of Hollywood's most powerful distributors: an empirical analysis', *Observatorio (OBS*) Journal*, 7(4): 45–62.

Staal, Gert and Van der Zwaag, Anne (2013) *Pastoe: 100 Years of Design Innovation*. Rotterdam: nai010 Publishers.

Stagis, Nikolaj (2012) *Den autentiske virksomhed*. Copenhagen: Gyldendal.

Standing, Guy (2011) *The Precariat*. London: Bloomsbury Academic.

Standing, Guy (2014) *A Precariat Charter: From Denizens to Citizens*. London: Bloomsbury Academic.

Stark, Tracey (1998) 'The dignity of the particular Adorno on Kant's aesthetics', *Philosophy and Social Criticism*, 24(2–3): 61–83.

Statista (2015) 'Number of worldwide active Amazon customer accounts from 1997 to 2014 (in millions)' (www.statista.com/statistics/237810/number-of-active-amazon-customer-accounts-worldwide, accessed 19/05/15).

Sternberg, Carolina Ana (2013) 'From "cartoneros" to "recolectores urbanos": the changing rhetoric and urban waste management policies in neoliberal Buenos Aires', *Geoforum*, 48: 187–95.

Stevenson, Deborah (2004) '"Civic gold" rush: cultural planning and the politics of the third way', *International Journal of Cultural Policy*, 10(1): 119–31.

Stewart, Kathleen (2011) 'Atmospheric attunements', *Environment and Planning D: Society and Space*, 29(3): 445–53.

Stiegler, Bernard (2010) *For a New Critique of Political Economy*. Cambridge: Polity Press.

Stoll, H.W. (1991) 'Design for manufacture: an overview', in J. Corbett, M. Dooner, J. Meleka and C. Pym (eds), *Design for Manufacture: Strategies, Principles and Techniques*. Wokingham, UK: Addison-Wesley. pp. 107–29.

Suchman, Lucy (1987) *Plans and Situated Actions: The Problem of Human–Machine Communication*. Cambridge: Cambridge University Press.

Sull, Donald and Turconi, Stefano (2008) 'Fast fashion lessons', *Business Strategy Review*, 19(2): 4–11.

Sullivan, Oriel and Gershuny, Jonathan (2004) 'Inconspicuous consumption work-rich, time-poor in the liberal market economy', *Journal of Consumer Culture*, 4(1): 79–100.

Sum, Ngai-Ling and Jessop, Bob (2013) *Towards a Cultural Political Economy: Putting Culture in its Place in Political Economy*. Cheltenham: Edward Elgar.

Sun, Wanning (2014) 'Regimes of healthy living: the reality of ageing in urban China and the cultivation of new normative subject', *Journal of Consumer Culture*, October: 1–18.

Sunley, P., Pinch, S., Reimer, S. and Macmillen, J. (2008) 'Innovation in a creative production system: the case of design', *Journal of Economic Geography*, 8(5): 675–98.

Sutton, Damian (2009) 'Cinema by design: Hollywood as network neighbourhood', in G. Julier and L. Moor (eds), *Design and Creativity: Policy, Management and Practice*. Oxford: Berg. pp. 174–90.

Swivel (2015) 'Designers' (www.swiveluk.com/uk/designers.html, accessed 02/06/15).

Swyngedouw, Erik (2005) 'Governance innovation and the citizen: the Janus face of governance-beyond-the-state', *Urban Studies*, 42(11): 1991–2006.

Teisman, Geert and Klijn, Erik-Hans (2002) 'Partnership arrangements: governmental rhetoric or governance scheme?', *Public Administration Review*, 62(2): 197–205.

Thackara, John (2006) *In the Bubble: Designing in a Complex World*. Cambridge, MA: MIT Press.

Thaler, Richard H. and Sunstein, Cass (2008) *Nudge: Improving Decisions about Health, Wealth and Happiness*. New Haven, CT: Yale University Press.

The Economist (2005) 'Global housing boom: in come the waves', 16 June (www.economist.com/node/4079027, accessed 17/08/15).

Thomas, Emily (2008) *Innovation by Design in Public Services*. London: Solace Foundation.

Thornton, Sarah (2009) *Seven Days in the Art World*. London: Granta.

Thorpe, Ann (2012) *Architecture and Design versus Consumerism: How Design Activism Confronts Growth*. London: Earthscan.

Thrift, Nigel (2000) 'Performing cultures in the new economy', *Annals of the Association of American Geographers*, 87(4): 674–92.

Thrift, Nigel (2004) 'Movement-space: the changing domain of thinking resulting from the development of new kinds of spatial awareness', *Economy and Society*, 33(4): 582–604.

Thrift, Nigel (2005) *Knowing Capitalism*. London: Sage.

Thrift, Nigel (2008) *Non-Representational Theory: Space, Politics, Affect*. London: Routledge.

Tien, James (2012) 'The next industrial revolution: integrated services and goods', *Journal of Systems Science and Systems Engineering*, 21(3): 257–96.

Timebanking UK (2015) (www.timebanking.org, accessed 20/12/15).

Tokatli, Nebahat (2008) 'Global sourcing: insights from the global clothing industry – the case of Zara, a fast fashion retailer', *Journal of Economic Geography*, 8(1): 21–38.

Tokatli, Nebahat and Kizilgün, Ömür (2004) 'Upgrading in the global clothing industry: Mavi jeans and the transformation of a Turkish firm from full-package to brand-name manufacturing and retailing', *Economic Geography*, 80(3): 221–40.

Tokatli, Nebahat and Kizilgün, Ömür (2009) 'From manufacturing garments for ready-to-wear to designing collections for fast fashion: evidence from Turkey', *Environment and Planning A*, 41(1): 146–62.

Tokatli, N., Wrigley, N. and Kizilgün, Ö. (2008) 'Shifting global supply networks and fast fashion: made in Turkey for Marks and Spencer', *Global Networks*, 8(3): 261–80.

Topman (2015) 'About Topman' (www.topman.com/en/tmuk/category/about-us-2706679/home?geoip=nore direct, accessed 17/08/15).

Törmikoski, Ilona (2009) 'Interview', in G. Julier and L. Moor (eds), *Design and Creativity: Policy, Management and Practice*. Oxford: Berg. pp. 241–51 and 243–55.

Towers Watson (2013) 'Global pension assets study' (www.towerswatson.com/en/Insights/IC-Types/Survey-Research-Results/2013/01/Global-Pensions-Asset-Study-2013, accessed 18/11/15).

Townley, Barbara and Beech, Nic (eds) (2010) *Managing Creativity: Exploring the Paradox*. Cambridge: Cambridge University Press

Townsend, A., Jeffery, L., Fidler, Devin and Crawford, M. (2011) 'The future of open fabrication' (www.iftf.org/member/OpenFab, accessed 08/02/16).

Transition Network (2015) 'Transition initiatives directory' (www.transitionnetwork.org/initiatives, accessed 12/10/15).

Turkle, Sherry (1984) *The Second Self: Computers and the Human Spirit*. London: Granada.

Umbral, Francisco (1987) *Guia de la Posmodernidad*. Madrid: Temas de Hoy.

UNCTAD (2010) 'Creative economy: a feasible development option' (report). Geneva: UNCTAD.

UNESCO (2015) 'Creative cities network: why cities?' (www.unesco.org/new/en/culture/themes/creativity/creative-cities-network/why-cities, accessed 27/02/15).

Unsworth, R., Ball, S., Bauman, I., Chatterton, P., Goldring, A., Hill, K. and Julier, G. (2011) 'Building resilience and well-being in the margins within the city: changing perceptions, making connections, realising potential, plugging resources leaks', *City*, 15(2): 181–203.

Urry, John (2007) *Mobilities*. Cambridge: Polity Press.

Urry, John (2014) *Offshoring*. Chicago, IL: Wiley.

Väliaho, Pasi (2014) *Biopolitical Screens: Image, Power, and the Neoliberal Brain*. Cambridge, MA: MIT Press.

Verganti, Roberto (2013) *Design Driven Innovation: Changing the Rules of Competition by Radically Innovating What Things Mean*. Boston, MA: Harvard Business Press.

Victorino, L., Ekaterina K. and Rohit V. (2009) 'Exploring the use of the abbreviated technology readiness index for hotel customer segmentation', *Cornell Hospitality Quarterly*, 50(3): 342–59.

Von Hippel, Eric (2005) *Democratizing Innovation*. Cambridge, MA: MIT Press.

Votolato, Gregory (1998) *American Design in the Twentieth Century: Personality and Performance*. Manchester: Manchester University Press.

Walker, Samuel (2015) 'Urban agriculture and the sustainability fix in Vancouver and Detroit', *Urban Geography*, July: 1–20.

Wallis, Cara and Qiu, Jack Linchuan (2012) 'Shanzhaiji and the transformation of the local mediascape in Shenzhen', in W. Sun and J. Chio (eds), *Mapping Media in China: Region, Province, Locality*. London: Routledge. pp. 109–25.

Walsh, James (2012) 'Mass migration and the mass society: Fordism, immigration policy and the post-war long boom in Canada and Australia, 1947–1970', *Journal of Historical Sociology*, 25(3): 352–85.

Wang, David and Ilhan, Ali O. (2009) 'Holding creativity together: a sociological theory of the design professions', *Design Issues*, 25(1): 5–21.

Weber, Cynthia (2010) 'Introduction: design and citizenship', *Citizenship Studies*, 14(1): 1–16.

Weber, Max (1978) *Economy and Society: An Outline of Interpretive Sociology*. London: University of California Press.

Weber, Max (2002 [1905]) *The Protestant Ethic and the Spirit of Capitalism: And Other Writings*. London: Penguin.

Weisbrot, Mark and Sandoval, Luis (2007) 'Argentina's economic recovery: policy choices and implications', *Center for Economic and Policy Research*, 1: 1–17.

Weisselberg, Lindsey (2009) '*Sui generis* genius: how the design protection statute could be amended to include entertainment pitch ideas', *The John Marshall Review of Intellectual Property Law*, 9: 184–201.

Wells, John (1989) 'Uneven development and de-industrialisation in the UK since 1979', in F. Green (ed.), *The Restructuring of the UK Economy*. Hemel Hempstead: Harvester Wheatsheaf. pp. 25–64.

Whitfield, Dexter (2001) *Public Services or Corporate Welfare: Rethinking the Nation State in the Global Economy*. London: Pluto Press.

Whitfield, Dexter (2006) *New Labour's Attack on Public Services: Modernisation by Marketisation? How the Commissioning, Choice, Competition and Contestability Agenda Threatens Public Services and the Welfare State: Lessons for Europe*. Nottingham: Spokesman Books.

Whitfield, Dexter (2012) *In Place of Austerity: Reconstructing the Economy, State and Public Services*. Nottingham: Spokesman Books.

Whitson, Risa (2011) 'Negotiating place and value: geographies of waste and scavenging in Buenos Aires', *Antipode*, 43(4): 1404–33.

Wilkinson, Adrian and Balmer, John (1996) 'Corporate and generic identities: lessons from the Co-operative Bank', *International Journal of Bank Marketing*, 14(4): 22–35.

Winograd, Terry and Flores, Flores (1986) *Understanding Computers and Cognition: A New Foundation for Design*. London: Intellect Books.

World Intellectual Property Organisation (WIPO) (2014) *World Intellectual Property Indicators*. Geneva: WIPO (www.wipo.int/edocs/pubdocs/en/wipo_pub_941_2014.pdf, accessed 12/02/15).

Wittel, Andreas (2001) 'Toward a network sociality', *Theory, Culture and Society*, 18(6): 51–76.

Witz, A., Warhurst, C. and Nickson, D. (2003) 'The labour of aesthetics and the aesthetics of organization', *Organization*, 10(1): 33–54.

Wood, Phil (1999) 'Cultural industries and the city: policy issues for the cultural industries at the local level', keynote speech to the *Cultural Industries and the City Conference*, Manchester Metropolitan University, 13–14 December.

Woodward, Ian (2001) 'Domestic objects and the taste epiphany: a resource for consumption methodology', *Journal of Material Culture*, 6(2): 115–36.

Work Foundation (2007) 'Staying ahead: the economic performance of the UK's creative industries' (report). London: The Work Foundation.

World Bank (2016) 'Global economic prospects – forecasts' (http://data.worldbank.org/country/india, accessed 08/12/16).

World Trade Organisation (WTO) (2013) *World Trade Report 2013 – Factors Shaping the Future of World Trade*. Geneva: WTO.

Zucman, Gabriel (2014) 'Taxing across borders: tracking personal wealth and corporate profits', *Journal of Economic Perspectives*, 28(4): 121–48.

Zukin, Sharon (1989) *Loft Living: Cultural and Capital in Urban Change*. New Brunswick, NJ: Rutgers University Press.

INDEX

Figures, Tables and Illustrations are indicated by page numbers in bold print.